THE ARAB NEWS

THE ARAB NEWS

Arabic-English Reader for Intermediate Students

with CDs, exercises and key

Fred Pragnell

Pragnell Books

First Edition 2003

Published by
Pragnell Books
3 Lower Teddington Road
Kingston Upon Thames
Surrey KT1 4ER

Tel/ Fax (44) 0208 943 9346
e-mail efprag@AOL.com

ISBN 0-9544606-0-X

Other books by the same author and available from the above address:

A Week in the Middle East An Arabic Language Reader with tapes and exercises, originally published in 1984 by Lund Humphries Publishers Ltd, London

Arabic in Action A Basic course in Spoken Arabic with tapes, originally published in 1992 by Lund Humphries Publishers Ltd, London

Contents

Section 2

Introduction

The Arab News is a dual-language progressively graded reader for intermediate students of Arabic wishing to familiarise themselves with the language of business and economics as found in the Arabic newspapers. The short and straightforward articles in the reader should also help those wanting to progress to more general topics.

A basic knowledge of the grammar and vocabulary of Modern Standard Arabic is assumed. The aim of this reader is to introduce and consolidate by subsequent repetition, the fifteen hundred or so lexical items commonly found in the business pages of an Arabic newspaper.

The articles, all taken from الشرق الاوسط Asharq al-Awsat newspaper, are loosely grouped together and cover the major topics - international trade, economic growth, trade agreements, company activity and results, the world stock and money markets.

The reader is divided into three sections:

1 - 42 Very short articles introducing the above topics;
43 - 72 Slightly longer articles, covering similar ground with wider vocabulary;
73 - 96 Full page articles, again covering similar topics, but with more extensive vocabulary.

The first occurrence of selected new words is put next to the Arabic article. The more extensive Word List at the end of the book is based on Hans Wehr *Dictionary of Modern Written Arabic*. This Word List may be used as a reference source, with the words themselves listed under their root. The student should be encouraged to add to both the vocabulary for each article and the Word List.

The vocabulary is consolidated by exercises every six articles. By doing these exercises, the student should gain both feedback on progress and a sense of satisfaction. There is a key to these exercises on page 140.

The answers to these exercises should be put on a separate sheet so that the student can repeat them as desired.

The following approach is suggested:

1. Initial learning of new vocabulary, checking the pronunciation in the dictionary and adding vowels where necessary;
2. Reading of the Arabic text with the English translation covered, noting words or phrases not understood;
3. Cross reference to the English translation.

A brief revision of the two or three preceding passages should be made before proceeding to the following one. In this way the student will get useful revision, gain confidence and speed in reading comprehension, as well as prepare himself for the following passage. Since the passages are grouped by subject area he will progressively internalise the core vocabulary for a particular area.

Using the CDs to develop listening skills

The set of 6 CD covers the 96 core articles. They are read by Muhammed Sultan, who has wide experience of professional recording. In section 1 the articles are read very slowly; the pace is gradually increased over sections 2 and 3. It is very important for the student to use the cassettes as he progresses through the course. The aim is to understand a complete article without reference to the text. This takes a lot of repetition and effort but is immensely rewarding in the transferable benefits it brings. In addition, dictation and transcription exercises can be very useful to further consolidate learning.

Acknowledgments

I wish to thank *Asharq al-Awsat* newspaper, "the international daily newspaper of the Arabs" for permission to use the articles.

I shall welcome any comments about the translations and exercises that will help to improve a subsequent edition.

ARTICLE 1

agreement	اتفاقية
signing	توقيع
stage	مرحلة *pl.* مراحل
to finance	مال
planning	تخطيط
development	تنمية
benefit	صالح
financing	تمويل
education	تعليم
health	صحة
infrastructure	بنية تحتية

اتفاقية بين اليمن والبنك الدولي

تم التوقيع أخيرا في واشنطن على الاتفاقية النهائية الخاصة بالمرحلة الثانية لمشروع الاشغال العامة الذي سيموله البنك الدولي بمبلغ قدره 50 مليون دولار.

وقال احمد محمد صوفان وزير التخطيط والتنمية اليمني في تصريح نقلته «ق.ن.أ» أمس بانه وقع على تلك الاتفاقية خلال زيارته الاخيرة للعاصمة الاميركية وستخصص لصالح تمويل مشاريع مختلفة في مجالات التعليم والصحة والبنية التحتية في مختلف محافظات الجمهورية.

ARTICLE 2

organisation	هيئة
investment	استثمار *pl.* ات
minister of state	وزير دولة
board	مجلس الادارة
development	انماء
headquarters	مقر *pl.* مقار
regional	اقليمي
performance	أداء *pl.* ات
belonging to	تابع
budget	ميزانية
activity	نشاط *pl.* انشطة

الهيئة العربية للاستثمار تجتمع في دبي

● افتتح الدكتور محمد خلفان ابن خرباش وزير الدولة للشؤون المالية والصناعة اليوم اجتماع مجلس ادارة الهيئة العربية للاستثمار والانماء الزراعي (الدورة 93) في المقر الاقليمي للهيئة بدبي. ونقلت وكالة (ق.ن.ا) «سيناقش المجلس خلال اجتماعه برئاسة عبد الكريم العامري رئيس المجلس اداء الشركات التابعة للهيئة في الدول العربية ونتائج اعمالها وميزانية العام الحالي ونشاط الشركات خلال الفترة المقبلة».

ARTICLE 3

size	حجم *pl.* حجوم
to reach	بلغ
to concentrate on	تركز على
participation	مساهمة
private sector	القطاع الخاص
capital	رأس مال *pl.* رؤوس اموال
to be linked to	تعلق ب
construction materials	مواد البناء

10 ملايين دولار استثمارات مغربية في مصر

الرباط: «الشرق الأوسط»

ذكر تقرير اقتصادي مصري ان حجم الاستثمارات المغربية في مصر بلغ 31 مليون جنيه (10 ملايين دولار) تتركز في ستة مشروعات في مجالات الصناعة والزراعة والخدمات.

وقال التقرير الصادر عن هيئة الاستثمار والمناطق الحرة المصرية ان مساهمة القطاع الخاص المغربي في المشروعات الستة التي تصل رؤوس اموالها الى 430 مليون جنيه تتعلق بالخصوص بمشروعين في مجال صناعة مواد البناء واخرى في مجال الصناعات الكيماوية ورابع في مجال الانتاج الزراعي فضلا عن استثمارات مغربية اخرى في بعض مجالات الخدمات والانشطة المالية.

Agreement between Yemen and the World Bank

The final agreement for the second stage of the public works project that the World Bank will finance to the sum of 50 million dollars was signed in Washington recently.

In a statement reported by QNA yesterday, the Yemeni minister of planning and development, Ahmed Mohammed Soufan, said that he had signed the agreement during his recent visit to the US capital and that it would be earmarked to finance various projects in the fields of education, health and infrastructure in different provinces in the republic.

Arab Investment Organisation meets in Dubai

The minister of state for financial affairs and industry, Dr. Mohammed Khalfan Ibn Kharbash, today opened the 93rd board meeting of the Arab Organisation for Agricultural Investment and Development in the organisation's regional headquarters in Dubai. The QNA agency said: "During its meeting headed by the chairman, Abdulkareem al-Amri, the board will discuss the performance of companies affiliated to the organisation in the Arab countries, the results of their operations, the budget for this year and the companies' activity over the coming period."

10 million dollars of Moroccan investment in Egypt

Rabat - *Asharq al-Awsat*: An Egyptian economic report said that Moroccan investments in Egypt totalled 31 million pounds, 10 million dollars, and focused on six projects in the industrial, agricultural and service sectors.

The report published by the Egyptian Organisation of Investment and Free Zones said that the participation of the Moroccan private sector in the six projects with capital of 430 million pounds was linked specifically to two projects in the field of the building materials industry, a third in the field of chemical industries. and a fourth in the area of agricultural production, besides other Moroccan investments in certain areas of services and financial activities.

ARTICLE 4

to ratify	ابرم
security	ضمان
safeguarding	حماية
signal	اشارة
investor	مستثمر
establishment	اقامة
partnership	شراكة
profitable	مثمر
during	فى ظل
improvement	اصلاح *pl.* ات
to be evident	تجلى

الجزائر تبرم اتفاقا لضمان الاستثمار مع الدنمارك

● ابرمت الجزائر والدنمارك اتفاقا حول ضمان الاستثمارات وحمايتها. ونقلت وكالة «واس» ان الاتفاق الذي وقع اول من امس يعد اشارة سياسية قوية من حكومتي البلدين للمستثمرين ورجال الاعمال لاقامة شراكة مثمرة في ظل الاصلاحات الاقتصادية الجارية في الجزائر وبفضل الخبرة الدنماركية. يشار الى ان الحضور الاقتصادي الدنماركي في الجزائر يتجلى في مصانع الاسمنت والصناعات الصيدلية واستغلال انابيب البترول وفي قطاع الغاز.

ARTICLE 5

fund	صندوق *pl.* صناديق
to obtain	حصل على
loan	قرض *pl.* قروض
to join	ربط
coastal	ساحلى
to aim	هدف
development	تطوير
land *adj.*	برى
facilitating	تسهيل

30 مليون دينار قرض من الصندوق العربي للإنماء لسورية

● حصلت سورية على ثلاثين مليون دينار كويتي قرضا من الصندوق العربي للانماء الاقتصادي والاجتماعي للمساهمة في تمويل مشروع طريق سريع يربط مدينة اللاذقية الساحلية بمنطقة اريحا التابعة لمحافظة حلب. وطبقا لوكالة «ق.ن.أ» فإن عبد اللطيف الحمد رئيس مجلس الادارة المدير العام للصندوق العربي، وعبد الرحيم السبيعي وزير التخطيط السوري، وقعا اتفاقية القرض الذي يهدف الى تمويل مشروع الطريق التي يبلغ طولها مائة كيلومتر وتطوير خدمات النقل البري بين ميناء اللاذقية ومدينة اريحا مما يسهم في ربط مناطق الانتاج الزراعي وموانئ التصدير وتسهيل حركة النقل والترانزيت في المناطق الشمالية والشرقية من سورية.

ARTICLE 6

loan	اقتراض
average	معدل
frame	اطار
interest rate	سعر الفائدة
grace period	فترة السماح
to fluctuate	تراوح
to repay	استحق
adviser	مستشار *pl.* ون
support	دعم
reconstruction	اعادة بناء
civil	أهلى
to last	دام

البنك الدولي يوافق على قروض للبنان بقيمة 600 مليون دولار

بيروت - رويترز: قال مسؤول بالبنك الدولي امس ان البنك وافق على اقراض لبنان 600 مليون دولار خلال السنوات الثلاث المقبلة. وذكر غسان الرفاعي مستشار البنك الدولي لشؤون الشرق الاوسط وشمال أفريقيا ان لبنان يستطيع الاقتراض بمعدل يصل الى 200 مليون دولار سنويا في اطار البرنامج.

واضاف الرفاعي ان سعر الفائدة على القروض، ألتي تتطلب موافقة البنك، يتراوح بين سبعة في المائة و7,5 في المائة فضلا عن فترة سماح مدتها خمس سنوات، وتستحق القروض بعد 15 عاما.

وقال مستشار البنك «هذا البرنامج استمرار لدعمنا للبنان. ويجب ان تبلغنا الحكومة السبب الذي ترغب في الاقتراض من أجله قبل ان نعطيها النقود».

وفي 1993 وافق البنك على قروض قيمتها 613,9 مليون دولار لمساعدة لبنان على اعادة بناء بنيته الاساسية بعد حرب أهلية دامت 15 عاما من 1975 الى 1990.

Algeria ratifies agreement with Denmark to secure investment

Algeria and Denmark have ratified an agreement concerning the securing and safeguarding of investments. The WAS agency said that the agreement signed the day before yesterday constituted a strong political signal from the governments of the two countries to investors and businessmen of the establishment of a profitable partnership in the wake of the current economic improvements in Algeria and which was down to Danish expertise. It points out that the Danish economic presence in Algeria was evident in the cement factories, pharmaceutical industries, the development of oil pipelines and in the field of gas.

30 million dollar loan from the Arab Development Fund for Syria

Syria has obtained a thirty million Kuwaiti dinar loan from the Arab Fund for Economic and Social Development as part of the financing for the highway project to join the coastal town of al-Ladhiqiyah to the area of Ariha in the province of Aleppo. According to the QNA agency, Abdulateef al-Hamad, chairman of the board of directors and director general of the Arab Fund, and Abduraheem al-Subeei, the Syrian minister for planning, signed the loan agreement to finance the project for the hundred kilometre road and to develop land transport services between the port of al-Ladhiqiyah and the town of Ariha. This project will help in linking the areas of agricultural production with the export ports and in improving transport and transit activity in the northern and eastern areas of Syria.

The World Bank agrees to lend Lebanon 600 million dollars

Beirut - *Reuters*: An official for the World Bank said yesterday that the bank had agreed to lend Lebanon 600 million dollars over the next three years. Ghassan al-Rafai, a World Bank adviser for Middle Eastern and North African affairs, said that Lebanon could borrow on average up to 200 million dollars a year under the programme.

Al-Rafai added that the interest rate on the loans, which required the bank's agreement, would range between 7% and 7.5%, in addition to a five year grace period, and that the loans would be repaid over 15 years.

The bank adviser said: "This programme is a continuation of our support for Lebanon, and the government must give us the reason it wants the loan before we give the money."

In 1993 the bank agreed loans of 613.9 million dollars to help Lebanon to rebuild its infrastructure after a civil war that had lasted 15 years from 1975 to 1990.

Exercises Articles 1 - 6

Exercise 1 Choose the best answer

١ تم الهدف/التوقيع/المجال/القطاع اخيرا على الاتفاقية النهائية.
٢ قال وزير الصندوق/الاقتراض/التخطيط/المستثمرين بانه وقع على الاتفاقية.
٣ افتتح وزير الصناعة اداء/انتاج/اجتماع/انماء مجلس الادارة.
٤ سيناقش الانماء/الاطار/القرض/المجلس اداء الشركات.
٥ ذكر التقرير ان مجال/انماء/حجم/قطاع الاستثمارات بلغ ٦٠ مليون دولار.
٦ قال المسؤول ان مساهمة الصندوق/القطاع/الدعم/الضمان الخاص مهمة.
٧ سيمول البنك الدولى مشروع/راس مال/اطار/تعليم الاشغال العامة.
٨ ابرم الوزراء سببا/اتفاقا/صندوقا/سعرا حول ضمان الاستثمارات.
٩ حصلت سورية على حجم/معدل/قطاع/قرض من الصندوق الدولى.
١٠ وافق البنك على استثمار/اجتماع/اشتغلال/اقتراض لبنان ٥٠٠ مليون دولار.
١١ حجم المناطق/الاستثمارات/الاشارات/الشركات بلغ ٣٥ مليون دولار.
١٢ سيناقش المجلس صحة/مرحلة/ميزانية/وكالة العام الحالى.
١٣ تصل محافظة/مجلات/صناعة/رؤوس اموال الشركات الى ٣٥ مليون دولار.
١٤ سعر الاقامة/القيمة/الفائدة/الاعادة على القروض يتراوح بين ٦ و ٧ فى المائة.
١٥ يجب ان تبلغنا المدة/الموافقة/الخبرة/الحكومة السبب.

Exercise 2 Match the following pairs

١	وزير	a	المقبلة
٢	العام	b	التخطيط
٣	الفترة	c	البناء
٤	مواد	d	زراعى
٥	انماء	e	الحالى

Exercise 3 Match the following pairs

١	رؤوس	a	السياسية
٢	الاشارة	b	الخاص
٣	القطاع	c	اقتصاضى
٤	رجال	d	اموال
٥	انماء	e	اعمال

Exercise 4 Put the following into the sentences below

طبقا   في ظل   برئـاسة   فضلا عن   بفضل   خلال

١ وقع الوزير الاتفاقية ________ زيارته لسورية.
٢ سيناقش المجلس ________ المدير العام اداء الشركة.
٣ ________ للحكومة فان وقع الوزراء اتفاقية.
٤ البلاد سيستطيع الاقتراض ________ البرنامج.
٥ ________ الاصلاحات الاقتصادية الجارية.
٦ مساهمة القطاع الخاص المغربى تتعلق بمشروعين، ________
استثمارات مغربية اخرى فى بعض مجلات الخدمات.

Exercise 5 Rearrange the following to make a sensible headline

رأسمال   المركزي   زيادة   العماني   البنك

Exercise 6 Rearrange the following to make a sensible headline

ريال   مواد   شركات   مشروعا   لإنتاج   تنشئ

بتروكيماوية   800 مليون   سعودية   بكلفة   وأجنبية

تونس تستضيف اجتماعات اللجنة العليا المشتركة التونسية المصرية

● تعقد في تونس الاسبوع الاول من مارس (آذار) المقبل اجتماعات اللجنة العليا المشتركة التونسية المصرية برئاسة رئيسي الوزراء في البلدين بهدف تطوير علاقات التعاون بين البلدين في مختلف المجالات خاصة التجارية والاقتصادية، حسبما ذكرت وكالة الأنباء القطرية امس.

ومن المقرر ان تسبق هذه الاجتماعات بيومين اجتماعات للجنة التحضيرية في تونس برئاسة منذر الزنايدي وزير التجارة التونسي وظافر البشري وزير الدولة للتخطيط والتعاون الدولي المصري لاعداد جدول اعمال اللجنة العليا وتقييم ما تم انجازه خلال الاجتماع السابق للجنة العليا المشتركة بالقاهرة في مارس الماضي.

ARTICLE 7

to host	استضاف
joint council	لجنة مشتركة
aim	اهداف *pl.* هدف
tie	ات *pl.* علقة
cooperation	تعاون
according to	حسبما
agenda	جدول اعمال
preparatory	تحضرى
assessment	تقييم
achievement	انجاز

توقيع عشر اتفاقيات تجارية بين مصر وتونس

القاهرة: «الشرق الأوسط»

اعلن الدكتور ظافر البشري وزير الدولة للتخطيط والتعاون الدولي انه سيتم توقيع عشر اتفاقيات في مجالات مختلفة خلال اجتماعات اللجنة العليا المصرية التونسية المشتركة التي ستعقد بتونس اليوم ويرأسها عن الجانب المصري الدكتور كمال الجنزوري رئيس الوزراء والجانب التونسي الدكتور حامد القروي رئيس وزراء تونس.

وقال الجنزوري قبل مغادرته القاهرة مساء اول امس متوجها الى تونس انه سيشارك في اجتماع اللجنة التحضيرية مع وزير التجارة والتعاون الدولي التونسي لبحث الامور التي ستعرض على اللجنة العليا المشتركة من بينها متابعة البرنامج التنفيذي للاتفاقيات السابقة والتي تشمل كل المجالات خاصة في ما يتعلق بتنمية التجارة بين البلدين وانشاء منطقة تجارة حرة بينهما.

ARTICLE 8

leaving	مغادرة
establishing	انشاء
to review	عرض

وزير التجارة الأميركي يزور كوريا الجنوبية أواخر مارس

سيول - رويترز: ذكرت كوريا الجنوبية امس ان وزير التجارة الاميركي وليام ديلي يعتزم زيارتها في المدة من 25 الى 28 مارس (آذار) لتوسيع التجارة الثنائية ومبادلات الاعمال بين البلدين. وقالت وزارة التجارة والصناعة والطاقة ان ديلي سيصحبه مديرون كبار من 15 شركة اميركية كبرى ستختارهم الولايات المتحدة في ما بعد، وقالت الوزارة في بيان ان ديلي ونظيره الكوري الجنوبي بارك تيأ يونج سيرأسان معا اجتماع لجنة التعاون التجاري الاميركية - الكورية الجنوبية. واضاف البيان قوله ان اللجنة عقدت اجتماعها الاول عام 1997 في واشنطن وحددت ثمانية قطاعات منها السيارات وتجارة الالكترونيات وتوسيع التعاون، وقال البيان ان يلي سيزور الصين بعد مغادرته كوريا الجنوبية.

ARTICLE 9

to be resolved	اعتزم
period	مدة
bilateral	ثنائـــي
exchange	مبادلة
to accompany	صحب
subsequently	فى ما بعد
counterpart	نظراء *pl.* نظير
communiqué	ات *pl.* بيان

Tunis to host meetings of the joint Egypto-Tunisian senior council

Meetings of the joint Egypto-Tunisian senior council will be held in Tunis in the first week of March chaired by the prime ministers of the two countries. The aim is to develop links of cooperation between the two countries in various fields, especially trade and the economy, according to an announcement from the Qatari News Agency yesterday.

Two days before these meetings, preparatory meetings of the council in Tunis headed by Mondhur al-Zanaidi, the Tunisian trade minister, and Dhafir al-Bashari, the Egyptian minister of state for planning and international cooperation, have been arranged in order to prepare the agenda for the senior council and to assess the achievements during the previous meeting of the joint senior council in Cairo last March.

Signing of ten trade agreements between Egypt and Tunisia

Cairo - *Asharq al-Awsat*: Doctor Dhafir al-Bashari, minister of state for planning and international cooperation, announced that ten agreements in various areas would be signed during the meetings of the joint Egypto-Tunisian senior council to be held in Tunis today and would be chaired on the Egyptian side by prime minister, Doctor Kamal al-Ganzouri, and on the Tunisian side by prime minister, Doctor Hammad al-Karoui.

Before leaving Cairo for Tunis the evening before last, al-Ganzouri said that he would be attending a meeting of the preparatory committee with the Tunisian minister of trade and international cooperation to discuss matters that would be submitted to the joint senior council. Among these matters would be those arising from the executive programme of the previous agreements, which covered all areas specifically relating to the development of trade between the two countries and the establishing of a free trade zone between them.

US trade minister to visit South Korea at the end of March

Seoul - *Reuters*: South Korea announced yesterday that the US trade minister, William Daley, was set to visit the country from 25th to 28th March to broaden bilateral trade and business exchanges between the two countries. The minister of trade, industry and energy said that Daley would be accompanied by senior managers from 15 of the largest US corporations to be chosen by the United States subsequently. In a statement the minister said that Daley and his South Korean counterpart, Park Tae-Young, would together head a meeting of the US-South Korean trade cooperation committee. The report added that the committee had held its first meeting in 1997 in Washington and had specified eight areas, among them automobiles, trade in electronics and the expansion of cooperation. The statement said that Daley would be visiting China after leaving South Korea.

وزير التجارة الكندي يزور السعودية الاثنين المقبل

الرياض: عبد العزيز حمدان

يبدأ وزير التجارة الدولية الكندي سيرجيو ماركي زيارة رسمية للسعودية الاثنين المقبل تستغرق يومين.

وسيبحث الوزير الذي يترأس وفدا كبيرا من رجال الأعمال الكنديين الخيارات المتاحة لتوسيع وتعميق الروابط التجارية، وتحسين التعاون بين القطاع الخاص في كلا البلدين، اضافة الى بحث بعض الاقتراحات المحددة حول التعاون في مجال الطرق والمواصلات والاتصالات.

ويرافق ماركي وفد يضم 35 رجل اعمال يمثلون 24 شركة يتركز نشاط معظمها في قطاع الزراعة، والمواد الغذائية والبناء والأعمار والتعليم والطاقة وتقنية المعلومات والاتصالات والمواصلات. هذا بالاضافة الى وجود ممثلين لثماني وكالات حكومية ومؤسسات تعليمية ضمن الوفد المرافق.

وقال السفير الكندي لدى السعودية دانيال هوبسون ان حجم التبادل التجاري بين البلدين قد ازداد في السنة الماضية عن 1,4 مليار دولار كندي (1,2 مليار دولار اميركي).

ARTICLE 10

to last	استغرق
option	خيار *pl.* ات
available	متاح
deepening	تعميق
tie	رابطة *pl.* روابط
improvement	تحسين
communications	مواصلات
links	اتصالات
to accompany	رافق
to consist of	ضم
to represent	مثّل
food *adj.*	غذائـــي
construction	اعمار

ارتفاع حجم التبادل التجاري بين الهند وإسرائيل

نيودلهي - ق.ن.أ: ارتفع حجم التجارة بين الهند واسرائيل الى 670 مليون دولار اميركي خلال عام 1998 مقارنة بحوالي 658 مليون دولار في عام 1997, ووصلت الصادرات الهندية الى اسرائيل لاول مرة منذ اقامة العلاقات بين البلدين في عام 1992 الى مستوى 343 مليون دولار وسجلت نموا بنسبة 17 في المائة مقابل الصادرات الاسرائيلية للهند التي وصلت الى 327 مليون دولار في عام 1998. وتركزت مجالات النمو في الصناعات الكيميائية بنسبة 28 في المائة والمنسوجات بنسبة 23 في المائة والماس بنسبة 22 في المائة. وانخفضت الصادرات الاسرائيلية بنسبة 10 في المائة اي الى 327 مليون دولار نتيجة لانخفاض صادرات الماس التي انخفضت بنسبة 25 في المائة نتيجة للازمة المالية والاقتصادية الآسيوية. وكانت اكثر من 60 في المائة من الصادارت الاسرائيلية للهند من خام الماس التي واجهت متاعب شديدة اثناء الازمة الآسيوية.

ARTICLE 11

rise	ارتفاع
compared with	مقارنة ب
level	مستوى *pl.* ات
to record	سجل
diamond	الماس
growth	نمو
as a result of	نتيجة
crisis	أزمة
raw, crude	خام
difficulties	متاعب

شركات من آيرلندا الشمالية تبحث عن فرص تجارية في السعودية

الرياض: «الشرق الأوسط»

تبدأ بعثة بريطانية تضم ثماني شركات من ايرلندا الشمالية اليوم زيارة الى الرياض للبحث عن فرص ابرام عقود تجارية مع رجال الأعمال السعوديين، في عدة قطاعات تشمل العصائر والمشروبات، والقماش، ومعدات الصناعات الكهربائية، والماكينات الصناعية، والرصف المعماري، والمعدات الأمنية والأجهزة والاتصالات، ومعدات التخزين، والأنابيب. وذكرت السفارة البريطانية في بيان أصدرته أن بيل ماجينز رئيس مجلس إدارة شركة سبرين ميتال برودكتس يترأس هذه البعثة التي ستزور في وقت لاحق كلا من جدة والبحرين.

ARTICLE 12

to look for	بحث عن
delegation	بعثة
opportunity	فرصة *pl.* فرص
ratification	ابرام
juice	عصير
fabrics	قماش
paving slab	رصف
building *adj.*	معماری
appliance	جهاز *pl.* اجهزة
materials	معدات
later on	فی وقت لاحق

The Canadian Minister of trade to visit Saudi Arabia on the second of next month

Riyadh - *Abdul Aziz Hamdan*: The Canadian minister for international trade, Sergio Marchi, will begin an official two day visit to Saudi on the second of next month.

The minister, who will head a large delegation of Canadian businessmen, will discuss the options available to broaden and deepen commercial ties, the improvement of cooperation between the private sectors in both countries, in addition to discussing some specific proposals regarding cooperation in the fields of roads, communications and links.

Accompanying Marchi will be a delegation consisting of 35 businessmen representing 24 companies, most of which concentrate their activity in the fields of agriculture, foodstuffs, building, construction, education, energy, information technology, communication and links. This is in addition to there being representatives of eight government agencies and educational establishments within the accompanying delegation.

The Canadian ambassador to Saudi, Daniel Hobson, said that trade between the two countries in the past year had exceeded 1.4 billion Canadian dollars, 1.2 billion US dollars.

Increase in trade between India and Israel

New Delhi - *QNA*: The volume of trade between India and Israel rose to 670 million US dollars in 1998 compared with around 658 million dollars in 1997 and for the first time since the establishment of relations between the two countries in 1992, Indian exports to Israel reached 343 million dollars and posted a record growth rate of 17% compared with Israeli exports to India which reaches 327 million dollars in 1998. The growth sectors were concentrated in the chemical industries, 28%, textiles, 23% and diamonds, 22%. Israeli exports fell 10% to 327 million dollars as a result of the 25% fall in diamond exports, brought about by the Asian economic and financial crisis. More than 60 % of Israeli exports to India, which faced severe difficulties during the Asian crisis, were uncut diamonds.

Companies from Northern Ireland look for trade opportunities in Saudi

Riyadh - *Asharq al-Awsat*: A British delegation of eight companies from Northern Ireland will begin a visit today to Riyadh to seek opportunities to conclude trade contracts with Saudi businessmen in a number of sectors including juices and drinks, fabrics, electrical appliances, industrial machines, building paving, security appliances, communications systems, storage products and pipes. In a statement it issued, the British embassy said that Bill Madgings, chairman of the board of Sperrin Metal Products, would lead this delegation, which will later visit both Jiddah and Bahrain.

Exercises   Articles 7 - 12

Exercise 1   Choose the best answer

١   يصل الى لبنان وزير التجارة الفرنسى لبحث توقيع/تعليم/توسيع/تعاون التجارة الثنائية.

٢   ناقش رؤساء الوزراء نمو/جانب/اعداد/مستوى جدول اعمال.

٣   وزير التخطيط يترأس جدولا/وجودا/هدفا/وفدا كبيرا.

٤   بحث رجال الاعمال فرص اقتراض/ابرام/اطار/اعمال عقود تجارية.

٥   سيبحث الوفد الخيارات المتاحة لتوقيع/لتمويل/لتعميق/لتخطيط الروابط التجارية.

٦   قال السفير المغربى قبل مغادرته/سفارته/فرصته/بعثته لبيروت انه سيشارك فى الاجتماع.

٧   سيناقش الوزراء علاقة/تنمية/بعثة/طاقة التجارة بين البلدين.

٨   تعقد اجتماعات بهدف تطوير علاقات/خيارات/اتصالات/مواصلات التعاون بين البلدين.

٩   سيزور السفير الامريكى الصين فى المدة/المدينة/المادة/العدة من ٢٠ الى ٢٣ مارس.

١٠   يتركز نشاط الشركة فى المواصلات/المعدات/البيانات/المعلومات الغذائية.

١١   بحث السفراء بعض الخدمات/الازمات/الاقتراحات/المواصلات المحددة حول التعاون.

١٢   الصادرات الفرنسية واجهت مبادلات/متاعب/معدات/اتصالات شديدة اثناء الازمة الآسيوية.

Exercise 2   Match the following pairs

١	لاول	a	التعاون
٢	توسيع	b	الخاص
٣	القطاع	c	بعد
٤	تجارة	d	مرة
٥	فى ما	e	ثنائية

Exercise 3   Match the following pairs

١	فى وقت	a	حكومية
٢	اللجنة	b	الاقامة
٣	وكالات	c	لاحق
٤	منذ	d	للازمة
٥	نتيجة	e	العليا

Exercise 4 Match the following pairs

١	السعودية والمغرب يستهدفان	a	الاستثمار في إيران
٢	عُمان توقع اتفاقا لاقتراض	b	للتنمية بنهاية 98
٣	شركات أميركية تعتزم	c	350 مليون دولار
٤	انخفاض صادرات السعودية بنسبة	d	زيادة الاستثمارات عام 99
٥	المغرب يتوقع	e	توسيع التبادل التجاري بينهما
٦	34 مليار دولار تمويلات البنك الأفريقي	f	22 في المائة خلال سبتمبر الماضي

ARTICLE 13

مصر تقترب من توقيع اتفاقية الشراكة مع أوروبا

القاهرة - رويترز: قال السفير جمال بيومي مساعد وزير الخارجية المصري لشؤون المشاركة المصرية الاوروبية انه يتوقع ان تستكمل المفاوضات التي تأخرت كثيرا بشأن اتفاق المشاركة مع الاتحاد الاوروبي في الاسبوع القادم.

وقال بيومي رئيس وفد مصر في المحادثات مع الاتحاد الاوروبي للصحافيين انه سيتوجه الى بروكسل يوم الاحد القادم لوضع اللمسات النهائية على الاتفاق التجاري وخاصة في مجالي المحاصيل الزراعية ومنتجات الصناعات الغذائية. واضاف بيومي انه يتوقع ان يستكمل الاتفاق خلال الاجتماع الذي يعقد في شتوتجارت بالمانيا يومي 15 و16 ابريل (نيسان) القادم بمشاركة 27 وزير خارجية من الاتحاد الاوروبي ودول حوض البحر المتوسط التي وقعت أو تتفاوض على اتفاقات مشاركة مماثلة.

to get near to	اقترب من
partnership	مشاركة
to expect	توقع
negotiation	مفاوضة
to complete	استكمل
to be late	تأخر
finishing touches	لمسات نهائية
production	محاصيل *pl.* محصول
rim	حوض
Mediterranean	البحر المتوسط
to negotiate	تفاوض
similar	مماثل

ARTICLE 14

fertilisers	مخصبات
chemical	كيماوى
ready	جاهز
to grant	منح
cooperative	تعاونى
to undertake	تعهد

مشروع مخصبات كيماوية بين الهند وسلطنة عمان

● توقع مسؤول هندي بان يكون مشروع المخصبات الكيماوية بين الهند وسلطنة عمان جاهزا للعمل بحلول عام 2002. ونقلت وكالة (ق. ن. ا) عن «يوناتيد نيوز» الهندية قولها بان سرجيت سينج وزير الصناعات الكيماوية الهندية قوله في البرلمان الهندي امس ان الموافقة على المشروع منحت في شهر ديسمبر (كانون الاول) من العام الماضي الى شركتي «راشتريا» للكيماويات والمخصبات وشركة كريشاك بهاراتي التعاونية اللتين تتعهدان تنفيذه.

ARTICLE 15

شركتان كندية وتركية تقيمان مصنع لأكسيد المغنيسيوم في الأردن

عمان: «الشرق الأوسط»

جرى أمس في العاصمة الأردنية التوقيع على اتفاقية بين شركة مغنيسيا الأردن المساهمة العامة المحدودة وائتلاف شركتي اجرا مونينكو الكندية واتيلا دوچان التركية لانشاء مصنع اكسيد المغنيسيوم في منطقة النميرة على البحر الميت بالقرب من مجمع صناعات شركة البوتاس العربية بكلفة (80) مليون دولار اميركي.

وقدرت مصادر مطلعة في شركة مغنيسيا الأردن ان المدة الزمنية لاقامة المشروع قد تصل الى (22) شهرا بطاقة انتاجية تقدر بحوالي 50 ألف طن سنويا من مادة اكسيد المغنيسيوم عالي الجودة الذي يدخل في صناعة الطوب الحراري والمستخدم في تبطين افران صهر الحديد والزجاج وانتاج الاسمنت اضافة الى 10 الاف طن سنويا من مادة هيدروكسيد المغنيسيوم التي تدخل في انتاج المواد المساعدة على اطفاء الحرائق ومعالجة الوقود والمياه والعديد من الصناعات الكيماوية.

ويذكر ان الدراسات التي خصصت لاقامة هذا المشروع ضمن مجمع الصناعات الكيماوية لاستغلال الخامات المتوفرة في البحر الميت بدأت منذ عام 1990 حيث باشرت شركة البوتاس العربية العديد من الدراسات الفنية والاقتصادية والتي تضمنت انشاء مصنع تجريبي في عام 1994 لاختبار ملاءمة المواد الخام المتوفرة لانتاج اكسيد المغنيسيوم.

corporation	مساهمة
agreement, coalition	ائتلاف
group	مجامع *pl.* مجمع
cost	كلفة
informed	مطلع
goodness	جودة
thermal	حرارى
molten	صهر
glass	زجاج
extinguisher	اطفاء
fire	حرائق *pl.* حريق
fuel	وقود
experimental	تجريبى
suitability	ملاءمة
available	متوفر

Egypt close to signing a partnership agreement with Europe

Cairo - *Reuters*: Ambassador Jamal Bioumi, the assistant Egyptian foreign minister for Egypto-European cooperation, said that he expected that negotiations that had been seriously delayed over an agreement with the European Union would be completed in the coming week.

Bioumi, head of the Egyptian delegation in discussions with the European Union, told journalists that he was going to Brussels next Sunday to put the finishing touches to the trade agreement and specifically in the two fields of agricultural production and the produce of the food industries. He added that he expected that the agreement would be concluded during the meeting to be held in Stuttgart, Germany, on 15th and 16th April, with the participation of 27 foreign ministers from the European Union and countries of the Mediterranean basin which had signed or were negotiating similar agreements of cooperation.

Chemical fertiliser project between India and the Sultanate of Oman

An Indian official expected that the chemical fertiliser project between India and the Sultanate of Oman would enter production by the beginning of 2002. The QNA agency reported the Indian United News as saying that Srajit Singh, minister for Indian chemical industries, had said in the Indian parliament yesterday that approval for the project had been granted last December to two companies, Rashtria for chemicals and fertilisers and Krishak Biharati Cooperative, which have undertaken to implement the project.

Two Canadian and Turkish companies set up magnesium oxide factory in Jordan

Amman - *Asharq al-Awsat*: The agreement between the Jordanian Magnesia Company Limited and a consortium of two companies, the Canadian Agra Munico and the Turkish Atila Dougan, to build a magnesium oxide factory in the region of Alnamera on the Dead Sea near the industrial complex of the Arab Potassium Company at a cost of 80 million dollars was signed yesterday in the Jordanian capital.

Informed sources at Jordanian Magnesia estimated that it might take 22 months to complete the project, with an annual output of around 50 thousand tons of high quality magnesium oxide. This is used in the thermal brick industry and in lining ovens of molten iron, glass and cement production. Ten thousand tons a year of magnesium hydroxide will also be produced, used to make products that help in extinguishing fires and treating fuel and water and a number of chemical industries.

It is to be mentioned that the studies to set up this project in a chemical industries complex to exploit the raw materials available in the Dead Sea began in 1990 when the Arab Potassium Company carried out a number of technical and economic studies. These included building a pilot factory in 1994 to test the suitability of the raw materials available to produce magnesium oxide.

ARTICLE 16

ارتفاع صادرات إسرائيل من الماس المصقول

● قالت وزارة التجارة والصناعة ان صادرات اسرائيل الصافية من الماس المصقول زادت بنسبة 3,2 في المائة في يناير (كانون الثاني) مقارنة مع الشهر نفسه من العام الماضي الى 379 مليون دولار.
واضافت الوزارة ان هناك علامات على انتعاش متواضع لصناعة الماس التي عانت من هبوط حاد في المبيعات العام الماضي بسبب الازمة المالية الاسيوية.
وطبقا لرويترز فقد هبطت صادرات الماس المصقول الاسرائيلية بنسبة 11,4 في المائة الى 3,6 مليار دولار في عام 1998.
ورغم الانتعاش الذي حدث في يناير الا ان مسؤولا كبيرا بالوزارة قال ان الاشهر القليلة المقبلة هي التي ستوضح هل تجاوزت صناعة الماس اسوأ مراحل الازمة.
والولايات المتحدة هي السوق الرئيسية لصادرات الماس الاسرائيلية، اذ تلقت 61 في المائة من اجمالي الصادرات العام الماضي.

polished, cut	مصقول
net	صافي
sign	علامة
revival	انتعاش
slight	متواضع
to suffer	عانى
fall	هبوط
sales	مبيع *pl.* ات
to exceed	تجاوز

ARTICLE 17

تراجع واردات دبي من الذهب

● أعلنت دائرة جمارك دبي في بيان أصدرته امس ان واردات دبي من الذهب تراجعت الى 377,4 طن عام 1998 من مستوى قياسي بلغ 660,3 طن قبل عام. ونقلت «رويترز» أن سويسرا صدرت 234 طنا من المعدن النفيس الى دبي تلتها جنوب أفريقيا 52,5 طن وبريطانيا 39,3 طن، وجاءت باقي كمية الواردات من كوريا الجنوبية وروسيا.

gold	ذهب
falling back	تراجع
department	دائرة
customs	جمرك *pl.* جمارك
record *adj.*	قياسي
metal	معدن
precious	نفيس
to follow	تلا
remainder	باقي

ARTICLE 18

مباحثات بين وزيري نفط السعودية وإيران في الرياض

دبي - رويترز: قال مصدر في صناعة النفط السعودية ان وزير النفط الايراني بيجان زانجانة عقد مباحثات مع نظيره السعودي علي النعيمي في الرياض امس. ووصل الوزير الايراني الى الرياض امس لبحث مسائل عالقة حول الحصص والتقيد بها من قبل الاعضاء.

ومن المتوقع ان يناقش الوزيران سبل التقريب بين وجهات نظرهما بشأن انقاذ اسعار النفط العالمية في احدث اجتماع بين الدولتين اللتين تتمتعان بثقل كبير في اوبك. وقال المصدر ان زانجانة سيصحبه الى السعودية مستشارون كبار في سياسة ايران في اوبك. وسئل المصدر هل سيعقد زانجانة محادثات مع النعيمي فقال «نعم». وقد توترت العلاقات بين ايران والسعودية بسبب الخلاف في مقدار النفط الذي يجب ان تخفضه ايران من انتاجها عملا باتفاق توصلت اليه اوبك للحد من المعروض النفطي من اجل دعم الاسعار. وتأتي مباحثات زانجانة والنعيمي قبل اجتماع وزاري مهم لاوبك في فيينا في 23 من مارس (آذار).

oil	نفط
observance	تقيد
member	عضو *pl.* أعضاء
point of view	وجهة النظر
preserving	انقاذ
to enjoy	تمتع ب
influence	ثقل
to be strained	توتر
disagreement	خلاف
according to	عملا ب
supply	معروض

Increase of Israeli exports of cut diamonds

The ministry of trade and industry said that Israeli net exports of cut diamonds had risen by 3.2% in January, compared with the same month last year to 379 million dollars. The ministry added that there were signs of a slight upturn in the diamond industry that had suffered a sharp drop in sales last year because of the Asian financial crisis.

According to Reuters, Israeli exports of cut diamonds fell by 11.4% to 3.6 billion dollars in 1998. In spite of the recovery that occurred in January, a high-ranking ministry official said that the next few months would show whether the diamond market had got through the worst stages of the crisis. The United States is the main market for Israeli diamond exports, taking 61% of all exports last year.

Fall in gold imports to Dubai

In a statement issued yesterday, the Dubai customs department announced that the country's gold imports had fallen back to 377.4 tons in 1998 from a record level of 660.3 tons the year before. Reuters reported that Switzerland had exported 234 tons of the precious metal to Dubai, followed by South Africa with 52.5 tons, and Britain with 39.3 tons. The remainder of the imports came from South Korea and Russia.

Discussions between the Saudi and Iranian oil ministers in Riyadh

Dubai - *Reuters*: A source in the Saudi oil industry said that the Iranian oil minister, Bijan Zangeneh, held discussions with his Saudi counterpart, Ali al-Naeemi, in Riyadh yesterday. The Iranian minister arrived in Riyadh yesterday to discuss related questions concerning the quotas and their observance by members.

The two ministers are expected to discuss ways of harmonising their positions on ways to maintain world oil prices in the latest meetings between the two countries, which enjoy great influence in OPEC. The source said that Zangeneh would be accompanied to Saudi by senior advisers on Iran's policy in OPEC. When asked whether Zangeneh would be holding discussions with al-Naeemi, the source confirmed this. Relations between Iran and Saudi have become strained over the dispute about how much Iran has to lower its oil production in line with the agreement OPEC reached to limit the supply of oil in order to support prices. The discussions between Zangeneh and al-Naeemi come ahead of an important ministerial meeting of OPEC in Vienna on 23rd March.

Exercises Articles 13 - 18

Exercise 1 Choose the best answer

١ يستكمل الاتفاق/الاطفاء/السماد/المجمع خلال الاجتماع المقبل.
٢ جرى التوقيع على اتفاقية لاطفاء/لانتعاش/لانجاز/لانشاء مصنع جديد.
٣ يناقش الوزيران سبل/ثقل/معروض/خلاف التقريب بين وجهات نظرهما.
٤ صادرات من البترول زادت ٢ فى المائة مراقبة/معالجة/مقارنة/علاقة مع فبراير.
٥ هذه المادة تدخل فى انتاج المواد المساعدة على انشاء/اطفاء/انقاذ/ابرام الحرائق.
٦ هناك واردات/مبيعات/علامات/اتصالات على انتعاش متواضع لصناعة الماس.
٧ عقد وزير النفط الايرانى خيارات/مباحثات/مبيعات/مخصصات مع نظيره السعودى.
٨ وضع رئيس الوزراء اللمسات/المبيعات/المواصلات/المبادلات النهائية على الاتفاق التجارى.
٩ سيكون مشروع المواصلات/المعلومات/الخيارات/المخصصات الكيماوية جاهزا بحلول ٢٠٠٢.
١٠ توترت العلاقات بين البلدين بسبب التبادل/الوجود/الخلاف/المعروض فى مقدار النفط.

Exercise 2 Match the following pairs

١	البحر	a	حاد
٢	هبوط	b	كبار
٣	الماس	c	مطلعة
٤	مستشارون	d	جمارك
٥	دائرة	e	الميت
٦	مصادر	f	المصقول

Exercise 3 Complete the following with a suitable word or phrase as in no.1

١	بسبب الازمة الاقتصادية	٢	منذ ______________
٣	رغم ______________	٤	بشأن ______________
٥	______________ فى المائة	٦	طبقا ______________
٧	فى ظل ______________	٨	فضلا عن ______________
٩	بفضل ______________	١٠	خلال ______________
١١	مقابل ______________	١٢	نتيجة ______________
١٣	مقارنة ______________	١٤	بحلول ______________

Exercise 4 Put the following words into the gaps

كمية

دائرة

تراجع

واردات

المعدن

مستوى

___ واردات دبي
من الذهب

● أعلنت ___ جمارك دبي في
بيان أصدرته امس ان ___
دبي من الذهب تراجعت الى
377,4 طن عام 1998 من
___ قياسي بلغ 660,3 طن
قبل عام. ونقلت «رويترز» أن
سويسرا صدرت 234 طنا من
___ النفيس الى دبي تلتها
جنوب أفريقيا 52,5 طن
وبريطانيا 39,3 طن، وجاءت
باقي ___ الواردات من كوريا
الجنوبية وروسيا.

Exercise 5 Put these verbs into the following headlines

يبحث يتوقع يزور

١ **وزير الطاقة الأردني ___ بغداد الأربعاء المقبل**
لبحث تجديد الاتفاقية النفطية

٢ **وزير التجارة الإيرلندي ___ في الرياض**
سبل تنمية التجارة مع السعودية

٣ **المكتب المغربي لاستغلال**
الموانئ ___ استثمار أكثر
من ملياري درهم عام 2000

ARTICLE 19

to cancel	الغى
import	استيراد *pl.* ات
supplier	مورد
to drop	انخفض
refinery	مصفاة *pl.* مصافى
extension	توسع
to compensate for	عوض
gap	فرق *pl.* فروق
to continue	تابع
message	خطاب
purchases	مشتريات
capacity	طاقة
present	حالى

الهند تلغي تعاقدات لاستيراد نفط من الشرق الأوسط

نيودلهي - رويترز: قال مسؤول كبير بالحكومة الهندية امس ان الهند ألغت عقودا حكومية لاستيراد زيت ديزل مع عدد من الموردين الرئيسيين في الشرق الاوسط.

وتتوقع الهند ان ينخفض الطلب على الواردات منه بنسبة 73 في المائة في السنة المالية 2000/1999 الى ثلاثة ملايين طن من أكثر من 11 مليون طن في السنة المالية التي تنتهي في مارس (اذار).

وقال مسؤولون حكوميون ان المصافي الجديدة والتوسع في المصافي الموجودة سيعوض الفرق.

وتابع المسؤول ان الهند لن تجدد عقودها مع الكويت وامارة ابوظبي والبحرين.

وصرح المسؤول الذي طلب عدم ذكر اسمه لرويترز «اصدرت شركة النفط الهندية خطابات للشركات الوطنية بانها لن تجدد عقود الديزل السنوية الا ان تلك الخاصة بالكيروسين مستمرة».

وتابع ان لجنة المشتريات اتخذت قرارا عدم تجديد العقود يوم الجمعة الماضي.

وجاء في تقرير حكومي حصلت علية رويترز ان الهند تتوقع رفع انتاج مصافيها الى 110,45 مليون طن (2,26 مليون برميل يوميا) بزيادة 48,9 مليون طن (مليون برميل يوميا) عن الطاقة الحالية.

ARTICLE 20

contraction	انكماش
product	ناتج
domestic	محلى
island	جزيرة *pl.* جزائر
speech	كلمة
firmness	ثبات
contrast	تناقض

انكماش الناتج المحلي في هونغ كونغ

هونغ كونغ - واس: ذكر وزير المالية في هونغ كونغ دونالد تسانج في حديث صحافي ان اجمالي الناتج المحلي في الجزيرة انكمش بنسبة 5,1 في المائة في عام 1998 مقابل الفترة ذاتها من العام الماضي، والقى وزير مالية هونغ كونغ كلمة امام البرلمان بشأن ميزانية السنة المالية 2000/1999 قال فيها: ان اجمالي الناتج المحلي في عام 1998 انخفض بنسبة 5,1 في المائة مع ثبات الاسعار، واشارت مصادر صحافية اقتصادية الى ان هذا يمثل تناقضا حادا مع نمو بنسبة 5,3 في المائة في عام 1997.

ARTICLE 21

quantity	مقدار
quarter	ربع
based on	بالاستناد الى
factor	عامل *pl.* عوامل
seasonal	موسمى
consideration	تقدير *pl.* ات
economist	اقتصادى
account	حسبة *pl.* ات
statistics	احصائية
to publish	نشر
federal	اتحادى

انكماش الناتج المحلي الألماني 0.4 في المائة

فرانكفورت - رويترز: انكمش اجمالي الناتج المحلي في المانيا بمقدار 0,4 في المائة في الربع الاخير من العام الماضي مقارنة بالربع الثالث بالاستناد الى بيانات معدلة وفق العوامل الموسمية، وأكدت هذه البيانات تقديرات اقتصاديين ذكروا ان اكبر اقتصاد في اوروبا انكمش في نهاية العام السابق عندما بدأت الازمات المالية في آسيا وروسيا تخفض نمو الصادرات.

ووفقا لحسابات «البوندسبنك» التي تستند جزئيا الى تقديرات فان اجمالي الناتج المحلي انكمش الى 797,1 مليار مارك في الربع الاخير من عام 1998 من 800,7 مليار مارك في الربع الثالث بالاستناد الى أسعار عام 1991، وقال «البوندسبنك» ان اجمالي الناتج المحلي في غرب المانيا انكمش بنسبة 0,6 في المائة في حين انكمش اجمالي الناتج المحلي في شرق المانيا بنسبة 0,9 في المائة، ومن المقرر ان ينشر مكتب الاحصائيات الاتحادية بيانات اجمالي الناتج المحلي للربع الاخير من عام 1998 في الرابع من مارس (آذار) المقبل.

India cancels contracts to import oil from the Middle East

New Delhi - *Reuters*: A senior official in the Indian government said yesterday that India had cancelled government contracts to import diesel oil with a number of the main suppliers in the Middle East.

India expects demand for imports of diesel to drop 73% in the financial year 1999/2000 to three million tons from more than 11 million tons in the financial year ending in March. Government officials said that the new refineries and expansion in the existing refineries would make up the difference.

The official went to say that India would not be renewing her contracts with Kuwait, the Emirate of Abu Dhabi and Bahrain. The official, who wished to remain anonymous, told Reuters: "The Indian Oil Company has issued statements to the national companies that it will not be renewing annual diesel contracts but that the contracts specifically for kerosene would be continuing." He went on to say that the purchasing committee had taken a decision not to renew the contracts last Friday.

A government report obtained by Reuters said that India was expecting an increase in the production of its refineries to 110.45 million tons, 2.26 million barrels a day, an increase of 48.9 million tons a day, from its present capacity.

Fall in Hong Kong GDP

Hong Kong - *WAS*: At a press conference the Hong Kong financial secretary, Donald Tsang, said that the island's gross domestic product had fallen by 5.1% in 1998 compared with the same period of last year. The Hong Kong financial secretary delivered a speech to parliament on the budget for the financial year 1999/2000 in which he said that GDP in 1998 had fallen by 5.1% at constant prices. Financial press sources pointed out that this represented a sharp contrast with a growth rate of 5.3% in 1997.

0.4% fall in German GDP

Frankfurt - *Reuters*: German GDP fell 0.4 % in the final quarter of last year compared with the third quarter on seasonally adjusted figures. These figures confirmed economists' estimates that the largest economy in Europe had contracted at the end of the previous year when the financial crises began in Asia and Russia and the growth in exports fell.

According to the figures of the Bundesbank, which are partly based on estimates, the GDP fell to 797.1 billion marks in the final quarter of 1998 from 800.7 billion marks in the third quarter, based on 1991 prices. The Bundesbank said that GDP in western Germany fell by 0.6%, while that in eastern Germany fell 0.9%. The federal statistics office is scheduled to publish figures for the GDP of the final quarter of 1998 on 4th March.

ARTICLE 22

deficit	عجز
to jump	قفز
analyst	محلل *pl.* ون
stock market	بورصة
recorded	مسجل
commodity, goods	سلعة *pl.* سلع
flourishing	ازدهار

ارتفاع العجز التجاري الأميركي إلى مستوى قياسي عام 98

واشنطن - رويترز: ذكرت وزارة التجارة الاميركية امس ان العجز التجاري الاميركي قفز الى مستوى قياسي بلغ 168,59 مليار دولار في العام الماضي بسبب زيادة الواردات وانخفاض الصادرات، وجاءت هذه الزيادة رغم تراجع العجز على نحو غير متوقع في ديسمبر (كانون الاول) الى 13,79 مليار دولار من الرقم المعدل لشهر نوفمبر (تشرين الثاني) عند 15,26 مليار دولار. وكان محللون في بورصة وول ستريت يتوقعون عجزا اكبر بكثير يصل الى 15,8 مليار دولار في ديسمبر بعد العجز المسجل في الشهر السابق في تجارة السلع والخدمات والذي ذكرت تقارير سابقة انه بلغ في الاصل 15,49 مليار دولار.

لكن العجز التجاري القياسي في عام 1998 الذي ارتفع بنسبة 53 في المائة عن عام 1997 عندما بلغ 110,21 مليار دولار كان متوقعا مع ازدهار الاقتصاد الاميركي.

ARTICLE 23

to make clear	اوضح
bank *adj.*	مصرفي
peak	قمة
to attribute to	عزا الى
slowdown	تباطوء
restraint	تقشف
expectation	ترقب
to dominate	ساد
developments	تطورات
capital	راس مال
coming into	وافد الى

تراجع النمو للاقتصاد اللبناني عام 98

بيروت - واس: تراجع النمو الاقتصادي في لبنان خلال العام 1998بنسبة 1,5 في المائة عنه في عام 1997، وأوضح تقرير مصرفي لبناني نشر في بيروت امس أن نسبة النمو الاقتصادي في العام 1998 قد تكون دون 2 في المائة بالمقارنة مع 3,5 في المائة في العام 1997 مشيرا الى أن قمة الناتج المحلي الاجمالي قد وصلت الى حوالي خمسة عشرة مليارا وسبعمائة مليون دولار اميركي في العام الماضي، وعزا اسباب التباطؤ في نمو الاقتصاد الى سياسة التقشف في القطاع العام والى حال الترقب التي سادت في القطاع الخاص بسبب التطورات السياسية الاخيرة في لبنان، وذكر أن نسبة التراجع في حركة الرساميل الوافدة الى لبنان قد بلغت في العام 1998 نحو 18 في المائة بحيث بقيت هذه النسبة دون المتوسط العالمي لتراجع حركة الرساميل والذي بلغ 35 في المائة بسبب ازمة الاسواق العالمية وبخاصة في اسيا وروسيا التي حدثت اخيرا.

ARTICLE 24

retail trade	تجزئة
wave	موجة
interest	اقبال
to take on	اكتسب
strength, force	قوة *pl.* ات ، قوى
pushing	دافع

نمو قوي لمبيعات التجزئة الأميركية

واشنطن - رويترز: قالت وزارة التجارة الاميركية امس الخميس ان مبيعات تجارة التجزئة الاميركية في شهر فبراير (شباط) قفزت بعد نتائج أقوى في يناير (كانون الثاني) عما كان متوقعا من قبل لان موجة الاقبال على الانفاق اكتسبت قوة دافعة.

وزاد اجمالي مبيعات التجزئة 0,9 في المائة الى مستوى معدل موسمياً بلغ 236,47 مليار دولار بعد قفزة بلغت واحدا في المائة في يناير اشارت تقارير سابقة الى انها ستبلغ فقط 0,2 في المائة.

Rise in the US trade deficit to a record level in 98

Washington - *Reuters*: The US trade ministry said that the US trade deficit had jumped last year to a record level of 168.59 billion dollars because of the increase in imports and the fall in exports. This increase came despite an unexpected fall in the deficit to 13.79 billion dollars in December from the November figure of 15.26 billion dollars. Wall Street analysts were expecting a much larger deficit of 15.8 billion dollars in December after the deficit recorded in the previous month in goods and services which previous reports had said had originally reached 15.49 billion dollars.

But the record deficit in 1998, up 53% from 110.21 billion dollars in 1997, was expected with the boom in the US economy.

Lebanon's economic growth drops back in 98

Beirut - *WAS*: Economic growth in Lebanon in 1998 fell 1.5% compared to 1997. A Lebanese bank report published in Beirut yesterday indicated that the rate of growth in 1998 might be under 2% compared with 3.5% in 1997, pointing out that GDP had peaked at around fifteen billion seven hundred million US dollars last year. It attributed the reasons for the slowdown in economic growth to the policy of restraint in the public sector and to the wait and see policy that had prevailed in the private sector because of the recent political developments in Lebanon. The report said that the flow of capital into Lebanon had fallen around 18% in 1998. This figure remained below the world average for the drop in capital movements, which reached 35% because of the recent crisis in the world markets, particularly in Asia and Russia.

Strong growth in US retail sales

Washington - *Reuters*: The US trade ministry said yesterday, Thursday, that US retail trade sales in February had jumped after stronger than expected results in January because of the wave of interest in spending had gained momentum. Total retail sales rose 0.9 per cent to an average seasonal level of 236.47 billion dollars, after a one per cent jump in January that previous reports had indicated would reach only 0.2 per cent.

Exercises Articles 19 - 24

Exercise 1 Choose the best answer

١ العجز القياسى فى عام ١٩٩٨ كان متوقعا مع ازدهار الاتحاد/الاتفاق/الاقتصاد/الانتعاش الامريكى.

٢ عزا محللون اسبابا العدم/الانقاذ/التباطؤ /التوسيع فى نمو الاقتصاد الى سياسة التقشف فى القطاع الخاص.

٣ زاد اجمالى تطورات/مبيعات/احصائيات/علامات التجزئية ١ فى المائة.

٤ الغت الهند هبوطا/ربطا/عقدا/انبوبا لاستيراد زيت ديزل.

٥ الشركة تتوقع رفع/انكماش/انخفاض/عجز انتاج مصافيها الى ١٠٠ من ٨٠ مليون طن.

٦ قفز الطلب/المعروض/الرقم/العجز التجارى الى مستوى قياسى.

٧ نسبة/خدمة/زيادة/قيمة النمو الاقتصادى كانت دون ٢ فى المائة.

٨ العجز التجارى قفز بسبب زيادة الواردات/الصادرات/التطورات/الاحصائيات.

٩ وفقا لمشتريات/لبورصات/لحسابات/لمبيعات البـنـك الدولى فان اجمالى الناتج المحلى انكمش الى ٨٠ مليون دولار.

١٠ القى وزير مالية لجنة/كلمة/محادثة/مرحلة امام البرلمان.

Exercise 2 Match the following pairs

١	واحد	a	متوقع
٢	العجز	b	المالية
٣	غير	c	التجارى
٤	وفقا	d	فى المائة
٥	السنة	e	لحسابات

Exercise 3 Choose the appropriate verb

١ الهند اعزت/الغت/انخفضت/اشارت عقودا.

٢ استغرقت/استكملت/استضافت/استطاعت الزيارة يومين.

٣ عزا/ذكر/جاء/اوضح اسباب التباطؤ الى سياسة التقشف.

٤ اجمالى الناتج المحلى انكمش/بلغ/وصل/توتر.

٥ العجز التجارى بلغ/عزا/قفز/نشر الى مستوى قياسى.

Exercise 4   Match the following pairs

١	التوقيع على اتفاقية منحة أميركية	a	عقد محطتي كهرباء
٢	ارتفاع الأسعار فى الأردن	b	لمشروعات القطاع الخاص
٣	الجزائر تمنح «شنايدر إلكتريك»	c	بنسبة 1,6٪ خلال العام الحالي
٤	بنك الاستثمار الأوروبي	d	لدعم قطاع الاتصالات في الأردن
٥	مصر تبحث إمكانية تمويل البنك الإسلامي	e	يقرض تونس 195 مليون يورو

Exercise 5   Match the following pairs

١	تراجع أسعار النفط وسط عدم	a	العامة لعام 2002
٢	البرلمان التركي يقر الميزانية	b	وقوداً للإصلاح الاقتصادي
٣	اليابان والصين	c	الاتفاق على خفض الإنتاج
٤	السعودية ترى في ثروة الغاز	d	للطلب العالمي للنفط في 2002.2001
٥	وكالة الطاقة الدولية لم تغير توقعاتها	e	تناقشان خلافا تجاريا غدا

ARTICLE 25

تباطؤ نمو الاقتصاد السويسري في الربع الأخير من 1998

لندن: «الشرق الاوسط»

تباطأ نمو اقتصاد سويسرا خلال الربع الاخير من العام الماضي في حين توقعت شركات صناعية سويسرية بقاء النشاط الاقتصادي راكدا في المدى القصير، وذلك طبقا للمعهد الفدرالي للتكنولوجيا في سويسرا.

وجاء في مسح للمعهد ان الانتاج الصناعي لم يشهد نموا في الربع الاخير من العام الماضي عن مستواه في الربعين الثاني والثالث في حين ترى الشركات ان الطلبيات على منتجاتها ليست بالمستوى المطلوب.

وقال المعهد ان تحليله للاقتصاد السويسري اعتمد على مسح اجراه لخمسة الاف شركة تعمل في مجالات الصناعة والبناء والهندسة وتجارة التجزئة والجملة والسفر.

continuation	بقاء
sluggish	راكد
short term	مدى قصير
institute	معهد *pl.* معاهد
survey	مسح
to witness	شهد
order	طلبية
desired	مطلوب
analysis	تحليل
to rely on	اعتمد على
wholesale	جملة

ARTICLE 26

انخفاض البطالة في منطقة اليورو الاوروبي في يناير

● أظهرت بيانات نشرها اليوم معهد الاحصاء الاوروبي (يوروستات) ان معدل البطالة في منطقة اليورو الاوروبي انخفض الى 10,6 في المائة في يناير (كانون الثاني) الماضي من 10,7 في المائة في ديسمبر (كانون الاول).

ونقلت رويترز عن المعهد قوله في بيانات بثها على موقعه على شبكة الانترنت ان معدل البطالة في الدول الاحدى عشرة التي تمثل أعضاء منطقة اليورو قد انخفض الى 10,6 في المائة. أما معدل البطالة في دول الاتحاد الاوروبي الخمس عشرة فقد بلغ 9,6 في المائة في يناير. وسجلت أسبانيا أعلى معدل في دول اليورو حيث بلغ معدل البطالة فيها 17,8 في المائة وسجلت لوكسمبورج أدنى معدل بنسبة 2,8 في المائة.

وبلغت البطالة في ألمانيا 9,1 في المائة وفي فرنسا 11,6 في المائة.

unemployment	بطالة
to transmit	بث
website	موقع شبكة
lowest	أدنى

ARTICLE 27

انخفاض قياسي في سعر الكاكاو

لندن ـ رويترز: قال متعاملون امس ان أسعار الكاكاو في بورصة لندن للتعاملات الآجلة هبطت الى مستويات قياسية جديدة خلال الاسابيع الاخيرة بسبب ضعف العوامل الفنية.

وقال محللون ان توقعات زيادة المعروض مع الارتفاع المنتظر في انتاج ساحل العاج في منتصف موسم الزراعة الذي بدأ فى مايو (أيار) 1998 وينتهي في يونيو (حزيران) 1999 ربما تدفع المستهلكين الى الاحجام عن الشراء انتظارا لاسعار أقل.

وسجلت التعاقدات الآجلة انخفاضات قياسية امس في حجم تعاملات ضعيف وتراجعت تعاقدات مارس (آذار) جنيهين استرلينيين عن ادنى سعر للتعاقد السابق الى 885 جنيها استرلينيا للطن في المعاملات المبكرة.

وهذا هو أدنى مستوى لتعاقدات مارس. وهبطت تعاقدات مايو (أيار) ثمانية جنيهات استرلينية عن السعر السابق الى 887 جنيها للطن. وقال محلل بشركة سمسرة ان الهبوط عن سعر 845 جنيها استرلينيا للطن سيمهد الطريق من الناحية الفنية للنزول الى 509 جنيها وهو أدنى مستوى للسعر وسجل في 1992.

trader, dealer	متعامل
future	الاجلة
technical	فنى
weakness	ضعف
coast	ساحل
ivory	عاج
consumer	مستهلك
abstention from	احجام عن
contract	تعاقد *pl.* ات
trading	معاملات
early	مبكر
brokerage	سمسرة
to pave the way	مهد الطريق
side	ناحية *pl.* نواح
fall	نزول

Slowdown in growth of the Swiss economy in the final quarter of 1998

London - *Asharq al-Awsat*: Growth in the Swiss economy slowed down during the final quarter of last year, as Swiss manufacturing companies expected economic activity to remain sluggish in the short term, according to the Federal Institute for Technology in Switzerland.

According to a survey by the institute, industrial production did nor show any growth in the final quarter of last year from its level of the second and third quarters, at a time when companies saw that orders for their products were not at the desired level.

The institute said that its analysis of the Swiss economy was based on a survey it had carried out of five thousand companies operating in the sectors of industry, construction, engineering, retail and wholesale trade and travel.

Fall in unemployment in the euro region in January

Figures published today by the European Institute of Statistics, Eurostat, showed that the unemployment rate in the euro region had dropped to 10.6% in January from 10.7% in December.

Reuters reported the institute as saying in reports it had put on its internet website that the unemployment rate in the eleven countries that are members of euroland had fallen to 10.6%. The unemployment rate in the fifteen countries of the European Union was 9.6% in January. Spain recorded the highest level of unemployment in the euro countries with 17.8% and Luxembourg recorded the lowest level with 2.8%.

Unemployment in Germany reached 9.1% and 11.6% in France.

Record fall in the price of cocoa

London - *Reuters*: Dealers yesterday said that cocoa prices on the London futures trading market had fallen to new record levels over recent weeks because of negative technical factors.

Analysts said that expectations of an increase in supply with the anticipated rise in the production of the Ivory coast in the middle of the farming season, which began in May 1998 and ends in June 1999, would probably encourage consumers not to buy in anticipation of lower prices.

Futures contracts showed a record fall yesterday in thin trading and March contracts dropped two pounds from the previous lowest contract price to 885 pounds a ton in early trading. This is the lowest level for March contracts. May contracts fell eight pounds from the previous price to 887 pounds per ton. An analyst for a firm of brokers said that the fall from 845 pounds per ton would pave the way from a technical standpoint for a drop to 509 pounds, the lowest price level, recorded in 1992.

ARTICLE 28

broker	سمسار pl. سماسرة
share	سحم pl. أسهم
to rise	صعد
index	مؤشر
point	نقطة pl. نقط
resolve	اعتزام
percentage	مئوى

ارتفاع البورصة التونسية بعد تخفيض أسعار الفائدة

● ذكر سماسرة ان الاسهم التونسية ارتفعت امس وقفز حجم المعاملات بعد اعلان الحكومة تخفيض أسعار الفائدة. وطبقا لوكالة رويترز فقد صعد مؤشر تونيندكس 0,35 في المائة الى 1023,71 نقطة ومؤشر بي.ڤي.ام.تي 0,41. في المائة الى 519,02 نقطة.

ومع اعلان الحكومة اعتزامها تخفيض سعر الفائدة في سوق النقد نقطة مئوية واحدة من 6,875 في المائة ارتفع حجم التعاملات الى 2,7 مليون دينار (2,39 مليون دولار) مقارنة مع 0,9 مليون دينار متوسط حجم التعاملات اليومي خلال 1998 ومقابل 1,443 مليون دينار في معاملات أول من امس.

الأسهم الأردنية تنخفض في معاملات هادئة

● تراجعت اسعار الاسهم الاردنية امس في معاملات محلية هادئة تركزت على عدد من الاسهم الصناعية الممتازة. وهبط مؤشر سوق عمان المالي حسب «رويترز» المكون من 60 سهما بنسبة 0,46 في المائة الى 182,28 نقطة بسبب الخسائر التي تعرضت لها اسهم البنوك.

ولم تتعد قيمة الاسهم التي تم تداولها 500 الف دينار (700 الف دولار) وهو من ادنى المستويات منذ عدة اسابيع. وتركز النشاط المحدود على عدد من اسهم الشركات الصناعية التي اغلقت ايضا على انخفاض. وهبط سهم دار الدواء 0,01 دينار الى 6,14 دينار في معاملات قيمتها 92 الف دينار. وكان السهم نشطا طوال الاسبوع بفضل شائعات بانه سيتم توزيع عائد للسهم قدره 0,35 دينار وربما تقسيم الاسهم عندما تعقد الشركة جمعيتها العمومية السنوية. وشهد سهما مصانع الاسمنت الاردنية ومناجم الفوسفات الاردنية نشاطا محليا لكنهما هبطا قليلا الى 3,73 دينار و2,32 دينار بالترتيب.

لكن سهم العربية للبوتاس ارتفع 0,04 دينار الى 4,04 دينار في معاملات هادئة للغاية قيمتها 12 الف دينار مما ساعد في تعويض الخسائر ودفع مؤشر اسهم الشركات الصناعية الى الارتفاع.

ARTICLE 29

quiet	هادىء
outstanding	ممتاز
according to	حسب
loss	خسارة pl. خسائر
to be faced with	تعرض ب
alternation, trading	تداول
a number of	عدة
all through	طوال
dividend	عائد
rumour	شائعة
distribution	توزيع
splitting	تقسيم
meeting	جمعية
general	عمومى
mine	منجم pl. مناجم
extremely	للغاية
compensation	تعويض

ARTICLE 30

profit	ربح pl. أرباح
to announce	افاد
audited	مدقق
total	مجمل
operation	تشغيل
to fall	نزل
costs	مصروفات
shareholdings	حقوق الاسهم
shareholder	مساهم pl. ون

نزول أرباح شركة إسمنت الشرقية السعودية عام 1998

● هبطت ارباح شركة اسمنت المنطقة الشرقية في المملكة العربية السعودية خلال عام 1998 الى 186 مليون ريال من 201 مليون ريال، حسبما افادت رويترز امس.

وقالت الشركة امس في بيانات غير مدققة ان مجمل ربح التشغيل خلال العام الماضي نزل الى 196 مليون ريال من 211 مليون ريال. ولم تتغير تقريبا المصروفات البالغة 21 مليون ريال.

وبلغت حقوق المساهمين في نهاية عام 1998 حوالي 1,242 مليار ريال مقابل 1,251 مليار ريال. والشركة احدى ثمان شركات اسمنت عاملة في السعودية.

Tunis stock market rises after lowering of interest rates

Brokers announced that Tunisian shares had risen yesterday and the turnover in trading had jumped after the government announced the lowering of interest rates. According to Reuters the Tunindax index rose 0.35% to 1023.71 points and the BPMT index 0.41% per cent to 519.02 points.

With the government announcement of its decision to reduce the interest rate in the money market one percentage point from 6.875 per cent, the turnover in trading rose to 2.7 million dinars (2.39 million dollars) compared with 0.9 million dinars, the average for daily trading during 1998, and compared with 1.443 million dinars in trading the day before yesterday.

Jordanian shares fall in thin trading

Jordanian share prices fell back yesterday in quiet local trading that concentrated on a number of blue chip industrial shares. According to Reuters, the Amman 60 share index fell 0.46% to 182.28 points because of losses faced by bank shares.

With a turnover of 500 thousand dinars, 700 thousand dollars, the value of the shares did not increase, one of the lowest levels for a number of weeks. The limited activity concentrated on a number of shares of industrial companies which also closed down. The price of Dar Aldowa fell 0.01 dinars to 6.14 dinars in trading of 92 thousand dinars. The share was active throughout the week because of rumours that there would be payment of a dividend of 0.35 dinars and perhaps a dividing of shares when the company held its annual general meeting. Shares in Jordanian Cement Factories and Jordanian Phosphate Mines experienced local activity but they fell slightly to 3.73 dinars and 2.32 dinars respectively.

However the price of Arab Potassium rose 0.04 dinars to 4.04 dinars in very quiet trading of 12 thousand dinars, thereby helping to make up for the losses and to push up the industrial share index.

Fall in profits of the Saudi Eastern Cement Company in 1998

Profits of the cement company for the eastern province in the Kingdom of Saudi Arabia in 1998 fell to 186 million riyals from 201 million riyals, according to a Reuters announcement yesterday.

In unaudited accounts the company said yesterday that the total operating profits fell last year from 211 million riyals to 196 million riyals, with expenditure of 21 million riyals hardly changing.

Shareholdings at the end of 1998 totalled around 1.242 billion riyals, compared with 1.251 billion riyals in 1997. The company is one of eight cement companies operating in Saudi Arabia.

Exercises Articles 25 - 30

Exercise 1 Choose the best answer

١ سيتباطؤ نمو الاقتصاد الفرنسى فى المدى/الاداء/الانماء/العدد القصير.
٢ تنفيذ/تمويل/تحسين/تحليل الاقتصاد الامريكى اعتمد على مسح اجراه المعهد الفدرالى للتكنولوجيا.
٣ الارتفاع فى انتاج الكاكاو تدفع المستهلكين الى الاعلان/الاحجام/الاقبال/الاتفاق عن الشراء.
٤ الطلبات/الاحصائيات/التطورات/العلاقات على منتجات صناعية ليست بالمستوى المطلوب.
٥ هبطت اسهم/ارباح/فرص/جمارك شركة اسمنت الاردنية الى ٢٠ مليون دينار.
٦ هذا ساعد فى تحسين/تخطيط/تطوير/تعويض الخسائر ودفع مؤشر الاسهم الى الارتفاع.
٧ تركز النشاط/المؤشر/النقد/الساعد المحدود على عدد من اسهم الشركات الصناعية.
٨ تراجعت صادرات/طالبيات/تعاملات/تعاقدات مارس جنيهين استرلينية.
٩ ارتفعت الاسهم بعد اعلان تخفيض اسعار/انتاج/اشغال/انجاز الفائدة.
١٠ معدل النقطة/البطالة/الموجة/القمة انخفض الى ١٠ فى المائة.
١١ اعتزمت الحكومة على تخفيض سعر الفائدة فى سوق الاسهم/الذهب/النقد/الماس.
١٢ انخفضت الاسهم فى معاملات/صادرات/طلبيات/تعاقدات هادئة.
١٣ مجمل مسح/نقد/ربح/مدى التشغيل نزل الى ٢٠ مليون ريال.
١٤ جاء فى مجلس/مسح/مؤشر/موسم المعهد ان الانتاج الصناعى لم يشهد نموا.

Exercise 2 Match the following pairs

١	مستوى	a	ارباح
٢	نزول	b	افادت الوكالة
٣	تجارة	c	الاحصاء
٤	حسبما	d	قياسى
٥	معهد	e	الجملة

Exercise 3 Match the following pairs

١	المدى	a	الفائدة
٢	اسعار	b	الانترنت
٣	معاملات	c	هادئة
٤	طوال	d	القصير
٥	شبكة	e	الاسبوع

Exercise 4 Choose the best answer

١ هبطت/سادت/اجتمعت/وقعت ارباح الشركة.
٢ خصصت/تراجعت/افتتحت/وصلت اسعار الاسهم امس.

٣ تركز/حصل/وصل/عزا النشاط المحدود على الاسهم الصناعية.

٤ بحث/ذكر/عقد/سجل سماسرة ان الاسهم ارتفعت امس.

٥ وصل/اصدر/صعد/شمل مؤشر دوو جونز ٩ نقطة.

٦ معدل البطالة حصل/هدف/انخفض/تراوح الى ١٠ فى المائة.

Exercise 5 Put the following into the sentences below

مقارنة طوال منذ دون للغاية طبقا بنسبة امام

١ زادت الصادرات ________ ٣ فى المائة.

٢ القى الوزير كلمة ________ البرلمان.

٣ ________ لوكالة رويترز فقد هبط مؤشر سوق عمان المالى.

٤ ارتفعت الاسهم فى معاملات هادئة ________.

٥ هذا من ادنى المستويات ________ عدة اسابيع.

٦ كانت نسبة النمو الاقتصادى ________ ٢ فى المائة.

٧ كان السهم نشاطا ________ الاسبوع.

٨ هبط ارباح فى الربع الاخير من العام الماضى ________ بالربع الثالث.

Exercise 6 Match the following pairs

١	6 ملايين دولار صافي الأرباح	a	نموا في أرباحها في 1998
٢	اليابان تساهم في إنشاء معهد	b	نصف السنوية لـ«البترول الأردنية»
٣	أرباح فرنسبنك اللبناني	c	بلغت 45 مليون دولار عام 1998
٤	«البحرين للسينما» تحقق 53%	d	الصناعات المعدنية بالأردن

توزيع أرباح على مساهمي «سافكو» السعودية

الرياض: «الشرق الأوسط»

اقر مجلس ادارة شركة الاسمدة العربية السعودية «سافكو» امس توصية من المقرر رفعها للجمعية العامة لتوزيع ارباح قدرها 165 مليون ريال على المساهمين تعادل 5,5 ريال للسهم الواحد.

وقال المهندس محمد بن حمد الماضي رئيس مجلس الادارة ان المجلس سعى من خلال هذه التوصية الى الاخذ بعين الاعتبار توازن مصلحة المساهمين والشركة الآنية والمستقبلية، وظروف السيولة المتاحة لديها، مشيرا الى انه رغم انخفاض ارباح الشركة 60 في المائة خلال العام الماضي، وارتفاع اسعار الغاز والتجهيزات الاساسية الا انه آثر عدم خفض الارباح الموزعة بنفس النسبة.

ARTICLE 31

fertiliser	أسمدة *pl.* سماد
recommendation	توصية
to equate	عادل
to strive	سعى
balance	توازن
interest	مصالح *pl.* مصلحة
present *adj.*	آني
conditions	ظروف *pl.* ظرف
liquidity	سيولة
equipment	تجهيزات

ارتفاع أرباح بنك بيبلوس اللبناني في 1998

● أعلن بنك بيبلوس اللبناني ارتفاع صافي الارباح بنسبة 45٪ في عام 1998 الى 50 مليون دولار من 34 مليون دولار قبل عام. وطبقا لرويترز فان البنك اكد في بيان أصدره امس ارتفاع أصوله 29 في المائة الى 3,466 مليار دولار مع زيادة الودائع الى 2,5 مليار دولار. وارتفعت القروض 122 مليون دولار في 1998 الى 976 مليون دولار. وذكرت ادارة بيبلوس انها ستوصي مجلس المديرين بتخصيص حوالي 43٪ من ايرادات 1998 لتوزيعات الارباح على الاسهم.

وفي 1997 بلغت توزيعات الارباح في البنك 42٪ وأوضح بيان البنك ارتفاع حصته في السوق الى 10٪ من تسعة في المائة في 1997. واحتفظ البنك بترتيبه الثاني بين البنوك اللبنانية من حيث حجم رأس المال وتبلغ حقوق المساهمين 276 مليون دولار.

ARTICLE 32

asset	اصول *pl.* اصل
deposit	ودائع *pl.* وديعة
to recommend	أوصى
allocation	تخصيص
profits	ايرادات
dividend	ارباح على الاسهم
position	ترتيب

ARTICLE 33

operating *adj.*	تشغيلي
cutting, deduction	اقتطاع
debt	ديون *pl.* دين
doubtful	مشكوك
revenue	تحصيل
to reflect	عكس
clarity	وضوح
competence	كفاءة
enthusiasm	حماس
merger	اندماج

انخفاض أرباح بنك الخليج الدولي إلى 82 مليون دولار في 98

المنامة ـ رويترز: اعلن بنك الخليج الدولي امس الخميس انه حقق 82,1 مليون دولار ارباحا صافية عام 1998 منخفضة عن أرباح العام السابق البالغة 86,4 مليون دولار.

وقال بيان للبنك ومقره البحرين ان الارباح التشغيلية قبل اقتطاع المخصصات بلغت 112,1 مليون دولار العام الماضي.

وخصص البنك 30 مليون دولار للديون المشكوك في تحصيلها عام 1998 مقابل 23 مليون دولار عام 1997.

وقال وزير المالية والاقتصاد البحريني ورئيس مجلس ادارة البنك ابراهيم عبد الكريم ان الاداء الممتاز للبنك يعكس وضوح استراتيجيته التي تركز على استغلال كفاءاته وقدراته في مجالات عمله.

واضاف يقول ان البنك ينظر بثقة وحماس للاندماج مع البنك السعودي العالمي الذي اعلن عنه في وقت سابق.

Earnings distribution to shareholders of the Saudi company Safco

Riyadh - *Asharq al-Awsat*: Yesterday the board of the Saudi Arab Fertiliser Company, Safco, confirmed the recommendation it had agreed to present to the general meeting to distribute dividends of 165 million riyals to shareholders, equivalent to 5.5 riyals per share.

Engineer Mohammad Bin Hamad al-Madi, chairman of the board of directors, said that through this recommendation the board had tried to take into account the balance of the present and future interest of the shareholders and the company, and the liquidity position it enjoyed, pointing out that despite a 60% drop in profits last year, and an increase in the price of gas and basic equipment, this had not led to a proportionate fall in distributed earnings.

Profits rise for the Lebanese bank Byblos in 1998

The Lebanese bank, Byblos, announced a 45% increase in net profits in 1998 to 50 million dollars from 34 million dollars for the year before. According to Reuters, in a statement it issued yesterday, the bank announced a 29% increase in assets to 3.466 billion dollars, with an increase in deposits to 2.5 billion dollars. Loans increased by 122 million dollars in 1998 to 976 million dollars. The Byblos management said that the board of directors would be recommending setting aside around 43% of 1998 profits for the distribution of dividends.

In 1997 distributions of the bank's earnings totalled 42% and its statement showed an increase in market share to 10% from 9% in 1997. The bank maintained its position as the second Lebanese bank in terms of capital, with shareholdings totalling 276 million dollars.

Fall in profits of the International Bank of the Gulf to 82 million dollars in 98

Manama - *Reuters*: The International Bank of the Gulf announced yesterday, Thursday, that it had made a net profit of 82.1 million dollars in 1998, down from the previous year's profit of 86.4 million dollars.

In a statement from its headquarters in Bahrain, the bank said that operating profits before provisions was 112.1 million dollars last year. The bank set aside 30 million dollars for doubtful debts in its income for 1998 against 23 million dollars in 1997.

Bahrain's finance and economy minister, and chairman of the board of the bank, Ibrahim Abdul Karim, said that the bank's outstanding performance reflected its clear strategy that focused on making best use of its abilities and expertise in the fields of its activity. He went on to say that the bank looked with confidence and enthusiasm to the merger with the Saudi International Bank that had been announced previously.

«نيسان» تنفي نبأ عن أن «ديملر كرايسلر» تعتزم شراء حصة أغلبية

● نفت شركة «نيسان موتور» اليابانية لصناعة السيارات امس تقريرا صحفيا قال ان مجموعة «ديملر كرايسلر» تعتزم شراء حصة تزيد عن 50 في المائة في «نيسان موتور».

ونقلت رويترز عن صحيفة ميانيتشي شيمبون اليابانية قولها امس ان «ديملر» لديها مثل هذه الخطط وان المفاوضات في مراحلها الاخيرة.

وقال متحدث باسم «نيسان»: «مازلنا ندرس تحالفا محتملا مع ديملر. لم يتقرر شيء حتى الان». ووصف المتحدث تقرير الصحيفة بانه تكهنات.

ARTICLE 34

conglomerate	مجموعة
spokesman	متحدث
alliance	تحالف
possible	محتمل
speculation	ات *pl.* تكهن

محطة «سي.بي.اس» التلفزيونية تعتزم شراء «ان.بي.سي»

نيو اورليانز - رويترز: قال ميل كرمازين رئيس شبكة «سي.بي.اس» للبث الاذاعي والتلفزيوني انه يريد شراء منافستها «ان.بي.سي» رغم ان هذا يقتضي تعديل اللوائح التي تحكم صناعة التلفزيون الأميركية.

وقال كرمازين في مؤتمر صحافي انه سيكون مستعدا لدفع «اكثر من ثمن» المحطة التابعة لشركة جنرال الكتريك.

وامتنع متحدث باسم «ان.بي.سي» عن التعقيب على اقوال كرمازين. وكان جاك ويلش رئيس جنرال الكتريك قد قال لمحللين في نيويورك في اواخر العام الماضي ان ان.بي.سي قيمتها 20 مليار دولار وذلك بعد ان كانت تساوي خمسة مليارات دولار فقط في عام 1997 .

ARTICLE 35

network	شبكة
dissemination	بث
broadcasting *adj.*	اذاعى
competitor	منافس
to mean	اقتضى
change	تعديل
rule	لوائح *pl.* لائحة
to refrain	امتنع
comment	ات *pl.* تعقيب
to equal	ساوى

اليمن يخصص شركة للأدوية

● وافقت الحكومة اليمنية امس على تخصيص شركة للادوية في اطار اصلاحات تهدف الى انعاش الاقتصاد المتداعي للبلاد.

ونقلت «رويترز» عن وكالة سبأ الرسمية للانباء ان اجتماعا وزاريا وافق على استراتيجية واسلوب تخصيص الشركة اليمنية لصناعة الادوية والتجارة. وصرح مسؤول في الشركة التي تأسست عام 1962 بأن الحكومة تمتلك 40 في المائة من اسهم الشركة ويملك القطاع الخاص النسبة الباقية.

واضافت سبأ ان الحكومة تريد اجتذاب مستثمرين استراتيجيين وتخطط لطرح اسهم للاكتتاب العام.

والتخصيص جزء اساسي من برنامج للاصلاح اوصى به البنك الدولي وصندوق النقد الدولي بهدف الحد من العجز الكبير في الميزانية وزيادة عوائد الضرائب وتعزيز النظام المالي

ARTICLE 36

to privatise	خصص
to agree to	وافق على
pharmaceuticals	ادوية *pl.* دواء
collapsing	متداعى
method	اساليب *pl.* اسلوب
to be founded	اس
to hold	امتلك
attraction	اجتذاب
to offer	طرح
registration	اكتتاب
taxes	ضرائب *pl.* ضريبة
strengthening	تعزيز

Nissan denies report that Daimler Chrysler is set to purchase a majority share

The Japanese car makers, Nissan Motors, denied yesterday a newspaper report that the Daimler Chrysler group was set to purchase a majority share in Nissan Motors.

Reuters reported the Japanese newspaper, Mainichi Shimbun, as saying yesterday that Daimler had such plans and that negotiations were in their final stages.

A spokesman for Nissan said: "We are still studying a possible merger with Daimler. Nothing has been decided yet." The spokesman described the newspaper report as speculation.

CBS television station to buy NBC

New Orleans - *Reuters*: Mel Karmazin, chairman of CBS, the radio and television broadcasting network, said that he wanted to buy its rival, NBC, despite the fact that this would mean a change in the regulations that governed the US television industry.

In a news conference Karmazin said that he would be prepared to pay "over the odds" for the station, a subsidiary of General Electric. A spokesman for NBC declined to comment on the words of Karmazin. Jack Welch, chief executive of General Electric, had told analysts in New York at the end of last year that NBC was worth 20 billion dollars compared with only five billion in 1997.

Yemen to privatise a pharmaceuticals company

The Yemeni government agreed yesterday to privatise a pharmaceuticals company as part of the reforms that aim to revitalise the country's collapsing economy.

Reuters reported the official news agency, Saba, as saying that a ministerial meeting had agreed on the strategy and methods for privatising the Yemeni Company for the Drugs Trade and Industry. An official in the company founded in 1962 said that the government held 40% of the shares in the company and that the private sector the remainder. Saba added that the government wanted to attract strategic investors and planned to offer shares for public subscription.

Privatisation is a fundamental part of a programme of reform recommended by the World Bank and the International Monetary Fund to limit the large budget deficit, increase tax revenues and strengthen the financial structure.

Exercises Articles 31 - 36

Exercise 1 Choose the best answer

١ المجلس سعى الى الاخذ بعين الاعتبار توزيع/توازن/تقسيم/تعزيز مصلحة المساهمين والشركة.
٢ اكد البنك ارتفاع اصوله/مصادره/طلبه/عجزه ٣٠ فى المائة.
٣ خصص البنك ١٠ مليون دولار للخسائر/للديون/للضرائب/للاساليب المشكوك فى تحصيلها.
٤ ينظر البنك بثقة/بناحية/بخسيرة/بشبكة الاندماج مع البنك الفرنسى.
٥ ستوصى الادارة مجلس المديرين بتخصيص ٣٠٪ من ايرادات/استثمارات/مشتريات/مصروفات ١٩٩٩ لتوزيعات الارباح على الاسهم.
٦ المجموعة تعتزم شراء حصة/جملة/كمية/جودة تزيد عن ١٥٪ فى المائة.
٧ وصف المتحدث تقرير الصحيفة بانه تكهنات/معلومات/اقتراحات/مواصلات.
٨ قال المتحدث ان كانت المفاوضات/الاحصائيات/التكهنات/المخصصات فى مراحلاتها الاخيرة.
٩ الارباح التشغيلية قبل اكتتاب/اقتطاع/اجتذاب/اقتراب المخصصات بلغت ١٠٠ مليون دولار.
١٠ الاداء الممتاز للبنك يعكس تحالف/حماس/اندماج/وضوح استراتيجيته.

Exercise 2 Match the following pairs

١	رأس	a	الخاص
٢	القطاع	b	الارباح
٣	مؤتمر	c	يدرس البرنامج
٤	صافى	d	المالى
٥	ما زال	e	صحافى

Exercise 3 Choose the suitable word

١ رغم / حوالى الانخفاض
٢ مقارنة / طبقا لتقرير
٣ بنسبة / حتى الان
٤ دون / خلال العام الماضى
٥ امام / منذ البرلمان

Exercise 4 Put the following words into the spaces

الضرائب العجز اسلوب انعاش طرح تخصيص

اليمن يخصص شركة للأدوية

● وافقت الحكومة اليمنية امس على شركة للادوية في اطار اصلاحات تهدف الى الاقتصاد المتداعي للبلاد.

ونقلت «رويترز» عن وكالة سبأ الرسمية للانباء ان اجتماعا وزاريا وافق على استراتيجية و تخصيص الشركة اليمنية لصناعة الادوية والتجارة. وصرح مسؤول في الشركة التي تأسست عام 1962 بأن الحكومة تمتلك 40 في المائة من اسهم الشركة ويملك القطاع الخاص النسبة الباقية. واضافت سبأ ان الحكومة تريد اجتذاب مستثمرين استراتيجيين وتخطط ل اسهم للاكتتاب العام.

والتخصيص جزء اساسي من برنامج للاصلاح اوصى به البنك الدولي وصندوق النقد الدولي بهدف الحد من الكبير في الميزانية وزيادة عوائد وتعزيز النظام المالي

Exercise 5 Match the following

١

وزير التنمية المصري يؤكد

a

جمعية أبوظبي التعاونية

٢

380.4 مليون درهم أرباح

b

تجارة وصناعة أبوظبي على الإنترنت

٣

البرلمان الإسرائيلي يقر موازنة

c

من خارج المنظمة قبل اجتماع مارس المقبل

٤

«أوبك» تسعى لعقد اجتماع للمنتجين

d

أن صناعة الدواء ببلاده في خطر

٥

موقع جديد باللغة العربية لغرفة

e

تعزيز التعاون النفطي والغازي

٦

وزير الطاقة الأميركي يبحث في السعودية

f

عام 1999 قيمتها 52.7 مليار دولار

ARTICLE 37

fair	معرض
confectionery	حلويات
to open	انطلق
to confirm	عزز
display	عرض *pl.* عروض
meal	وجبة
almond	لوز
ground *adj.*	مسحوق
egg white	زلال
pastry	عجائن

5 شركات سعودية تشارك في المعرض العالمي للحلويات

الرياض: «الشرق الأوسط»

تشارك خمس شركات سعودية من جدة في المعرض العالمي للحلويات والبسكويت «أي. إس. إم» المقرر أن ينطلق يوم الأحد المقبل في مدينة كلونجي الألمانية.

وذكر مكتب الاتصال الألماني السعودي للشؤون الاقتصادية في بيان أصدره أخيرا أن قائمة المشاركين السعوديين تشمل مصنع بدره، والشركة السعودية للمنتجات الغذائية، ومصنع «غندور» ومصنع باطوق، والشركة الوطنية للبسكويت والحلويات المحدودة. وأوضح البيان أن الشركات السعودية المشاركة ستعزز خبراتها في هذا المعرض، سواء في ما يتعلق بمبيعاتها التجارية المتعددة، أو بزيادة حجم مشتريات التشغيل.

ويشتمل المعرض الذي يستمر حتى الرابع من فبراير (شباط) المقبل على عروض للشيكولاته ومنتجاتها، والكاكاو، والحلويات السكرية، والبسكويت، والوجبات الخفيفة، والآيسكريم، وحلويات مسحوق اللوز، والسكر، وزلال البيض، والعجائن، ويعتبر أكبر معرض من نوعه في العالم.

ARTICLE 38

proceeds	واردات
perfume	عطور
preparations	مستحضرات
to compete	تنافس
appointed	منتدب
to win	اكتسب
fame	شهرة
reservation	حجز
space	مساحة
campaign	حملة

178 مليون دولار واردات الكويت من العطور ومستحضرات التجميل

الكويت: «الشرق الأوسط»

تتنافس 80 شركة ومؤسسة ووكيل محلي للعطور وأدوات التجميل على تسويق منتجاتها في معرض الكويت الدولي للعطور الذي افتتح اخيرا ويتوقع ان يصل عدد زائريه الى 150 ألف زائر.

وقال الوكيل المساعد بوزارة التجارة والصناعة لدى افتتاحه المعرض ان الكويت تعتبر من الدول المستهلكة كثيرا للعطور حيث بلغت وارداتها منه ومن مستحضرات التجميل عام 1997 حوالي 178 مليون دولار، في حين بلغت تلك الواردات في الأشهر الخمسة الأولى من العام 1998 نحو 92,4 مليون دولار.

من جهته قال رئيس مجلس الادارة والعضو المنتدب لشركة ارض المعارض الدولية محمد احمد الغربللي ان المعرض الذي نظمته الشركة للمرة الرابعة عشرة قد اكتسب شهرة واسعة، وقد تم حجز المساحات المحددة للعرض بالكامل مع بدء الحملة التسويقية لاقامته. وأضاف ان المعرض هذا العام شهد حضورا للمنتجات المحلية، والوكلاء والشركات الخليجية الى جانب المشاركة الدولية.

ARTICLE 39

air *adj.*	جوى
ticket	تذكرة *pl.* تذاكر
flight	رحلة *pl.* ات
step	اجراء *pl.* ات
in line with	متماش مع
fluctuation	تقلب *pl.* ات
to include	تضمن
support	دعم

«الجوية اليمنية» ترفع أسعار رحلاتها المحلية 20%

● ذكر مسؤول بشركة الخطوط الجوية اليمنية امس ان الشركة رفعت اسعار تذاكر السفر على رحلاتها المحلية بنسبة 20 ٪ وعلى رحلاتها الدولية بنسبة ثمانية في المائة. ونقلت رويترز بان هذا الاجراء اتخذ لجعل اسعار السفر على الرحلات المحلية متماشية مع الاسعار الدولية وللتعويض عن التقلبات في قيمة الريال اليمني امام الدولار.

وفي ابريل (نيسان) من العام الماضي رفعت الشركة اسعار تذاكر السفر على رحلاتها المحلية بنسبة 50٪ في اطار اصلاحات اقتصادية بدأتها الحكومة عام 1990 تتضمن خفض الدعم الحكومي.

Five Saudi companies to participate in the international confectionery fair

Riyadh - *Asharq al-Awsat*: Five Saudi companies from Jeddah are participating in the international fair for confectionery and biscuits, ASM, due to open next Sunday in the German city of Cologne.

In a statement it issued recently the Saudi-German liaison office for economic affairs said that the list of Saudi participants included the Badrah firm, the Saudi Company for Food Products, the Ghandoor firm, the Batooq firm and the National Company for Biscuits and Confectionery Limited. The statement said that the Saudi companies participating would confirm their expertise in this fair, whether through their various commercial sales or by an increase in outlays on operating acquisitions.

The fair, which continues until 4th February, includes displays of chocolates and their by-products, cocoa, sugared confectionery, biscuits, snacks, ice-cream, pastries of ground almond, sugar, egg white and dough. It is considered to be the largest fair of its kind in the world.

Kuwait imports 178 million dollars worth of perfumes and beauty preparations

Kuwait - *Asharq al-Awsat*: 80 companies, organisations and a local agency for perfumes and beauty products are competing in marketing their products at the Kuwaiti international fair for perfumes that has opened recently and where 150,000 visitors are expected.

When he opened the fair, the assistant under-secretary of state for trade and industry said that Kuwait was considered a high consumer of perfumes, with imports of the latter and of beauty preparations totalling some 178 million dollars in 1997, and with imports in the first five months of 1998 reaching 92.4 million dollars.

For his part, the chairman of the board and member appointed by the international company, Ard al-Ma'arid, Mohammad Ahmad al-Gharbaly, said that the fair organised by the company for the fourteenth time had gained a wide reputation, and reservations for the spaces allocated for the fair were booked at the start of the marketing campaign to launch it. He added that this year the fair had seen the appearance of local products, with agents and companies from the Gulf in addition to international participation.

Yemenia Airways increases its fares on domestic flights by 20%

An official for Yemenia Airways announced yesterday that the company had raised fares on its domestic flights by 20%, and on its international flights by 8%. Reuters said that this step had been taken to put travel prices on domestic flights in line with world prices and to compensate for fluctuations in the value of the Yemeni riyal against the dollar.

In April last year the company raised the prices of its domestic flights by 50% as part of the economic reforms instituted by the government in 1990 that included reducing government support.

ARTICLE 40

power	طاقة
organisation	منظمة
except for	باستثناء
to stabilize	استقر
noticeable	يذكر
productivity	انتاجية
to pump	ضخ

وكالة الطاقة: نمو إنتاج أويك في فبراير إلى 27.55 مليون برميل يوميا

لندن - رويترز: قالت وكالة الطاقة الدولية امس ان انتاج منظمة أويك من النفط الخام زاد بمقدار 150 ألف برميل يوميا الى 27,55 مليون برميل في اليوم في فبراير (شباط) الماضي نتيجة لارتفاع الانتاج العراقي. وقالت الوكالة في تقريرها الشهري عن سوق النفط ان انتاج دول أويك باستثناء العراق في فبراير الماضي استقر دون تغيير يذكر عند 24,98 مليون برميل في اليوم أي بما يقل 2,01 مليون برميل في اليوم عن مستوى الانتاج الاساسي لشهر فبراير 1998 الذي احتسبت على أساسه تخفيضات اويك الانتاجية.

ويمثل ذلك نسبة 77 في المائة من التخفيضات المستهدفة البالغة 2,6 مليون برميل يوميا. وقد ضخ العراق 2,57 مليون برميل في اليوم خلال الشهر الماضي ارتفاعا من 2,41 مليون برميل يوميا في يناير (كانون الثاني) الماضي لتتجاوز صادراته مليوني برميل في اليوم. وبلغ المعروض النفطي من الدول المنتجة غير الاعضاء في أويك 44,77 مليون برميل يوميا انخفاضا من 44,97 مليون في يناير الماضي.

وبلغ اجمالي الانتاج العالمي في فبراير الماضي 75,25 مليون برميل يوميا مقارنة مع 75,29 مليون برميل يوميا في يناير ومع متوسط عام 1998 البالغ 75,27 مليون برميل في اليوم.

ARTICLE 41

well *n.*	آبار *pl.* بئر
idle	معطل
to lead to	افضى الى
reserves	احتياطيات
liable	قابل
cover	تغطية
at the start of	بحلول
cost	تكاليف *pl.* تكليف
entitlements	مستحقات
need	افتقار
condensed	مكثف

روسيا تتوقع انخفاضا جديدا في إنتاج النفط

موسكو - رويترز: ذكر سيرجي جنرالوف وزير الطاقة الروسي امس ان من المتوقع تراجع انتاج بلاده من النفط بما يتراوح بين خمسة وسبعة ملايين طن سنويا خلال السنوات القليلة المقبلة، وفي مؤتمر صحافي قال جنرالوف: ارتفع عدد الآبار المعطلة بشكل حاد وربما يفضي ذلك الى خسارة بعض الاحتياطيات القابلة للتغطية.

وأضاف ان 35 ألف بئر نفطي تمثل 26,3 في المائة من اجمالي عدد آبار البلاد تعطلت بحلول أول يناير (كانون الثاني) 1999.

وحدد الوزير مشكلات قطاع الطاقة الروسي في ارتفاع تكاليف الانتاج وتأخر دفع المستحقات والافتقار الى الاستثمارات. وفي 1998 هبط الانتاج الروسي من النفط الخام والغاز المكثف الى 303 ملايين طن من 305 ملايين في العام السابق عليه. وبلغ انتاج الاتحاد السوفياتي السابق في أعلى مستوياته 600 مليون طن في أواخر الثمانينات.

ARTICLE 42

to fail	فشل
exchange	مقايضة
principle	مبادىء *pl.* مبداء
attempt	محاولة
to stumble	تعثر
insistence	اصرار
inspection	تفتيش
complex *adj.*	معقد
wasting	مضيع
normal	معتاد
condition	شروط *pl.* شرط
payment	سداد
to stretch	امتد

تايلاند تفشل في الاتفاق مع إيران على مقايضة الأرز بالنفط

بانكوك - رويترز: قال مسؤول كبير بوزارة التجارة التايلاندية ان تايلاند فشلت امس الخميس في التوصل الى اتفاق بشأن مبيعات الارز لايران. وصرح براتشا تشاروتراكولتشيا مدير عام التجارة الخارجية بالوزارة لرويترز بعد الاجتماع مع مفاوضين ايرانيين بأنهم اتفقوا من ناحية المبدأ على محاولة دعم حجم التجارة بين البلدين.

لكنه قال ان المحادثات تعثرت بسبب اصرار ايران على نظام تفتيش معقد ومضيع للوقت على المنتجات. وقال «موقف تايلاند هو أننا نريد بيع الارز بالشروط المعتادة وليس بشروط ايران. واذا قبلت ايران فاننا كنا سنعرض بيع الارز بفترة سداد تمتد عامين أو ثلاثة اعوام».

وقال براتشا انه كان من الممكن التوصل الى اتفاق يشمل مقايضة منتجات تايلاندية مثل الارز والسكر بنفط ايراني.

Energy agency: OPEC production in February rises to 27.55 million barrels a day

London - *Reuters*: The International Energy Agency yesterday said that OPEC's crude oil production had increased by 150 thousand barrels a day to 27.55 million barrels a day last February as a result of the increase in Iraqi production. In its monthly report on the oil market, the agency said that the production of the OPEC countries, Iraq apart, had stabilised this past February without noticeable change at 24.98 million barrels a day, that is 2.01million barrels less than the basic level of production for February 1998, the basis for which OPEC calculated reductions in its production.

This represents 77% of the projected reduction of 2.6 million barrels a day. Iraq pumped 2.57 million barrels a day last month, an increase from 2.41 million barrels a day last January, with exports exceeding 2 million barrels a day. The oil supply of the non OPEC oil producing countries totalled 44.77 million barrels a day, a drop from 44.97 million in January.

World-wide production in February reached 75.25 million barrels a day, compared with 75.29 million barrels a day in January and with the average in 1998 of 75.27 million barrels a day.

Russia anticipates a new drop in oil production

Moscow - *Reuters*: Sergio Janralov, the Russian energy minister, said yesterday that a fall in his country's oil production of between 5 and 7 million tons a year was expected over the next few years, and in a news conference Janralov said: "The number of wells that are mothballed has risen sharply and this will probably lead to losses of some reserves that act as cover."

He added that 35 thousand oil wells which were mothballed at the beginning of January 1999 represented 26.3% of the total number of wells in the country.

The minister specified the problems of the Russian energy sector as the rise in production costs, the delay in paying money that was due and the need for investment. In 1998 production of Russian crude oil and condensed gas fell to 303 million tons from 305 million tons in the previous year. The production of what was previously the Soviet Union reached a maximum of 600 million tons in the late eighties.

Thailand fails to reach agreement with Iran on the exchange of rice for oil

Bangkok - *Reuters*: A senior official in the Thai trade ministry said yesterday, Thursday, that Thailand had failed to reach an agreement on sales of rice to Iran. Pratcha Tsharootrakoolitshia, director general of foreign trade in the ministry, told Reuters after the meeting with Iranian negotiators that they had agreed in principle to try to maintain the volume of trade between the two countries.

But he said that the discussions had faltered because of Iran's insistence on the complicated and time-wasting system of inspection of the products. He said: "Thailand's position is that we want to sell rice under normal terms not Iran's. If Iran agrees, we will offer to sell the rice with a payment period stretching over two or three years."

Pratcha said that it was possible to reach an agreement that included exchanging Thai products like rice and sugar for Iranian oil.

Exercises Articles 37 - 42

Exercise 1 Choose the best answer

١ تشارك خمس شركات فى عطور/دعم/معرض/سداد الحلويات.
٢ اكتسب المعرض حملة/شهرة/رحلة/تغطية واسعة.
٣ شهد المعرض وضوحا/انكماشا/حضورا/حجزا المنتجات المحلية.
٤ رفعت الشركة اسعار شروط/رحلات/خطوط/تذاكر السفر.
٥ بلغ العجز/التقلب/المعروض/الحجز النفطى ٦٠ مليون برميل.
٦ ذكر الوزير ان من المتوقع عروض/سداد/شرط/تراجع الانتاج من النفط.
٧ فشلت فرنسا فى الاصرار/الاجراء/السداد/التوصل الى اتفاق.
٨ تعثرت الاحتياطيات/المحادثات/الرحلات/الوجبات بسبب اصرار على تفتيش معقد.
٩ امتدت طاقة/فترة/حملة/سيولة السداد عامين.
١٠ هذا الاجراء اتخذ للتعويض عن التقلب فى طاقة/خسيرة/ناحية/قيمة النقد.

Exercise 2 Match the following pairs

١	الدول	a	الجوية
٢	الانتاج	b	اصلاحات الاقتصادية
٣	الخطوط	c	المستهلكة
٤	فى اطار	d	يذكر
٥	دون تغيير	e	العالمى

Exercise 3 Choose the appropriate verb

١ يتوقع/يعتبر/يمثل/ينشر اكبر معرض فى العالم.
٢ احتسبت/ارتفعت/اقتربت/اكتسبت الشركة شهرة واسعة.
٣ يتوقع/يدخل/يشارك/يمثل ذلك ٦٠٪ من التخفيضات.
٤ أبار كثيرة تاخرت/تعطلت/ارتفعت/وصلت العام الماضى.
٥ انتاج من النفط الخام زاد/امتد/تراوح/زار ٥٠٪ فى المائة.

Exercise 4 Match the following

a

١ المغرب يتسلم 7 طائرات

من الاحتياطي لمواجهة ارتفاع الدولار أمام الجنيه

b

٢ بوينج بحلول عام 2001

المركزي المصري يعتزم طرح 500 مليون دولار

c

٣ الاتحاد العربي للنقل الجوي يبحث في بيروت

مقابل الين وتراجع الأسهم الأوروبية

d

٤ تعزيز تعاون شركات الطيران العربية

المكسيك مستعدة لبحث تخفيض إنتاج النفط

e

٥ الدولار يقترب من أعلى مستوياته

مع السعودية وفنزويلا قبل اجتماع أوبك

ARTICLE 43

session	دورة
realisation	تحقيق
integration	تكامل
formation of blocs	تكتل *pl.* ات
work force	قوة عاملة
phenomenon	ظاهرة
to touch	مس
stability	استقرار
to review	استعرض
horizon	افق *pl.* آفاق
challenge	تحد *pl.* تحديات
edge	طرف *pl.* اطراف
IT	عولمة

وزراء العمل العرب يجتمعون في القاهرة

القاهرة - واس: يعقد مؤتمر العمل العربي دورته السادسة والعشرين يوم 6 مارس (آذار) المقبل في القاهرة بمشاركة وزراء العمل العرب. وسيناقش المؤتمر موضوع السوق العربية المشتركة لتحقيق التكامل الاقتصادي العربي في ظل التكتلات الاقتصادية العالمية والاقليمية. كما يبحث المؤتمر سبل تحقيق التنمية البشرية لمواجهة البطالة العربية والتي تصل الى 14 في المائة من حجم القوى العاملة خاصة بعد ان اصبحت ظاهرة خطيرة تمس الاستقرار الامني والسياسي والاقتصادي والاجتماعي بالدول العربية. ويستعرض المؤتمر الذي يستمر اسبوعاً تقرير المدير العام لمنظمة العمل العربية حول الآفاق المستقبلية لدور المنظمة في ضوء المتغيرات والتحديات التي تفرضها ظاهرة العولمة وآثارها المختلفة على اطراف الانتاج بالدول العربية.

ARTICLE 44

to support	ايد
to occupy	تولى
occasion	مناسبة
candidate	مرشح
attainment of	حصول على
unanimity	اجماع
consisting of	موءلف من

فرنسا تؤيد المغربي أبو أيوب لرئاسة منظمة التجارة

باريس - رويترز: قالت فرنسا امس انها تريد ان يتولى حسن ابو ايوب وزير التجارة المغربي السابق رئاسة منظمة التجارة العالمية عندما يترك الرئيس الحالي الايطالي ريناتو روجييرو منصبة في أبريل (نيسان) المقبل.

وجاء في بيان لوزارة الخارجية الفرنسية «تعرب فرنسا مجددا عن تأييدها للسيد أبو أيوب، وهو ما سبق ان أعلنته في جنيف في عدة مناسبات».

وأضاف البيان «يتمتع هذا المرشح حاليا بتأييد واسع النطاق في منظمة التجارة العالمية وبامكانه الحصول على اجماع. ليس لبلدنا سوى مرشح واحد هو السيد أبو أيوب». وهناك ثلاثة مرشحين آخرين لرئاسة المنظمة المؤلفة من 133 دولة هم روي مكلارين سفير كندا لدى بريطانيا ومايكل مور وهو رئيس وزراء سابق لنيوزيلندا وسوباتشاي بانيتشباكدي النائب الاول لرئيس وزراء تايلاند.

Arab ministers of labour to meet in Cairo

Cairo - *WAS*: The Arab conference on employment is holding its twenty-sixth session on 6th March in Cairo attended by Arab ministers of labour. The conference will discuss the subject of the Arab common market to achieve Arab economic integration in the face of worldwide and regional economic blocs. It will discuss ways of promoting human development to counter Arab unemployment that has reached 14% of the workforce, all the more so after becoming a serious phenomenon that is affecting the security and the political, economic and social stability of the Arab countries.

The week-long conference will review a report of the director-general of the Arab Labour Organisation on the future prospects of the organisation's role in the light of the changes and challenges posed by the advent of information technology and its various effects on areas of production in the Arab countries.

France supports the Moroccan Abuyoub as director-general of the World Trade Organisation

Paris - *Reuters*: France said yesterday that it wanted Hassan Abuyoub, the former Moroccan minister of trade, to become director-general of the World Trade Organisation when the current Italian director-general, Renato Ruggiero, left his post next April.

A statement by the French foreign ministry said: "Once more France declares its support for Mr Abuyoub, which it has already announced on a number of occasions in Geneva."

The statement added: "This candidate presently enjoys widespread support in the World Trade Organisation and he may have the support of everyone. The only candidate for our country is Mr Abuyoub." There are three other candidates to head the organisation which is made up of 133 countries - Roy Maclaren, Canadian ambassador to Britain, Michael Moore, former premier of New Zealand and Supachai Panitchpakdi, first deputy prime minister of Thailand.

ARTICLE 45

urgent	عاجل
to realise	شعر ب
dispute	نزاع
anger	غضب
restriction	قيود *pl.* قيد
fair, just	عادل
to harm	ضر
endeavour	سعى

لندن وواشنطن تتفقان على إجراء محادثات عاجلة بشأن الموز

شيفننج - رويترز: ذكر روبن كوك وزير الخارجية البريطاني ان بريطانيا والولايات المتحدة اتفقتا على ضرورة اجراء محادثات عاجلة بين واشنطن والاتحاد الاوروبي للتوصل الى حل للخلاف التجاري بشأن تجارة الموز.

واضاف كوك بعد اجتماع مع مادلين اولبرايت وزيرة الخارجية الامريكية ان الجانبين شعرا بضرورة ايجاد حل للنزاع المتنامي بشأن واردات الموز باسرع ما يمكن.

وتشعر بريطانيا بغضب بسبب قرار الولايات المتحدة فرض قيود على الصادرات قبل حكم منظمة التجارة العالمية بشأن نظام الاتحاد الاوروبي المعدل لتجارة الموز والتي تقول المنظمة انه يدعم بشكل غير عادل الدول الصغيرة المنتجة للموز في الكاريبي على حساب الدول الاخرى في اميركا اللاتينية. وقال كوك للصحافيين بعد المحادثات: اتفقنا على ان المطلوب هو اجراء محادثات عاجلة. لا يمكن ان نسمح بان يضر هذا الخلاف بالعلاقات بيننا. كلانا يحتاج الى قرار عاجل وكلانا متفق على السعي الى التوصل لهذا القرار.

أميركا تقدم قمحا مجانيا إلى الأردن

عمان: «الشرق الأوسط»

وقعت الحكومتان الأردنية والاميركية على اتفاقية تقدم بموجبها الحكومة الاميركية منحة مجانية مقدارها 100 الف طن متري من القمح الاميركي الى الاردن، وتقدر قيمة هذه المنحة بحوالي 13 مليون دولار وهي قيمة المساعدات الغذائية المقررة للأردن للعام الحالي والتي تقدمها وزارة الزراعة الاميركية بموجب برنامج 416 ب.

وتأتي هذه المنحة في اطار مساهمة الحكومة الاميركية في دعم الخزينة الاردنية حيث سيتم شحن الكمية على دفعتين، الاولى خلال شهري ابريل (نيسان) ومايو (ايار) المقبلين، والثانية خلال شهري مايو ويونيو (حزيران) المقبلين.

وكانت هذه المنحة قد تقررت في اكتوبر (تشرين الاول) عام 1998 بموجب الجزء 416 ب من مرسوم الزراعة لعام 1949 والذي تقوم وزارة الزراعة الاميركية من خلاله بتقديم القمح كمساعدة غذائية للبلدان المؤهلة من خلال المنظمات التطوعية الخاصة او من خلال الاتفاقيات الثنائية بين الحكومة الاميركية وحكومة البلد المعني بالمنحة.

ARTICLE 46

wheat	قمح
free	مجاني
according to	بموجب
gift	منح *pl.* منحة
food *adj.*	غذائـــي
treasury	خزينة
loading	شحن
decree	مراسيم *pl.* مرسوم
deserving	موءهل
voluntary	تطوعي
interested in	معني ب

London and Washington agree to hold urgent discussions on the banana issue

Chevening - *Reuters*: The British foreign secretary, Robin Cook, said that Britain and the United States had agreed on the need to hold urgent discussions between Washington and the European Union to reach a solution to the trade dispute concerning the banana trade.

After a meeting with US secretary of state, Madeleine Albright, Cook added that the two sides felt the need to find a solution as quickly as possible to the growing dispute over the imports of bananas.

Britain feels anger at the decision of the United States to impose export restrictions before the ruling of the World Trade Organisation on the European Union's system for quotas for the banana trade, which the organisation says unfairly favours the small banana growing countries in the Caribbean at the expense of the other countries in Latin America. Cook told journalists after the discussions: "We agreed that urgent discussions were required. We cannot allow this disagreement to harm relations between us. We all need an urgent decision and we are all agreed on striving to reach this decision."

America to supply Jordan with free wheat

Amman - *Asharq al-Awsat*: The Jordanian and US governments have signed an agreement by which the US government will provide a free gift of 100 thousand metric tons of US wheat to Jordan. The value of this gift is estimated at around 13 million dollars, the value of the food assistance agreed for Jordan for the present year, which the US agricultural ministry provides in accordance with Program 416B.

The gift comes as part of the US government's contribution in supporting the Jordanian treasury. The shipment will be carried out in two stages, the first during April and May, and the second in May and June.

This gift had been agreed in October 1998 in accordance with section 416B of the Agricultural Act of 1949, according to which the US ministry of agriculture undertakes to provide wheat as food assistance to qualifying countries through private voluntary organisations or through bilateral agreements between the US government and that of the country receiving the gift.

ARTICLE 47

lawyer	محامون *pl.* محام
post	مناصب *pl.* منصب
to elect	انتخب
after	خلفا
to spend *(time)*	امضى
justice	عدالة
advantage	مزايا *pl.* مزية
part	ارجاء *pl.* رجا
society	مجتمع
proportion	معادلة
ordinary	عادى

محام من تشيلي يتولى منصب مدير عام منظمة العمل الدولية

● تولى جوان سومافيا وهو محام ودبلوماسي من تشيلي امس منصب مدير عام منظمة العمل الدولية.

وانتخب مجلس المنظمة سومافيا لهذا المنصب في العام الماضي خلفا لميشيل هانسن وهو وزير بلجيكي سابق امضى عشر سنوات من حياته العملية رئيسا لمنظمة العمل التابعة للامم المتحدة التي تعمل على اقرار العدالة الاجتماعية وحقوق العمال.

وقال سومافيا في بيان انه يرغب في التأكد من ان مزايا العولمة تصل الى كافة ارجاء المجتمع واضاف «اتفقنا دوليا على تشجيع المجتمعات الحرة والاقتصادات الحرة. وهذا الاجماع لن يستمر اذا لم تدخل في المعادلة المزايا الحقيقية التي يشعر بها الناس العاديون واسرهم».

وتأسست المنظمة عام 1919 ويبلغ عدد أعضائها 174 دولة.

ARTICLE 48

unemployed	عاطل
prevailing	سائد
compulsorily	قسرا
proceedings	محاضر *pl.* محضر
improvement	تحسن
apprehension	مخاوف
aggravation	تفاقم
returns	مداخيل *pl.*
contracting	تخليص
expenditure	ات *pl.* نفقة
stagnation	ركود

أعلى معدل بطالة في اليابان منذ 50 عاما

لندن: «الشرق الأوسط»

ارتفع عدد العاطلين عن العمل في اليابان خلال يناير (كانون الثاني) الماضي الى 2,98 مليون شخص أي بزيادة 25 في المائة عما سجل خلال نفس الشهر من العام الماضي. واعتبرت الحكومة اليابانية هذا العدد منخفضا بالمقارنة مع الأوضاع الاقتصادية السائدة على المستوى العالمي، ولكنه مؤشر الى أن الانخفاض في الأداء الاقتصادي الياباني سيستمر هذا العام. وتبين آخر البيانات أن عدد الاشخاص الذين تركوا العمل قسرا بلغ هذا العام مليون شخص، تتراوح اعمارهم بين 35 و55 سنة. واظهرت كذلك إن هذا العام شهد أعلى عدد للعاطلين عن العمل في اليابان منذ نصف قرن. وكان بنك اليابان المركزي قد نشر محضر الاجتماع الذي عقدته لجنة السياسة المالية في يناير مشيرا الى أن أغلبية أعضاء اللجنة لا يرون أي أفق لتحسن اقتصادي بل أن البعض عبر عن مخاوفه من تفاقم الانكماش الاقتصادي. ويذكر أن الحكومة اليابانية كانت قد وافقت على استخدام حوالي 24 مليار ين (126 مليار دولار أميركي) من مداخيل ضرائب هذا العام وتقليص النفقات بهدف إخراج البلاد من حالة الركود الاقتصادي.

A judge from Chile to hold the position of director-general of the World Labour Organisation

A Chilean lawyer and diplomat, Juan Sumafiya, yesterday took up the position of director-general of the World Labour Organisation.

The committee of the organisation elected Sumafiya to this post last year to succeed a former Belgian minister, Michel Hansan, who spent ten years of his working life as head of the World Labour Organisation, affiliated to the United Nations, which works to establish social justice and labour rights.

In a statement Sumafiya said he wanted assurance that the benefits of information technology were reaching all parts of society and he added: "World-wide we have agreed to encourage free societies and free economies. This agreement will not continue unless real advantages that ordinary people and their families can feel enter the equation."

The organisation was established in 1919 and has 174 member countries.

Highest unemployment rate in Japan for 50 years

London - *Asharq al-Awsat*: The number of jobless in Japan rose last January to 2.98 million people, a 25% increase over the number registered in the same month of last year. The Japanese government considered this number low against the economic conditions prevailing world-wide, but a sign that the fall in the Japanese economic performance would continue this year. The conclusion of the data made clear that the number of people aged between 35 and 55 made redundant this year had reached a million. The figures also showed that this year witnessed the highest number of unemployed for half a century. The Central Bank of Japan has published the minutes of the meeting held by the financial policy committee in January which showed that the majority of the committee members did not see any prospect of economic improvement; indeed some of them expressed their concern that the economic recession would get worse. It is to be mentioned that the Japanese government has agreed to use around 24 billion yen, 126 million US dollars, from tax receipts this year and to reduce expenditure with the aim of getting the country out of the situation of economic stagnation.

Exercises Articles 43 - 48

Exercise 1 Choose the best answer

١ سيناقش المؤتمر موضوع السوق العربية المشتركة لتحقيق التقلب/التفتيش/التكامل/التغيير الاقتصادى.
٢ يبحث المؤتمر اطراف/اثار/سبل/افاق تحقيق التنمية البشرية.
٣ اصبحت البطالة عولمة/ظاهرة/مناسبة/منحة خطيرة فى العالم العربى.
٤ ظاهرة العولمة تتعرض لمساعدات/لتحديات/لمحاولات/لتغطيات كثيرة.
٥ يتمتع المرشح بتاييد/باجتماع/بتعزيز/بتسويق واسع.
٦ سيتم شحن الكمية/القيمة/الاقامة/الكلفة على دفعين.
٧ اطراف/خطوط/عوائد/مزايا العولمة لم تصل الى كافة ارجاء المجتمع.
٨ ارتفع عدد المسؤولين/الاقتصاديين/العاطلين/المستهلكين عن العمل.
٩ الانخفاض فى الاجراء/الايجاد/الاتحاد/الاداء الاقتصادى سيستمر هذا العام.
١٠ عبر البعض عن مخاوفه تكامل/تراجع/تفاقم/تباطؤ الانكماش الاقتصادى.
١١ استخدمت الحكومة ٥٠ مليار ين من مداخيل مزايا/ضرائب/افاق/لوائح.
١٢ خرج البلاد من حالة التحقيق/الركود/التفاقم/التكليف الاقتصادى.

Exercise 2 Match the following pairs

١	عاطل	a	الى انخفاض
٢	مؤشر	b	من حالة الركود
٣	مزايا	c	عن التقلبات
٤	تعويض	d	العولمة
٥	اخراج	e	عن العمل

Exercise 3 Match the following pairs

١	على المستوى	a	غير عادل
٢	بشكل	b	التحديات
٣	باستثناء	c	بحوالى ٦٠ مليون دولار
٤	فى ضوء	d	وكالة الطاقة
٥	مقارنة	e	العالمى

Exercise 4 Choose the appropriate verb

١ يسجل/يعقد/يشهد مؤتمر العمل دورته السادسة.
٢ يستضيف/يستعرض/يستغرق المؤتمر تقرير المدير العام.

٣ يحتاج/يتمتع/يعرب المرشح بتاييد واسع.
٤ تبلغ/تقفز/تقدم الحكومة منحة مجانية.
٥ ارتفع/اعتزم/انتخب الرئيس الوزير السابق لهذا المنصب.

Exercise 5 Put the words in these headlines in the correct order

١ الإجمالي تتجاوز ديون الإسرائيلية الحكومة المحلي الناتج

٢ لليوم الثاني الانخفاض الكويت أسهم تواصل

٣ في الرياض والكويت الإمارات وركود عام في ارتفاع

٤ ريال الاستثمارات 4.6 مليار العام اليمن قيمة الأجنبية في الماضي

٥ أميركا «طفيفا» يتوقع صندوق النقد ركودا في

ARTICLE 49

to borrow	اقترض
on behalf of	نيابة عن
supervisor	مشرف
resources	موارد *pl.* مورد
governor	محافظ
provision	توفير
worth pointing out	تجدر الاشارة
land	اليابسة

عُمان تقترض 250 مليون دولار أميركي من بنك الصادرات والواردات الياباني

مسقط : من سامر حامد

وقعت سلطنة عمان وبنك الصادرات والواردات الياباني في طوكيو امس على اتفاقية قرض بمبلغ 250 مليون دولار اميركي. وقع الاتفاقية نيابة عن حكومة السلطنة احمد بن عبد النبي مكي وزير الاقتصاد الوطني المشرف على وزارة المالية ونائب رئيس مجلس الشؤون المالية وموارد الطاقة، ووقعها نيابة عن بنك الصادرات والواردات الياباني هيروشي ياسودا محافظ البنك. يأتي التوقيع على اتفاقية القرض استكمالا للخطوات التي اتخذتها حكومة سلطنة عمان في توفير البنية التحتية لمشروع انشاء ميناء صحار.

ويتوقع الانتهاء من تنفيذ المشروع في نهاية عام 2002.

تجدر الاشارة الى ان فترة القرض تبلغ 16,5 سنة متضمنة فترة سماح مدتها ثلاث سنوات ويتم تمويل 50 في المائة من القرض بالدولار الاميركي والـ50 في المائة الأخرى بالين الياباني. وتبلغ مساحة ميناء صحار الجديد الاجمالية 47 كيلومترا مربعا منها 14 كيلومترا مربعا على اليابسة و8 كيلومترات لحوض داخل البحر.

ARTICLE 50

family *adj.*	عائلى
bonds	اوراق مالية
maintenance	ابقاء
active	نشط
to reflect	انعكس
revenue	*pl.* ايرادات

خبراء يدعون لإخراج الشركات العائلية من البورصة المصرية

القاهرة - رويترز: انتقد خبراء مصريون كثرة عدد الشركات المغلقة او العائلية التي تمثل أكثر من ثلثي عدد الشركات الموجودة في البورصة المصرية للاوراق المالية والتي يبلغ عددها 891 شركة حاليا، وطالبوا باخراجها والابقاء على الشركات نشطة التعامل فحسب. وقال منير هندي استاذ الادارة المالية بكلية التجارة بجامعة طنطا «لا توجد بورصة بالاسواق الناشئة تسجل الشركات المغلقة فلا مكان عندها للشركات العائلية. والمهم وجود تعامل نشط على اسهم الشركة». وأضاف ان كثرة عدد الشركات المقيدة ادى الى انخفاض متوسط رأس المال للشركة في البورصة المصرية مقارنة مع نظيره في الدول العربية. وقال انه اذا كانت الشركات المغلقة تدخل البورصة من اجل الحصول على مزايا ضريبية فان هذا ينعكس على الايرادات الضريبية باعتباره مال الشعب.

Oman borrows 250 million US dollars from the Export-Import Bank of Japan

Muscat, *by Samir Hamid*: The Sultanate of Oman and the Export-Import Bank of Japan in Tokyo yesterday signed a loan agreement for 250 million US dollars. The agreement was signed by Ahmed Bin Nabi Macki, minister of the national economy, head of the finance ministry and deputy head of the council of financial affairs and energy resources, on behalf of the Omani government, and by Hiroshi Yasooda, governor of the bank, on behalf of the Export-Import Bank of Japan. The signing of the loan agreement completes the steps taken by the Omani government to providing the infrastructure for a project to build a port at Suhar.

The project is expected to be completed by the end of 2002. It is worth pointing out that the loan is for 16.5 years which includes a grace period of three years with fifty per cent of financing in US dollars and the other fifty per cent in Japanese yen. The overall surface of the new port of Suhar is 47 square kilometres with 14 square kilometres on land and 8 kilometres for the sea basin.

Exports call on family companies to leave the Egyptian stock market

Cairo - *Reuters*: Egyptian experts criticised the large number of close or family companies that make up more than a third of the companies on the Egyptian securities market, presently totalling 891, calling for their removal and for trading to be left to companies. Mounir Hindy, professor of financial administration at the faculty of commerce at the university of Tanta said: "There is not one developing market that lists close companies and there is no place for family companies. The important thing is that there should be active trading in company shares." He added that the high number of companies registered had led to an average reduction in the capital of companies on the Egyptian stock market compared with his counterparts in Arab countries. He said that if close companies entered the market to obtain tax advantages, this would rebound on tax revenues, the nation's assets.

ARTICLE 51

to be sorry	اسف
comment	ات *pl.* تعليق
guaranteed	مضمون
owner	ارباب *pl.* رب
to be preoccupied	عانى من
job	وظائف *pl.* وظيفة
perils	مخاطر
to struggle	جاهد
through	وسط
competitive	تنافسي
strong	مرير
time	آجال *pl.* اجل
to value of	بواقع
to recede	انحسر
pressure	ضغوط *pl.* ضغط
time	اونة *pl.* اوان

اتحاد الصناعة البريطاني يأسف لتثبيت أسعار الفائدة

لندن: «الشرق الأوسط»

اعرب اتحاد الصناعة البريطاني امس عن اسفه لقرار بنك انجلترا (البنك المركزي البريطاني) تثبيت اسعار الفائدة عند مستوياتها الحالية.

وفي تعليق حول قرار البنك قالت كيت باركر، المستشارة الاقتصادية في الاتحاد في بيان امس «ان العديد من الشركات ستأسف لقرار البنك بالابقاء على معدلات الفائدة عند مستوياتها. فعلى الرغم من مؤشرات على ان الاقتصاد البريطاني لم يعد يسير في طريق الانخفاض، الا ان الافاق لا تزال غير مضمونة. فأرباب الصناعة لا يزالون يعانون من ركود يعرض الوظائف للمخاطر. ويجاهد المصدرون وسط قوة الجنيه الاسترليني وفي سوق تنافسية مريرة».

وكان بنك انجلترا المركزي قد قرر امس ترك أسعار الفائدة الرئيسية للاجال القصيرة دون تغيير بواقع 5,50 في المائة بعد ان انحسرت الضغوط عليه في الاونة الاخيرة لخفض الفائدة.

ARTICLE 52

to exceed	فوق
expectation	ات *pl.* توقع
measurement	مقاييس *pl.* مقياس
to be in tune with	اتفق مع
inflation	تضخم
to disappear	تلاشى

نمو الاقتصاد الأميركي أواخر 98 فاق التوقعات

واشنطن - رويترز: قالت الحكومة الاميركية امس ان الارتفاع الحاد في معدل النمو الاقتصادي الاميركي خلال الشهور الثلاثة الاخيرة من 1998 فاق توقعات سابقة. وافادت وزارة التجارة ارتفاع معدل النمو السنوى للناتج المحلي الاجمالي وهو المقياس الاوسع نطاقا لصحة الاقتصاد الى 6,1 في المائة خلال الربع الاخير من العام. وقبل شهر توقعت تقديرات ان يسجل معدل النمو 5,6 في المائة في الربع الاخير من 1998.

وأظهرت بيانات أعلنت اخيرا ارتفاع حجم الاستثمارات في المشروعات والمعدات بنحو يفوق تقديرات سابقة لوزارة التجارة كما تجاوز حجم الصادرات التوقعات. وقال محللون ان هذين العاملين ساهما الى حد بعيد في ارتفاع معدل نمو اجمالي الناتج المحلي بما يتفق مع توقع اقتصاديين في وول ستريت بنيويورك ان يصل المعدل الى ستة في المائة. وتلاشى التضخم تقريبا مع نهاية العام الماضي رغم الارتفاع الحاد في النمو.

الا أن ارتفاع تقديرات وزارة التجارة للربع الأخير لم يؤثر على معدل النمو الاجمالي لعام 1998 الذي سجل 3,9 في المائة متفقا مع توقعات الوزارة قبل شهر. ويعتبر معدل النمو الذي شهده الربع الأخير من العام الماضي أقوى معدل شهده ربع سنة خلال فترة التسعينات.

Confederation of British Industry regrets the holding of interest rates

London - *Asharq al-Awsat*: The CBI yesterday expressed its regret about the decision by the Bank of England to hold interest rates at their present levels.

In a comment about the bank's decision, the confederation's economic adviser, Kate Barker, said in a statement yesterday: "Many companies will regret the bank's decision to hold interest rates at the same levels. Although the signs are that the British economy is no longer deteriorating, nevertheless the prospects remain uncertain. Business leaders are still concerned about a sluggishness that threatens jobs. Exporters are struggling because of the strong pound and in a bitterly competitive market."

Yesterday the Bank of England decided to leave short term base interest rates on hold at 5.50% after recent pressures to lower the rate had receded.

US economic growth at the end of 98 exceeded expectations

Washington - *Reuters*: The US government said yesterday that the sharp rise in the rate of US economic growth for the last three months of 1998 had exceeded previous expectations. The trade ministry reported a rise in the annual growth rate of GDP, the most commonly used indicator of the economy's health, to 6.1% over the last quarter of 1998.

Figures published recently showed an increase in investment in projects and capital equipment that exceeded previous estimates of the trade ministry. Exports also exceeded expectations. Analysts said that these two factors had contributed to a large extent to the increase in the growth rate of GDP, in line with the expectation of Wall Street economists that the rate should reach six per cent. Inflation virtually disappeared at the end of last year in spite of the sharp increase in growth.

However the rise in expectations of the ministry of trade for the final quarter did not affect the overall rate of growth for 1998 of 3.9%, in line with the ministry's expectations a month ago. The growth rate recorded in the final quarter of last year is thought to be the strongest rate that a quarter has seen during the nineties.

ARTICLE 53

to fall	هوى
to sink	تدنى
nominal	اسمى
decline	تدنى
peak	ذروة
foot	قدم *pl.* اقدام
cubic	معكب

إيرادات النفط البريطانية تهوي بمقدار الثلث في عام 1998

لندن - رويترز: اعلن رويال بنك اوف اسكوتلند في تقرير امس ان ايرادات بريطانيا من النفط هبطت بمقدار الثلث في العام الماضي رغم الزيادة في انتاج النفط.

وتدنت الايرادات مرة اخرى في ديسمبر (كانون الاول) الى 15,9 مليون جنيه استرليني يوميا وهو اقل دخل في 25 عاما في مؤشر رويال بنك اوف اسكوتلند لأيرادات النفط والغاز.

وهبط متوسط سعر النفط في ديسمبر بواقع 8,4 في المائة الى 9,81 دولار للبرميل.

وفي العام الماضي هبطت ايرادات النفط اليومية الى 19,6 مليون جنية استرليني فقط (32,19 مليون دولار) وهو ما يمثل ادنى مستوى من الناحية الاسمية في عشر سنوات.

ويعكس الانخفاض السنوى تدني سعر النفط الى 12,78 دولار للبرميل في المتوسط. وقال رويال بنك اوف اسكوتلند ان ايرادات بريطانيا في العام الماضي كانت أقل بمقدار الخمس من قيمتها الحقيقية في سنة الذروة في 1984.

وهبطت ايرادات النفط والغاز معا هبوطا حادا في العام الماضي الى 33,9 مليون جنيه استرليني يوميا منخفضة بنحو الربع تقريبا عن عام 1997. وانخفضت ايرادات الغاز بواقع 2,9 في المائة على مدى العام.

لكن انتاج بريطانيا من النفط في العام الماضي زاد بنسبة 1,1 في المائة الى 2,54 مليون برميل يوميا في اول زيادة سنوية في ثلاث سنوات واقل بمقدار 2,1 في المائة من ذروة الانتاج في عام 1985.

وزاد انتاج النفط بنسبة 3,9 في المائة في ديسمبر الى 2,71 مليون برميل يوميا، بينما ارتفع انتاج الغاز على مدى الشهر الى 11,062 مليون قدم مكعب يوميا.

ARTICLE 54

absolutely	على الاطلاق
to occupy	احتل
grade	مرتبة *pl.* مراتب
generosity	سخاء
successively	على التوالى
birth *adj.*	انجابى
aid	معونة
donor	مانح
to be behind	تخلف
group	مجموعة
performing	وفاء
duty	التزام *pl.* ات
population	سكان

انخفاض في المساعدات المقدمة من منظمة التعاون الاقتصادي والتنمية

لندن: «الشرق الأوسط»

اظهرت ارقام صدرت اخيرا عن منظمة التعاون الاقتصادي والتنمية انخفاضا ملموسا في حجم المساعدات التنموية التي قدمتها البلدان الاعضاء الى الدول النامية.. فقد هبط حجم هذه المساعدات الى 252,1 مليار دولار في عام 1997 من اعلى مستوى لها على الاطلاق سجلته عام 1996 عند 282,6 مليار دولار.

وطبقا لارقام المنظمة فقد احتلت النرويج والدنمارك المرتبتين الاولى والثانية في قائمة الدول الاكثر سخاء من بين بلدان منظمة التعاون. فقد جاءت نسب المعونات التنموية الى الناتج المحلي الاجمالي والتي قدمتها الدنمارك والنرويج عند 0,97 في المائة و 0,86 في المائة على التوالي، في حين احتلت المساعدات التنموية التي قدمتها الولايات المتحدة كنسبة الى الناتج المحلي الاجمالي المرتبة الاخيرة بواقع 0,09 في المائة.

وكانت دراسة صدرت اخيرا شملت 20 دولة من الدول المانحة قد اظهرت ان النرويج والدنمارك تتقدمان بقية دول العالم في تمويل برامج الصحة الانجابية في الدول النامية بينما تتخلف الولايات المتحدة كثيرا عن الدول الاخرى المانحة. وأفادت الدراسة التى أصدرتها امس مجموعة الضغط «بوبيوليشين اكشن انترناشيونال» ان الدول المانحة ابعد ما تكون عن الوفاء بالتزامات تمويل برامج السكان التي وضعت أثناء المؤتمر الدولي للسكان والتنمية في القاهرة عام 1994.

وبلغ حجم المساعدات المقدمة من الدولتين لبرامج السكان الدولية 1,4 مليار دولار او نحو ربع المبلغ المتفق عليه في القاهرة ويصل الى 5,7 ميار دولار بحلول عام 2000.

UK oil revenues fall by a third in 1998

London - *Reuters*: The Royal Bank of Scotland announced in a report yesterday that UK oil revenues had fallen by a third last year despite an increase in oil production.

Revenues dropped once again in December to 15.9 million pounds a day, the lowest revenue for 25 years according to the Royal Bank of Scotland index for oil and gas revenues.

The average price for oil in December fell 8.4% to 9.81 dollars a barrel. Last year daily oil revenues fell to just 19.6 million pounds, 32.19 million dollars, the lowest level in cash terms for ten years. The annual fall reflects the decline in the average price of oil to 12.78 dollars a barrel. The Royal Bank of Scotland said British revenues last year were around five times lower than their value in real terms in the peak year of 1984.

Oil and gas revenues together fell sharply last year to 33.9 million pounds a day, a fall of around a quarter from 1997. Gas revenues fell by 2.9% over the year. But UK oil production last year rose 1.1% to 2.54 million barrels a day in the first annual increase in three years and was 2.1% less than the peak production in 1985. Oil production rose by 3.9% in December to 2.71 million barrels a day, while gas production over the month rose to 11.062 million cubic feet per day.

Fall in aid provided by the Organisation for Economic Cooperation and Development

London - *Asharq al-Awsat*: Figures published recently by the Organisation for Economic Cooperation and Development showed a marked drop in the volume of development aid the member countries gave to the developing countries. This aid fell to 252.1 billion dollars in 1997 from its highest ever level recorded in 1996 of 282.6 billion dollars.

According to the organisation's figures, Norway and Denmark held first and second place in the list of the most generous countries in the OECD. The rates of development aid related to GDP, of which Denmark and Norway gave 0.97% and 0.86% respectively, while development aid that the US gave as a percentage of GDP was in last place at 0.09%.

A study recently published that included 20 of the donor nations had shown that Norway and Denmark headed the other countries of the world in financing programmes on childbirth health in the developing nations, while the United States lagged a long way behind the other donor nations. The study published yesterday by the pressure group, Population Action International, pointed out that the donor nations were further than ever from fulfilling the commitments of financing the population programmes set up during the international conference on population and development in Cairo in 1994.

Aid given by the two countries to the international population programmes totalled 1.4 billion dollars or around a quarter of the amount agreed in Cairo, which will reach 5.7 billion dollars by the start of 2000.

Exercises Articles 49 - 54

Exercise 1 Choose the best answer

١ يتوقع الانتهاء من تعليق/توقيع/تثبيت/تنفيذ المشروع الشهر المقبل.
٢ فترة النظير/التوفير/المعرض/القرض تبلغ ١٥ سنة.
٣ الشركات المغلقة تدخل البورصة من اجل الحصول على افاق/اوضاع/موارد/مزايا ضريبية.
٤ الوزيرون لا يزالون يعانون من انتعاش/انماء/ركود/انعاش يعرض الوظائف للمخاطر.
٥ كان البنك قرر ترك/عامل/ابقاء/نزاع اسعار الفائدة دون تغيير.
٦ ارتفع معدل النمو السنوى للركود/للتضخم/للناتج/للانتعاش المحلى الاجمالى الى ٦ فى المائة.
٧ تلاشى الانتعاش/المخاوف/الركود/التضخم تقريبا رغم الارتفاع الحاد فى النمو.
٨ هبطت توقعات/نفقات/ايرادات/خطوات من البفط العام الماضى.
٩ احتلت الولايات المتحدة الفرصة/الفترة/المساعدة/المرتبة الاخيرة
١٠ الدول المانحة ابعد ما تكون عن الوفاء بتوقعات/ببيانات/بتقديرات/بالتزامات تمويل البرامج.

Exercise 2 Match the following pairs

١	تجدر	a	السماح
٢	فترة	b	للاجال القصيرة
٣	على رغم	c	مكعب
٤	قدم	d	الاشارة
٥	مقارنة	e	من مؤشرات
٦	اسعار الفائدة	f	مع الايرادات

Exercise 3 Choose the most suitable adjective

١ انخفاض انجابى/ مشكوك/ملموس
٢ الناتج الحاد/المحلى/الهادىء
٣ مزايا راكدة/حقيقية/مطلعة
٤ انكماش تطوعى/سياسى/اقتصدى
٥ قرار ملموس/معطل/عاجل
٦ بنية تحتية/اسمية/عادلة
٧ اللجنة الخامة/الجاهزة/التحضيرية
٨ انتعاش متواضع/مشترك/تجريبى

Exercise 4 Put the words of these headlines in the correct order

١ تخفض تدني الكويت بسبب الإنفاق الحكومي النفط أسعار

٢ سوق أميركا السعودية على الأغذية تنافس فرنسا

٣ صناعة النفط مليار دولار في نيجيريا شل تعرض

لتنشيط استثمار 8.5

Exercise 5 Match the following

١ القطاع المصرفي والمالي في الجزائر

a لدى صندوق النقد لمعالجة الأزمات المالية

٢ اختتام مؤتمر سيدات

b يشهد دفعا خاصا خلال عام 1998

٣ هل أسواق الأسهم العالمية في

c مستويات عالية من التفاؤل؟

٤ خبير بنكي يدعو إلى توفير 300 مليار دولار

d العمل في بريطانيا للربع الأخير

٥ ازدياد عدد العاطلين عن

e الأعمال العربي في القاهرة

ARTICLE 55

to take possession of	استحاذ على
priority	اولية
concern	اهتمام
needs	ات *pl.* احتياج
district	احياء *pl.* حي
competition	منافسة
attraction	جذب
shopper	متسوق
creation	استحداث
to accompany	تواكب
specifications	مواصفات
pattern	نقلة
concept	مفهوم
luxurious	ترفيهي
to attract	استقطب

10 مليارات ريال حجم الاستثمارات في أكثر من 600 مجمع تجاري بالرياض

الرياض: «الشرق الأوسط»

وصل حجم الاستثمارات في انشاء الأسواق والمراكز التجارية في العاصمة السعودية الرياض إلى نحو 10 مليارات ريال، حيث يبلغ عدد الأسواق والمراكز التجارية أكثر من 600 سوق ومركز تجاري.

وأشارت دراسة حديثة الى أن القطاع الخاص يستحوذ على 95 في المائة منها. ويحتل هذا القطاع أولويات اهتمام رجال الأعمال والمستثمرين، إضافة الى احتياجات بعض الأحياء الحديثة إلى مثل هذه الأسواق.

ويرجع متعاملون في السوق إقبال المستثمرين على انشاء مثل هذه الاسواق التجارية بمدينة الرياض إلى النمو السكاني المتزايد الذي وصل الى 3,11 مليون نسمة بنسبة نمو 3,7 في المائة سنوياً إضافة الى زيادة دخل الأسرة الذي يبلغ حوالي 123 ألف ريال سنوياً.

وقد شهدت الأسواق والمراكز التجارية بالرياض منافسة كبيرة بغرض جذب المتسوقين، مما دفع إدارات المجمعات التجارية إلى استحداث أساليب تسويقية جديدة تتواكب والرغبات المتجددة للمتسوقين.

يذكر أن أحدث هذه الأسواق مركز الوزير «ابن سليمان» التجاري، الذي نفذ في وسط مدينة الرياض بأحدث التقنيات والمواصفات المعمارية، والذي يعتبر نقلة حقيقية ومرحلة جديدة في مفهوم التسوق بالمراكز التجارية، وذلك للاهتمام بمستوى الخدمات وتوفير الوسائل الترفيهية المصاحبة لعملية التسوق، حيث يتوقع أن يستقطب المركز عدداً كبيراً من المتسوقين.

ARTICLE 56

operation	عملية
preparatory to	تمهيدا
ownership	ملكية
front	مقدمة
to contain	حوى
building	مبان *pl.* مبنى
reserve	رديف
support *adj.*	مساند
floor	طوابق *pl.* طابق
first results	بواكير *pl.* باكورة
to intend	نوى
permit	تراخيص *pl.* ترخيص
insurance	تامين
cooperative spirit	تعاونية

اكتمال إنشاء أول مركز طبي متخصص بعمليات اليوم الواحد في الرياض

الرياض: من عدنان جابر

اكتملت في الرياض الأعمال الإنشائية لأول مركز طبي من نوعه في السعودية يخصص لعمليات اليوم الواحد تمهيدا للبدء بتشغيله في منتصف الشهر المقبل. وذكر الدكتور صالح قنباز أن المشروع الذي يحمل اسم المركز الطبي التخصصي تكلف 140 مليون ريال (37,3 مليون دولار). وتشارك في ملكيته مجموعة من المستثمرين المحليين تأتي في مقدمتهم مجموعة الراشد، وشركة الثماد.

ويعد هذا المشروع الذي يقع على مساحة 15 ألف متر مربع، ويحوي 12 دورا، إضافة الى مبنى رديف للخدمات المساندة مكون من ثلاثة طوابق، باكورة المشاريع الطبية الجديدة التي ينوي القطاع الخاص إضافتها في العاصمة السعودية خلال الفترة المقبلة، إذ تشير الأوساط المطلعة الى أن هناك 10 تراخيص صدرت لإقامة مستشفيات ومراكز صحية جديدة في الرياض بدأ تنفيذ أربعا منها حتى الآن.

وأوضح قنباز أن المركز التخصصي الطبي سيكون مشاركا في الضمان الطبي التعاوني المتبع حاليا من قبل العديد من المستشفيات الخاصة، حيث أجرت عدة شركات تأمين اتصالاتها لإبرام عقود مع المركز الجديد، من بينها مجموعة بوبا، والشركة الوطنية للتأمين التعاوني «التعاونية للتأمين».

Investment in more than 600 commercial centres in Riyadh totals 10 billion riyals

Riyadh - *Asharq al-Awsat*: Investment in the construction of commercial centres and markets in the Saudi capital, Riyadh, has reached around 10 billion riyals, with the number of commercial markets and centres topping 600.

A new study showed that the private sector controlled 95% of them. This sector is of prime interest for businessmen and investors. In addition some modern districts need such markets. Traders in the market attribute the demand of the investors for constructing such commercial centres in the city of Riyadh to the increasing growth of the population, which reached 3.11 million, at an annual rate of growth of 3.7%, in addition to an increase in income per family which is now around 123,000 riyals a year.

The commercial markets and centres in Riyadh have seen intense competition to attract shoppers. This has led the management of the commercial centres to develop accompanying new marketing strategies and renewed desires for the shoppers. It is to be mentioned that the newest of these markets is the commercial centre, al-Wazir Ibn Suliman. Built in Riyadh city centre to the most up to date building techniques and specifications, it constitutes a genuine model and new stage in the concept of selling in commercial centres in terms of the concern for the level of services and the luxurious facilities that accompany the selling process. The centre is expected to attract a large number of shoppers.

Completion of the construction of the first medical centre specialising in same-day operations in Riyadh

Riyadh, *from Adnan Jabr*: Building works have recently been completed in Riyadh of the first medical centre of its kind in Saudi specialising in same-day operations prior to its opening in the middle of next month. Doctor Salah Qanbaz said that the project, which carries the name of the National Specialist Centre, cost 140 million riyals, 37.3 million dollars. Ownership is shared by a group of local investors, headed by the Rashad group and the al-Thamad company.

This project, situated in an area of 15,000 square metres and on twelve floors, in addition to a back-up building for reserve services on three floors, may be seen as the first signs of new medical schemes that the private sector is proposing to add in the Saudi capital in the immediate future; informed circles point out that ten permits have been issued to set up new clinics and health centres in Riyadh, and up to now building has begun on four.

Qanbaz said that the specialist medical centre would be a partner in cooperative medical insurance used at present by many private clinics, with a number of insurance companies having made contact to set up contracts with the new centre, among them BUPA, and the national company for cooperative insurance, Cooperative Insurance.

9.5 مليون ريال أرباح «الشيكات السعودية»

الرياض: «الشرق الأوسط»

حققت شركة الشيكات السياحية السعودية خلال العام الماضي أرباحا بلغت 9,5 مليون ريال بانخفاض طفيف عن أرباح العام الأسبق البالغة 11 مليون ريال.وأبلغ عبد العزيز العجروش مدير عام الشركة «الشرق الأوسط» أن «الشيكات السعودية» تمكنت من رفع مبيعاتها خلال العام الماضي بواقع 13 في المائة لتصل الى 170 مليون ريال مقابل مبيعات قدرها 150 مليون ريال للعام الأسبق.

وعزا العجروش انخفاض الأرباح خلال العام الماضي رغم ارتفاع حجم مبيعاتها الى أسباب تتعلق بقصر مدة صرف الشيكات التي تمت خلال العام الماضي مقارنة بالعام الأسبق 1997 والذي شهد تسجيل مبيعات شيكات لعدد من الحجاج الذين لم يتمكنوا من الحضور الى الحج، وبالتالي زادت فترة احتفاظهم بالشيكات نفسها، إذ تسجل أرباح الشركة نتائج إيجابية كلما زادت مدة الاحتفاظ.

ARTICLE 57

shortness	قصر
money changing	صرف
hence	بالتالى
retention	احتفاظ

179 مليون ريال أرباح شركة إسمنت القصيم خلال عام 1998

الرياض: «الشرق الأوسط»

أوصى مجلس ادارة شركة اسمنت القصيم بتوزيع أرباح للمساهمين بنسبة 34٪ من رأس المال، وبما يعادل 17 ريال للسهم الواحد، ليبلغ ما سيتم توزيعه من ارباح على المساهمين نحو 153 مليون ريال لعام 1998، مقارنة بـ144 مليون ريال، تم توزيعها ارباحا للمساهمين لعام 1997.

وبهذا يكون مجمل ما تم توزيعه أرباحا للمساهمين من عام 1980 حتى العام الماضي 1,120 مليار ريال، مقارنة بـ300 مليون ريال تم دفعها بواسطة المساهمين كرأس مال أساسي للشركة.

وقال الأمير عبد الرحمن العبد الله الفيصل رئيس مجلس الادارة ان أرباح الشركة لعام 1998 بلغت 179 مليون ريال، مقارنة بالارباح المتحققة في عام 1997 والبالغة 181 مليون ريال.

واشار في البيان الذي وزعته الشركة يوم امس الأربعاء ان الشركة حققت مستويات جيدة في انتاج مادة الكلنك بلغت 1,400 مليون طن من خلال خطي الانتاج الاول والثاني بنسبة انخفاض 6 في المائة، وذلك بسبب زيادة كمية مخزون الكلنك وانخفاض الاستهلاك المحلي للاسمنت.

واضاف بان مبيعات الشركة بلغت حوالي 1,500 مليون طن أسمنت بنوعيه العادي والمقاوم بزيادة طفيفة عن مبيعات العام المالي 1997, واكد رئيس مجلس الادارة بان الشركة سوف تعمل بكل ما لديها من جهد وطاقة وعطاء لتحقيق المزيد من القفزات التطويرية والانتاجية خلال العام المالي 1999 .

ARTICLE 58

sum	مجمل
by	بواسطة
stored	مخزون
gift	عطاء *pl.* اعطية
developmental	تطويرى

9.5 million riyal profits for Saudi Cheques

Riyadh - *Asharq al-Awsat*: Saudi Travellers Cheques posted profits of 9.5 million riyals last year, down slightly from the previous year of 11 million riyals. Abdul-Aziz al-Ajroosh, director-general of the company, told Asharq al-Awsat that Saudi Cheques had been able to raise its sales last year by 13% to 170 million riyals compared with sales of 150 million riyals the previous year.

Al-Ajroosh attributed the fall in profits last year despite increased sales to reasons connected with the short period the cheques were held for compared with the previous year 1997, which saw sales of cheques to a number of pilgrims who were unable to attend the Hajj. This meant they held the cheques for a longer period, and company profits rise whenever the period the cheques are held increases.

179 million riyal profits of al-Qaseem Cement Company in 1998

Riyadh - *Asharq al-Awsat*: The board of directors of the cement company, al-Qaseem, recommended distribution of profits to shareholders of 34% of capital, equivalent to 17 riyals per share. Profits distributed to shareholders will reach 153 million riyals for 1998, compared with 144 million riyals distributed to shareholders in 1997.

Thus the total distributed to shareholders from 1980 up to last year is 1.12 billion riyals, compared to 300 million riyals paid by shareholders as start-up capital to the company. Prince Abdulrahman Abdullah al-Faisal, chairman of the board, said that company profits for 1998 totalled 179 million riyals, compared to profits for 1997 of 181 million riyals.

In a statement issued by the company yesterday, Wednesday, he pointed out that the company had achieved excellent levels of production of clinker of 1.4 million tons in the first and second stages of production, a 6% reduction. This was because of an increase in the amount of clinker stored and a fall in local cement consumption. He added that company sales had reached around 1.5 million tons of cement of its ordinary and enhanced types, a slight increase in sales from the financial year 1997. The chairman of the board gave an assurance that the company would do everything in its power to bring about the greatest leaps in development and productivity during 1999.

انخفاض أرباح «النقل البحري» السعودية إلى 30 مليون ريال

باناجة أكد لـ الشرق الأوسط أن الانخفاض حدث نتيجة المنافسة وانخفاض النفط

الرياض: محمد الخضري

عزا احمد سليمان باناجة رئيس مجلس إدارة الشركة السعودية للنقل البحري انخفاض أرباح الشركة الى 30 مليون ريال الى حدة التنافس والتاثير المباشر للأوضاع الاقتصادية في العالم، وانخفاض الطلب على النفط. واوضح باناجة في تصريح لـ «الشرق الأوسط» ان هذه الأرباح لا تتواءم مع راس مال الشركة البالغ ملياري ريال وموجوداتها التي تقدر بحوالي 4 مليارات ريال، مبيناً أن مجالات النقل التي تعمل فيها الشركة هي نقل البترول ونقل البتروكيماويات ونقل البضائع. موضحاً مدى التاثير المباشر للنواحي المالية على قطاع النقل البحري نظراً لكلفته العالية، الأمر الذي يستوجب البحث عن افضل الطرق والأساليب لمصادر التمويل والنظر في هيكلة هذا التمويل حتى لا يشكل عبئاً على كاهل الشركة ويؤثر في معدلات نمو الأرباح. وأضاف باناجة تطلعات مجلس الادارة الجديدة الى تحقيق أرباح متنامية خلال المرحلة المقبلة في ظل وجود هذه المنافسة الحادة التي ستزداد في المستقبل بعد اتمام انضمام السعودية الى منظمة التجارة العالمية وليس لنا من سبيل لمواجهة هذه المنافسة سوى تقديم الخدمة الأفضل.

ARTICLE 59

sharpness	حدة
to tally with	توئم
goods	بضاعة *pl.* بضائع
to deserve	استوجب
structuring	هيكلة
burden	عبء *pl.* اعباء
back	كاهل
aim	تطلع
completion	اتمام
entry	انضمام

3.6 في المائة زيادة في عدد الوجبات التي أنتجها تموين «السعودية»

جدة: «الشرق الأوسط»

قال عبد الرحمن الهلالي مدير عام تموين «السعودية» ان الوجبات التي انتجها تموين الخطوط الجوية العربية السعودية بوحداته الثلاث في كل من جدة - الرياض - القاهرة خلال العام الماضي بلغت 981, 525, 12وجبة بزيادة 3,6 في المائة مقارنة بعام 1997 في حين ارتفع عدد الرحلات الممونة خلال عام 98 الى 091, 79 رحلة لـ«السعودية» وشركات الطيران الاخرى العاملة في السعودية والتي يصل عددها الى 45 شركة طيران بنسبة زيادة 5,6 في المائة لوحدتي جدة والرياض. وسجلت وحدة تموين «السعودية» بالقاهرة زيادة في عدد الوجبات المنتجة بنسبة 2,2 في المائة مقارنة بعام 97 وهو ما يدل على مرونة خطوط الانتاج واستجابتها لمختلف الضغوط والمتطلبات التشغيلية.

واضاف ان وحدة تموين «السعودية» بجدة انتجت 370, 495, 6 وجبة لخدمة 36544 رحلة في حين انتجت وحدة تموين الرياض 120, 558, 5 وجبة لخدمة 36544 رحلة، فيما انتجت وحدة تموين القاهرة 472491 وجبة لخدمة 1979 رحلة.

ARTICLE 60

catering	تموين
line	خط *pl.* خطوط
aviation	طيران
to show	دل على
flexibility	مرونة
responding	استجابة
requirements	متطلبات

Fall in profits of Saudi Marine Transportation to 30 million riyals

Banaja told the Sharq al-Awsat that the fall came about as a result of competition and the fall in oil demand

Riyadh - Mohammad al-Khadri: Ahmad Suleiman Banaja, chairman of the board of the Saudi Company, Marine Transportation, attributed the drop in company profits to 30 million riyals to intense competition, the direct effect of worldwide economic conditions and the drop in oil demand. In a statement to the Sharq al-Awsat, Banaja said that these profits were not in line with the considerable capital of the company of two billion riyals and its assets calculated at around 4 billion riyals.

He explained that the transport sectors in which the company operated were oil, petrochemicals and goods transportation and he made clear the extent of the direct effect of financial aspects on the marine transportation sector in view of its high costs. This will mean searching out better ways and means for sourcing finance and looking at the structuring of this finance so as not to prove a burden on the company and thereby affect the rate of growth in profits. Banaja added that it was the aim of the new board to achieve higher profits in the next phase in spite of this intense competition that was set to intensify in the future after Saudi joined the World Trade Organisation and that the only way to face that competition was to offer a better service.

3.6 per cent increase in the number of meals produced by Saudi Catering

Jeddah - *Asharq al-Awsat*: Abdulrahman Al-Halali, general manager of Saudi Catering, said that the meals prepared by the catering section of Saudi Arabian Airlines in the three branches of Jeddah, Riyadh and Cairo last year totalled 12,525,981 - an increase of 3.6% compared with 1997, while the number of flights supplied on Saudia and the 45 other airline companies operating in Saudi rose to 79,091 in 1998. This was a 5.6 increase for the Jeddah and Riyadh branches. Saudi Catering in Cairo showed a 2.2% increase in the number of meals produced compared with 97. This shows the flexibility of the production lines and their response to different pressures and operational requirements.

He added that the catering branch in Jeddah produced 6,495,370 meals to serve 36,544 flights, while the Riyadh catering branch produced 5,558,120 meals to serve 36,544 flights and the Cairo catering branch produced 472,491 meals to serve 1,979 flights.

Exercises Articles 55 - 60

Exercise 1 Choose the best answer

١ شهدت الاسواق مساعدة/معادلة/مناسبة/منافسة كبيرة بغرض جذب المتسوقين.

٢ هذا دفع الادارة الى استحداث عوامل/اساليب/نواح/اصول تسويقية جديدة.

٣ تشير الاحياء/الطوابق/الاوساط/الاعباء الى ان الاعمال الانشائية ستكتمل الشهر المقبل.

٤ صدرت ٢٠ تراخيص/بواكر/وظائف/موارد لاقامة مستشفيات خديدة.

٥ اجرت عدة شركات تامين ايراداتها/اتصالاتها/اجتماعاتها/اتفاقاتها لابرام العقود.

٦ حققت الشركة نتائـــج/ارباح/مبان/اوراق بلغت ٢٠ مليون ريال.

٧ اوصى مجلس الادارة بتعليق/بتوزيع/بتثبيت/بتوقيع ارباح للمساهمين بنسبة ٣٠٪ من رأس المال.

٨ اكد رئـــيـــس مجلس الادارة بان الشركة سوف تعمل لتحقيق/لتعقيب/لتوزيع/لتعويض المزيد من القفزات التطويرية.

٩ انخفاض الارباح حدث نتيجة المرونة/المنافسة/النفقة/الخزينة الحادة.

١٠ ليس لنا من سبيل لمواجهة هذه المنافسة سوى تمويل/تخفيض/تشغيل/تقديم الخدمة الافضل.

Exercise 2 Match the following pairs

١	الدول تتمتع	a	عن التعقيب
٢	امتنع المتحدث	b	عن الدول الاخرى
٣	يعتمد التحليل	c	من توقيع اتفاقية
٤	تقترب فرنسا	d	على مسح جديد
٥	تتخلف الولايات المتحدة	e	بثقل كبير

Exercise 3 Put the following into the passage

بزيادة انخفاض ارباح

للسهم بتوزيع البيان الاستهلاك

مستويات القفزات جهد كراس

179 مليون ريال ــــ شركة إسمنت القصيم خلال عام 1998

الرياض: «الشرق الأوسط»

أوصى مجلس ادارة شركة اسمنت القصيم ــــ أرباح للمساهمين بنسبة 34٪ من رأس المال، وبما يعادل 17 ريال الواحد، ــــ ليبلغ ما سيتم توزيعه من ارباح على المساهمين نحو 153 مليون ريال لعام 1998، مقارنة بـ144 مليون ريال، تم توزيعها ارباحا للمساهمين لعام 1997.

وبهذا يكون مجمل ما تم توزيعه أرباحا للمساهمين من عام 1980 حتى العام الماضي 1,120 مليار ريال، مقارنة بـ300 مليون ريال تم دفعها بواسطة المساهمين ــــ مال أساسي للشركة.

وقال الأمير عبد الرحمن العبد الله الفيصل رئيس مجلس الادارة ان أرباح الشركة لعام 1998 بلغت 179 مليون ريال، مقارنة بالارباح المتحققة في عام 1997 والبالغة 181 مليون ريال.

واشار في ــــ الذي وزعته الشركة يوم امس الأربعاء ان الشركة حققت ــــ جيدة في انتاج مادة الكلنك بلغت 1,400 مليون طن من خلال خطي الانتاج الاول والثاني بنسبة انخفاض 6 في المائة، وذلك بسبب زيادة كمية مخزون الكلنك و ــــ المحلي للاسمنت.

واضاف بان مبيعات الشركة بلغت حوالي 1,500 مليون طن أسمنت بنوعيه العادي والمقاوم ــــ طفيفة عن مبيعات العام المالي 1997, واكد رئيس مجلس الادارة بان الشركة سوف تعمل بكل ما لديها من ــــ وطاقة وعطاء لتحقيق المزيد من ــــ التطويرية والانتاجية خلال العام المالي 1999 .

Exercise 4 Put the words of these headlines in the correct order

١ في واردات ارتفاع دبي طفيف من الذهب

٢ تعاوناً مع «ايرفرانس» في ابريل «طيران تبدأ الشرق الأوسط»

٣ في المائة «التعاونية للتأمين» نمواً تحقق السعودية السعودية قدره 6

Exercise 5 These three passages are continuations of articles 55-60; match them

١

كما سيناقش مجلس الادارة خلال اجتماعه المقبل خلال الشهر الجاري بحث كافة الجوانب والنظر في الايجابيات ومحاولة تدعيمها والنظر في السلبيات ومحاولة تلافيها والتقليل من نقاط الضعف لأن هذا هو أنسب طريق لنجاح أي منشأة أو شركة، مشيراً

٢

واشار الى انضمام الخطوط القطرية والخطوط البحرينية لقائمة شركات الطيرن المتعاملة مع تموين «السعودية»، كما تمت عودة شركة الطيران الايطالية للتزود بالوجبات من وحدة تموين جدة، وذلك في بداية شهر أبريل 98، وهناك مباحثات جارية مع الخطوط الفرنسية لمعاودة التزود بالوجبات من وحدة تموين «السعودية» في الرياض.

٣

وتشكل مبيعات الشركة الخارجية والموجهة للحجاج القادمين الى الأماكن المقدسة الحصة الأكبر، إذ تصل الى نحو 97 في المائة وتشمل الشيكات السياحية، وشيكات خدمات الحج الخاصة بمكتب الوكلاء الموحد

ARTICLE 61

to be wary of	تحفظ
individual	منفرد
detail	تفصيل *pl.* تفاصيل
resistance	اعتراض
reservation	تحفظ *pl.* ات
decided	مزمع
merging	دمج
basis	صعيد

الكويت تتحفظ على اندماج هوكست ورون بولنك

الكويت - رويترز: تحفظت الكويت امس على خطط اندماج شركة رون بولنك الفرنسية مع مجموعة هوكست الالمانية للكيماويات والادوية. وقال وزير النفط الكويتي الشيخ سعود ناصر الصباح لرويترز «هذا الاندماج لا يخدم مصالحنا».

ويرأس الشيخ سعود ايضا مؤسسة البترول الكويتية التي تمتلك اكبر حصة منفردة من اسهم هوكست. وبذا تمتلك الحكومة الكويتية بطريق غير مباشر 24,5 في المائة من اسهم هوكست.

ولم يوضح الوزير تفاصيل الاعتراضات الكويتية لكنه قال «لدينا تحفظات» على الاندماج. وكانت هوكست قد امتنعت أول من امس عن التعقيب على تقارير صحافية عن عدم تأييد الكويت لاندماجها المزمع. وكانت هوكست ورون بولنك قد اعلنتا عزمهما على دمج عمليات علوم الحياة لديهما في شركة تسمى افنتيس. ونقلت صحيفة «فرانكفورتر ألجماينه تسايتونج» عن مصادر لم تسمها قولها ان الكويت لديها شكوك في ان الاندماج سيضمن قدرة هوكست التنافسية على الصعيد الدولي.

ARTICLE 62

more prominent	ابرز
intermediary	وساط

المجموعة المالية تدخل البورصة

● ذكر عبد الستار بكري عضو مجلس ادارة بورصة القاهرة والاسكندرية امس انه تم قيد أربع شركات جديدة بالبورصة بلغت رؤوس أموالها 3, 383 مليون جنيه ليصل عدد الشركات المقيدة بها الى 883 شركة. واضافت وكالة رويترز انه تمت زيادة رأسمال شركة أيضا بنحو 99 مليون جنيه. وفي نهاية العام الماضي بلغ عدد الشركات المقيدة بالبورصة 861 شركة.

والشركات الجديدة هي المصرية للمنتجات السياحية (اكتتاب عام) برأسمال 350 مليون جنيه موزع على 5, 3 مليون سهم بقيمة اسمية 100 جنيه للسهم مدفوع بنسبة 25 في المائة. والمجموعة المالية هرميس القابضة (اكتتاب مغلق) برأسمال 3, 29 مليون جنيه موزع على 86, 5 مليون سهم. وهي تعد من أبرز شركات الوساطة بسوق المال المصرية. والمصرية للتنمية والآليات (ايكاد) وهي من شركات الاكتتاب المغلق برأسمال مليوني جنيه موزع على ألفي سهم.

Kuwait cautious of the merger of Hoechst and Rhône-Poulenc

Kuwait - *Reuters*: Kuwait expressed its caution about merger plans of the French company Rhône-Poulenc with the German chemical and pharmaceutical conglomerate Hoechst. The Kuwaiti oil minister, Sheikh Saud Nasser al-Sabah, told Reuters: "This merger does not serve our interests."

Sheikh Saud also heads the Kuwaiti Oil Organisation, which holds the largest individual block of shares in Hoechst. The Kuwaiti government thereby indirectly holds 24.5% of Hoechst shares.

The minister did not give details of the Kuwaiti objections, saying: "We have reservations" about the merger. The day before yesterday Hoechst had declined to comment on newspaper reports about the lack of Kuwaiti support for the prospective merger. Hoechst and Rhône-Poulenc had announced their determination to merge their life sciences business into a firm called Aventis. The newspaper, Frankfurter Allgemeine Zeitung, reported unnamed sources as saying that Kuwait had doubts about whether the merger would guarantee Hoechst's ability to compete at an international level.

Financial group enters the stock market

Abdul Satir Bakri, member of the board of the Alexandria Cairo stock exchange, announced yesterday that four new companies had been listed on the stock market with capital of 383.3 million pounds, to take the number of companies listed to 883. Reuters agency added that the company capital had increased by around 99 million pounds. At the end of last year there were 861 companies listed on the stock market.

The new companies are the Egyptian company for Travel Products, by public subscription, with 350 million pounds of capital, made up of 3.5 million shares with a nominal value of 100 pounds per share, with 25% paid up; the financial holding group Hermes, by close subscription, with a capital of 29.3 million pounds, made up of 5.86 million shares, considered one of the foremost financial intermediaries on the Egyptian stock market, the Egyptian company for development and instruments, Ikad, a company of close subscription with a capital of two million pounds made up of two thousand shares.

توقع انخفاض حاد للدولار العام الحالي

دافوس (سويسرا) ـ رويترز: قال الاقتصادي الاميركي فريد بيرجستن انه يتوقع ان يشهد الدولار انخفاضا حادا في عام 1999 حيث تشير جميع الاعتبارات الهيكلية والدورية الى انه سيسير في هذا الاتجاه.

وذكر بيرجستن في بحث سيقدمه الى الاجتماع السنوي لمنتدى الاقتصاد العالمي اليوم (الجمعة) «من المرجح أن يكون بين الاحداث الاقتصادية العالمية الرئيسية لعام 1999 الانخفاض الحاد في سعر صرف الدولار».

وقال ان أسعار التكافؤ الاساسية التي يحسبها معهد الاقتصاد الدولي الذي يرأسه بيرجستن توحي بأن سعر التعادل لليورو سيتراوح بين 1,25 دولار و1,30 دولار. وبلغ اليورو ظهر امس في اوروبا 1,1422/1,1425 دولار.

كما توحي نفس الاساسيات بأن سعر الدولار سيبلغ 100 ين. وبلغ سعر الدولار امس 115,55/115,60 ين.

واضاف انه نظرا لان اسعار السوق مرتفعة فان «الدولار يمكن ان ينخفض لمستويات اقل من ذلك في تراجعه الاول». وأي تحرك في هذا الاتجاه من شأنه ان يضر بالنمو في اليابان ويزيد معدل البطالة في أوروبا.

ويمكن لانخفاض الدولار ان يؤدي في نهاية الامر الى رفع أسعار الفائدة الاميركية في وقت يبدو ان الاقتصاد يتباطأ فيه.

وقال بيرجستن المستشار السابق للبيت الابيض ان الآثار يمكن ان تشمل تباطؤ النمو في دول رئيسية وزيادة الحاجة الى قيام مجموعة الثلاث (منطقة اليورو واليابان والولايات المتحدة) بادارة اسعار الصرف بشكل أنشط.

ARTICLE 63

structural	هيكلي
cyclical	دوري
gathering	منتدى *pl.* ات
likely	مرجح
equivalence	تكافوء
to suggest	أوحى
noon	ظهر
movement	تحرك
to slow down	تباطوء
carrying out	قيام

اليورو يفقد «بريقه» أمام الدولار وبورصات أوروبا ترتفع بعد تعثر

لندن: «الشرق الأوسط» ووكالات الأنباء

هبط اليورو الاوروبي الى ادنى مستوياته أمام العملة الاميركية منذ طرحه في بداية العام الجديد وذلك بعد أن لاقت العملة الاميركية دعما امام جميع العملات الرئيسية الاخرى بفضل توقعات نمو الاقتصاد الاميركي. وانخفضت معظم اسواق الاسهم الاوروبية عند بدء المعاملات امس متأثرة بانخفاض وول ستريت واسواق آسيا في الليلة قبل الماضية. لكن بورصة لندن عاودت ارتفاعها ومعها بورصة الاسهم السويدية التي اكتسبت قوة دافعة بعد انباء بأن شركة «ڤولڤو» باعت وحدة صناعة السيارات الى شركة «فورد» الاميركية مقابل 50 مليار كرونة.

وساعدت توقعات متفائلة بشأن الاقتصاد الاميركي الدولار على أن يرتفع في بداية المعاملات الاوروبية امام جميع العملات الرئيسية. وسادت السوق توقعات بان النمو الاقتصادي الاميركي سيظل أفضل من معدلات النمو في كل من أوروبا واليابان. وهبط اليورو في المعاملات الاوروبية ظهر أمس الى 1,1388 دولار بالمقارنة مع 1,1478 دولار في أواخر المعاملات الاوروبية أمس الاول.

واتجهت انظار الاسواق الى بيان الان چرينسپان رئيس مجلس الاحتياطي الفدرالي (البنك المركزي الاميركي) امام الكونچرس وبعض الاحصائيات الاميركية من بينها مؤشر تكاليف البطالة الاميركية في الربع الاخير من العام الماضي.

ARTICLE 64

to lose	فقد
shine	بريق
currency	عملة
to attain	اكتسب
optimistic	متفائل

Sharp reduction in the dollar expected this year

Davos, Switzerland - *Reuters*: The US economist, Fred Bergsten, said that the dollar was expected to see a sharp fall in 1999, with all the structural and cyclical indicators pointing to its heading in this direction.

In a paper he will present to the annual meeting of the World Economic Forum today, Friday, Bergsten says: "A sharp decline in the dollar will probably be one of the major international economic events in 1999." He said that fundamental equilibrium rates calculated by the Institute of International Economy headed by Bergsten suggested that the equilibrium rate of the euro would range between 1.25 and 1.30 dollars. At midday yesterday in Europe, the euro reached 1.1422/1.1425 dollars.

The same calculations indicated that the dollar would reach 100 yen. The dollar yesterday reached 115.55/155.60 yen. He added that in view of the fact that market rates were high, "the dollar may drop to levels lower than in its first downturn." Any movement in this direction will harm growth in Japan and raise the unemployment rate in Europe. The fall in the dollar may lead in the end to an increase in US interest rates at a time when her economy seems to be slowing down.

Bergsten, former adviser to the White House, said that the effects may include a slowdown of growth in the major nations and an increase in the need for the group of three (euro-zone, Japan and the US) to start managing currency rates more actively.

The euro loses its shine against the dollar and the European markets rise after a stutter

London - *Asharq al-Awsat and news agencies*: The euro fell to its lowest levels against the US currency since its launch at the beginning of the new year, after the US currency received support from all the other major currencies through expectations of US economic growth. Most European stock markets fell at the start of trading yesterday under the effect of Wall Street and the Asian markets the night before last. But the London market resumed its rise and with it the Swedish stock market, which gained momentum on the news that Volvo had sold its car making division to the US corporation Ford for 50 billion kronor.

Optimistic forecasts about the US economy helped the dollar to rise at the start of European business against all the major currencies. Expectations dominated the market that US economic growth would continue to be higher than growth rates in both Europe and Japan. On the European markets the euro fell at noon yesterday to 1,1388 dollars compared with 1.1478 dollars at the close of European trading the day before yesterday.

Attentions of the market turned on the report of Alan Greenspan, the chairman of the Federal Reserve (the US central bank), to Congress and some US statistics, among them the US index of unemployment costs for the final quarter of last year.

صعود قوي للبورصات الأوروبية بفضل عروض اندماج

لندن: «الشرق الأوسط» ووكالات الأنباء

دفعت انباء عن عرضي اندماج في باريس ولندن ببورصات الاسهم الاوروبية الى الارتفاع بقوة امس حيث قفزت أسعار الاسهم في جميع انحاء القارة وفتح مؤشر «فاينانشال تايمز» المؤشر الرئيسي لبورصة لندن اكبر بورصات القارة على ارتفاع اكثر من واحد في المائة. وانتعش اليورو قليلا في بداية المعاملات الاوروبية بعد ان سجل مستويات منخفضة قياسية امام الدولار في وقت سابق، غير ان المحللين يقولون ان العملة الاوروبية الجديدة لا تزال معرضة لضغوط.

وانتعشت بورصات الاسهم الاوروبية بعد ان اعلنت مجموعة «سوسيتيه جنرال» المصرفية الفرنسية انها قدمت عرضا تقدم بمقتضاه خمسة اسهم جديدة لكل ثمانية اسهم في بنك «پاريبا» في مشروع اندماج يشكل اكبر مجموعة مصرفية في فرنسا تتفوق على بنك كريدي اجريكول». وفي لندن قالت شركة التأمين البريطانية «چارديان رويال اكستشينج» انها وافقت على عرض شراء من جانب صن «لايف اند بروفينشال هولدينچز» التي تسيطر مجموعة «اكسا» الفرنسية على اغلبيتها وذلك بقيمة 3,4 مليار جنيه (5,6 مليار دولار).

وارتفعت اسهم البنوك البريطانية وكان من بين اكبر الرابحين بنوك «باركليز» و «ناتوست» و «لويدز». وارتفع سهم شركة «رويال اند صن اليانس» للتأمين 5,1 في المائة بينما هبط سهم «صن لايف» 3,6 في المائة. وفتح مؤشر «فاينانشال تايمز» على صعود حاد وواصل ارتفاعه في المعاملات المسائية ليتجاوز 6 آلاف نقطة بارتفاع يزيد عن 130 نقطة.

ARTICLE 65

continent	قارة *pl.* ات
to recover	انتعش
banking *adj.*	مصرفي
in accordance with	بمقتضى
to control	سيطر
winner	رابح
balanced	مسائي

ندوة تقيّم آثار اليورو على الأسواق الأوروبية

أبوظبي - ق. ن. ا: اختتمت في ابوظبي أول من امس ندوة حول اسواق باريس المالية واثر عملة (اليورو) على الاسواق العالمية، نظمتها مجموعة «تشرشل» وشركة «يوروبلاس» بالتعاون مع غرفة تجارة وصناعة ابوظبي ومصرف الامارات المركزي وبعض المؤسسات المعنية في اوروبا.

وافتتح خليل فولاذي العضو المنتدب لبنك ابوظبي الاسلامي الندوة التي حضرها عدد من كبار المسؤولين بالمؤسسات المالية والمصرفية والاقتصادية بالدولة بكلمة اشار فيها الى ان الندوة تهدف الى دراسة الوضع المالي والاستفادة من الواقع الاقتصادي الجديد في اوروبا في ظل وجود اليورو الذي اصبح ذات فعالية مالية كبرى لنحو ثلاثمائة مليون اوروبي.

كما القى سلطان السويدي محافظ المصرف المركزي كلمة حول الاثر الاقتصادي والمالي لليورو الذي وضع حدا لسيطرة الدولار، مشيرا الى ان الفرصة لاتزال متاحة لدولة الامارات ودول الخليج للتطور اقتصاديا وسياسيا وحماية مصالحها المشتركة من خلال الوضع الاقتصادي الجديد.

ومن جانبه اكد جان فرانسوا ثيودور رئيس بورصة باريس خلالها على ان الندوة تفتح المجال للاستثمارات الفرنسية مستعرضا اهم النقاط القوية التي يتمتع بها السوق الاوروبي الجديد وفرنسا على وجه الخصوص، مشيرا الى ثورة اليورو في الاسواق العالمية.

ARTICLE 66

seminar	ندوة
to conclude	اختتم
chamber of commerce	غرفة التجارة
bank	مصرف
use	استفادة
reality	واقع
effectiveness	فعالية
supremacy	سيطرة
revolution	ثورة

Strong rise on the European markets on merger bids

London - *Asharq al-Awsat and news agencies*: News of two merger bids in Paris and London pushed European stock markets strongly up yesterday, with share prices jumping throughout the continent and the Financial Times index, the main index of the London stock market, the largest market in the continent, opening up more than one per cent. The euro recovered slightly at the start of European trading after previously recording record low levels against the dollar, although analysts say that the new European currency is still exposed to pressures.

European stock markets recovered after the French banking group Société Générale, announced that it had launched a bid by which it will offer five new shares for every eight shares in the bank Paribas in a merger plan that will form the largest banking group in France, bigger than Crédit Agricole. In London the British insurance company, Guardian Royal Exchange, said that it accepted an acquisition offer of 3.4 billion pounds (5.6 billion dollars) from Sun Life and Provincial Holdings, in which the French group AXA has a majority holding.

Shares in British banks rose and among the largest gainers were Barclays, NatWest and Lloyds. Shares in the Royal and Sun Alliance insurance company rose 5.1% while Sun Life fell 3.6%. The Financial Times opened up sharply and continued its rise in balanced trading to pass 6,000, up more than 130 points.

Seminar assesses influence of the euro on the European markets

Abu Dhabi - *QNA*: A seminar in Abu Dhabi on the Paris stock market and the effect of the euro on world markets ended the day before yesterday. It was organised by the Churchill group and Europlus, with the cooperation of the Abu Dhabi chamber of commerce and industry, the central bank of the Emirates and some organisations involved in Europe.

Khalil Fouladi, the member representing the Islamic Bank of Abu Dhabi, opened the seminar attended by a number of senior officials of the financial, banking and economic organisations of the country with a talk in which he said that the seminar was aiming to study the financial situation and the benefits to be derived from the new economic reality in Europe where the launch of the euro had given huge financial efficiency to some 300 million Europeans. The governor of the central bank, Sultan Soueedi, also gave a talk on the economic and financial effect of the euro which has restricted the supremacy of the dollar. He pointed out that the Emirates and the Gulf states still had the opportunity to develop economically and politically and protect the common interests through the new economic situation.

For his part, the chairman of the Paris Bourse, Jean-François Théodore, confirmed during the seminar that it was opening the way for French investment, citing the main advantages enjoyed by the new European market and by France in particular, and pointing to the revolution of the euro in the international markets.

Exercises Articles 61 - 66

Exercise 1 Choose the best answer

١ تحفظت الكويت على خطوط/خطط/تخطيط/خطوات الاندماج.
٢ سيضمن الاندماج الفرصة/القدرة/القارة/القفزة التنافسية للشركة على الصعيد الدولى.
٣ تم قيد/قرض/قطاع/قيام اربع شركات جديدة بالبورصة.
٤ تشير جميع الاعتراضات/الاحتياجات/الاحتياطات/الاعتبارات الهيكلية الى انخفاض.
٥ اى تحرك الدولار فى هذا الاتجاه سيزيد معهد/معدل/معادلة/معظم البطالة.
٦ الاثار يمكن ان تشمل تحرك/تكليف/تباطؤ /تكافـؤ النمو فى دول رئـيـسيـة .
٧ انخفض معظم اسواق الاسم عند بدء المعاملات/العملات/العمليات/التعاملات.
٨ ساعدت تحديات/تغييرات/تقسيمات/توقعات متفائلة الدولار على ان يرتفع.
٩ يقولون المحللون ان اليورو لا تزال معرضة لشروط/لضغوط/لخطوط/لوجود.
١٠ الفرصة لا تزال متاحة للتامين/للتطور/للتقريب/للتسويق اقتصاديا.

Exercise 2 Match the following pairs

١	الفرصة لا تزال	a	الخصوص
٢	فى جميع	b	متاحة
٣	اول من	c	الدولى
٤	على الصعيد	d	امس
٥	على وجه	e	انحاء القارة

Exercise 3 Choose the appropriate verb

١ تشكل/تمتلك/تكلف/تسجل المؤسسة اكبر حصة منفردة من الاسهم.
٢ اكتسبت/اعتزمت/انتقدت/انتخبت البورصة قوة دافعة بعد الانباء.
٣ احتاجت/اختتمت/اتجهت/احتللت انظار الاسواق الى بيان الاقتصادى.
٤ امتنع/امتدد/التزم/انتعش الدولار قليلا فى بداية المعاملات.
٥ تبحث/تسجل/تفتح/تحقق الندوة المجال للاستثمارات الفرنسية

Exercise 4 Match the following pairs

١	بطرق	a	عن التعقيب
٢	الاعتبارات	b	غير مباشرة
٣	امتنع الوزير	c	البطالة
٤	تكاليف	d	الاقتصادى
٥	الواقع	e	الدورية

Exercise 5 Put the following words into the sentences below

ينظم عملات تختتم الفرص

١

الأسهم الخليجية ___ الأسبوع
بانخفاض في كل من الرياض والكويت

٢

ندوة حول تمويل ___ الاستثمارية في منطقة نجران
تنظمها المجموعة السعودية للأبحاث والتسويق في مايو المقبل

٣

محللون يتساءلون حول مستقبل ارتباط ___ الخليج بالدولار

٤

مجلس الصادرات البريطاني ___ ندوة
في بيروت عن التخصيص بلبنان

تراجع قيمة صادرات السعودية إلى فرنسا خلال 98

باريس: ميشال أبو نجم

تراجع فائض المبادلات التجارية بين السعودية وفرنسا الى 2,109 مليار فرنك العام الماضي مقابل 6,841 مليار عام 1997. وتفيد ارقام رسمية من ادارة الجمارك الفرنسية ان صادرات السعودية الى فرنسا بلغت العام الماضي 10,5 مليار فرنك بعد ان كانت قد وصلت العام الذي قبله الى 15,317 مليار فرنك. وبذلك تكون قد هبطت بنسبة 31,14 في المائة.

ويعود السبب في ذلك الى انهيار أسعار النفط حيث ان السواد الأعظم من الصادرات السعودية الى فرنسا يتشكل من النفط الخام ومشتقاته. وقد بلغت قيمة خامات النفط التي اشترتها فرنسا من السعودية 10,2 مليار فرنك، مما يعني انها تشكل 96,73 في المائة من اجمالي المشتريات الفرنسية. الا ان قيمتها للعام 97 كانت تقترب من سقف الـ15 مليار فرنك. والجدير تسجيله ان مشتريات فرنسا من الزيوت السعودية لم تتراجع من حيث الحجم. وبشكل عام، فإن قيمة الفاتورة الفرنسية من النفط ومشتقاته هبطت العام الماضي بنسبة 29 في المائة، في حين ان الكميات المستوردة ارتفعت بنسبة 5,1 في المائة. وتبلغ قيمة اجمالي ما تستورده فرنسا من هذه المواد 71 مليار فرنك، منها 14,36 في المائة قيمة مشترياتها من النفط ومشتقاته من السعودية. وبالاضافة الى مواد الطاقة، فإن ما يتبقى من الواردات الفرنسية يتشكل من المواد البلاستيكية وخلافها.

ARTICLE 67

surplus	فوائض *pl.* فائض
collapse	انهيار
largest part	سواد
greater	اعظم
derivatives	مشتقات
ceiling	سقوف *pl.* سقف
bill	فواتير *pl.* فاتورة
imports	مستوردات
to import	استورد
to be left	تبقى

برنامج التجارة العربية يوسع قاعدة التمويل ويخفف الشروط أمام الشركات الصغيرة

ابوظبي: عبد العزيز الصديقي

قال الدكتور جاسم المناعي الرئيس التنفيذي لبرنامج تمويل التجارة العربية ان البرنامج يتجه الى اضفاء مزيد من المرونة في اجراءات تمويل التجارة العربية البينية.

وقال الدكتور المناعي الذي كان يتحدث امام لقاء المصدرين والمستوردين العرب في قطاع المنتجات الزراعية والصناعية الغذائية الذي يواصل اعماله بابوظبي، انه في اطار هذا التوجه سيقوم البرنامج بتوفير آليات تمويل تتوافق مع متطلبات الشركات الصغيرة والمتوسطة والتي تشكل النسبة الاكبر من الشركات في العالم العربي. واضاف ان البرنامج يبحث تطوير اساليب تمويلية جديدة لكنه لم يحدد طبيعة او نوعية تلك الاساليب.

واكد الدكتور المناعي ان البرنامج يسعى لتوسيع وتطوير شبكة معلومات التجارة العربية التي ترتبط مع عدد كبير من مؤسسات تنمية التجارة في الدول العربية مثل غرف التجارة ومؤسسات ترويج الصادرات بهدف توفير المعلومة الدقيقة والمفيدة للتاجر العربي. واوضح ان البرنامج يقوم بتنفيذ مشروع اقليمي واسع النطاق لترويج التجارة العربية البينية.

ARTICLE 68

to widen	وسع
basis	قواعد *pl.* قاعدة
granting	اضفاء
meeting	لقاء
attention	توجه
instruments	آليات
to be linked	ارتبط
spreading	ترويج

Fall in the value of Saudi exports to France in 98

Paris - *Michel Abu Najam*: The balance of trade surplus between Saudi and France dropped to 2.109 billion francs last year compared with 6.841 billion francs in 1997. Official figures from the French customs authority report that Saudi exports to France last year totalled 10.5 billion francs, after reaching 15.317 billion francs the year before, a fall of 31.14 per cent.

The reason for this was the fall in oil prices as the vast majority of Saudi exports is made up of crude oil and its derivatives. The value of crude oil that France bought from Saudi totalled 10.2 billion francs, which meant that it made up 96.73% of all French purchases. However its value for 97 had come close to the ceiling of 15 billion francs. It should be pointed out that French purchases of Saudi oil had not fallen in quantity, but more generally, and the value of the French bill for oil and its derivatives fell last year by 29% at a time when imports had risen by 5.1%. French imports of these materials totalled 71 billion francs, 14.36% of this being the value of her purchases of oil and its derivatives from Saudi. Apart from energy materials, the remainder of French imports was made up of plastics and the like.

Arab trade programme to broaden base for financing and lighten conditions for small companies

Abu Dhabi - *Abdul Aziz al-Sadiqi*: Doctor Jasim al-Manai, executive director of the programme for financing Arab trade, said that the programme was aiming to give added flexibility in the provisions for financing inter-Arab trade.

Speaking at a meeting of Arab exporters and importers in the field of agricultural produce and food processing which is continuing in Abu Dhabi, Doctor al-Manai said that to this end the programme would undertake to provide financial instruments that would meet the demands of small and medium sized companies that form the greater proportion of companies in the Arab world. He added that the programme was seeking to develop new methods of financing but he did not specify the nature or kind of these methods.

Doctor al-Manai said that the programme would strive to broaden and develop the Arab trade information network that was linked up to a large number of organisations for trade development in the Arab countries, like the chambers of commerce and organisations for promoting exports, with the aim of providing accurate and useful information for the Arab businessman. He indicated that the programme would undertake a comprehensive regional project to promote inter-Arab trade.

وزير الصناعة الفرنسي يبحث في القاهرة مساهمة فرنسا في برنامج التخصيص

القاهرة: «الشرق الاوسط»

في اطار تنامي العلاقات التجارية الاقتصادية بين البلدين في الفترة الاخيرة يزور كريستيان بييريه وزير الدولة الفرنسي للصناعة القاهرة في الفترة من 21 الى 23 فبراير (شباط) الجاري. وقالت مصادر السفارة الفرنسية بالقاهرة ان الزيارة تأتي تلبية لدعوة قدمتها السلطات المصرية للوزير ممثلة في الدكتور عاطف عبيد وزير قطاع الاعمال العام المصري خلال زيارة الرئيس مبارك لفرنسا في مايو(ايار) الماضي.

ومن المقرر ان يجري بييريه اتصالات مع عدد من اعضاء الحكومة المصرية حول مستقبل التعاون الفرنسي - المصري في مجالات التنمية الاقتصادية والصناعية، فيما تأتي قطاعات الطاقة والكهرباء والبترول والاتصالات اللاسلكية على رأس الموضوعات محل البحث، كما يولي وزير الصناعة الفرنسي اهتماما خاصا بسير عملية التخصيص في مصر وامكانية مساهمة الجانب الفرنسي في هذا المجال.

ARTICLE 69

in compliance with	تلبية ل
invitation	دعوة
representative	ممثل
radio	لاسلكي
progress	سير
possibility	امكانية

باعت 82 ألف سيارة في دول مجلس التعاون الخليجي

مبيعات قياسية لـ«نيسان» اليابانية بمنطقة الخليج في العام الماضي

أبوظبي: «الشرق الأوسط»

قالت شركة سيارات «نيسان» اليابانية المصنعة للسيارات انها حققت مبيعات قياسية لعام 1998 في دول مجلس التعاون الخليجي، حيث باعت ما مجموعه 82 الف سيارة.

وذكرت الشركة في بيان لها وزع في أبوظبي امس الاول ان هذه أعلى نسبة مبيعات تحققها الشركة في المنطقة منذ 13 عاما رغم الظروف الصعبة التي تشهدها الأسواق والمنافسة الشديدة بين الشركات الأخرى المصنعة للسيارات، وحسب الشركة فان المبيعات زادت بنسبة 50 في المائة مقارنة بعام 1997.

وحسب الشركة فان مبيعات سيارة «نيسان باترول» الجديدة التي طرحت للمرة الأولى في نوفمبر (تشرين الثاني) الماضي، حققت ارتفاعا كبيرا في أسواق دول مجلس التعاون الخليجي عام 1998 بلغت نسبته 80 في المائة مقارنة بنفس الفترة من العام الذي سبقه.

وقال كيوسوكي ميوشي، المدير العام لشركة «نيسان الشرق الأوسط» ومقرها المنطقة الحرة بجبل علي «أشعر بسعادة بالغة للأداء المتميز الذي شهدته الشركة في عام 1998». وعزا هذا النجاح الى عدة عوامل أهمها تنوع المنتجات التي يتم توزيعها في دول مجلس التعاون الخليجي بالاضافة الى وجود شبكة واسعة من الموزعين تلبي احتياجات العملاء في مجال المبيعات وخدمات ما بعد البيع. وذكر أن الأولوية القصوى بالنسبة لنيسان كانت تعزيز الالتزام اتجاه متطلبات ابناء مجلس التعاون الخليجي وقد أثمر ذلك عن تقدير عال لدى العملاء.

ARTICLE 70

to launch	طرح
happiness	سعادة
success	نجاح
variety	تنوع
distributor	موزع
customer	عميل *pl.* عملاء
extreme	أقصى *fem.* قصوى
to bear fruit	اثمر

The French minister for industry will discuss in Cairo French involvement in the privatisation programme

Cairo - *Asharq al-Awsat*: As part of the recent development of economic trade relations between the two countries, the French minister for industry, Christian Pierret, is to visit Cairo from 21 to 23 February. French ambassadorial sources in Cairo said that the visit came following an invitation made by the Egyptian authorities representing Doctor Atif Abeed, Egyptian minister of public works, during a visit by President Mubarak to France last May.

Pierret is scheduled to make contacts with a number of the members of the Egyptian government regarding the future of Franco-Egyptian cooperation in the fields of economic and industrial development, with the energy, electricity, oil and radio communications sectors coming at the head of the topics for discussion. The French industry minister is showing a special interest in the course of the privatisation programme in Egypt and the possibility of French involvement in this area.

Sales of 82,000 cars in the countries of the Gulf Cooperation Council

Record sales for Nissan in the Gulf last year

The Japanese car manufacturer, Nissan, said that it had achieved record sales for 1998 in the countries of the Gulf Cooperation Council, with a total of 82,000 cars being sold.

In a statement issued in Abu Dhabi the day before yesterday, the company said that this was the highest rate of sales the company had achieved in the area for 13 years in spite of the difficult conditions that the markets faced and the severe competition from the other car manufacturers. According to the company, sales rose 50% compared to 1997.

According to the company, sales of the new Nissan Patrol, which was launched last November, achieved a large increase in the markets of the Gulf Cooperation Council, 80% up over the same period for the previous period.

Kiusuki Miushi, the general manager of Nissan Middle East, which has its headquarters of the free zone in Jebel Ali, said: "I feel very pleased with the excellent performance the company has seen in 1998." He attributed this success to a number of factors, the most important of them the range of the products distributed in the countries of the Gulf Cooperation Council, in addition to the wide network of distributors to meet the requirements of customers in the area of sales and after-sales services. He said that the highest priority for Nissan had been to strengthen the commitment to meeting the requirements of the people of the Gulf Cooperation Council and this had borne fruit through the high regard customers had for the company.

رئيس «شيفرون» في السعودية لبحث فرص الاستثمار في مجال البترول

الرياض: «الشرق الأوسط»

وصل رئيس شركة شيفرون الأميركية كينيث دير أمس الى الرياض في زيارة تستمر عدة أيام يبحث خلالها مع المسؤولين السعوديين سبل الاستثمار في مجال البترول والغاز.

وتكتمت مصادر الشركة بالرياض عن الخوض في طبيعة المقترحات التي يحملها رئيس الشركة لتقديمها الى المسؤولين السعوديين،الا أن وكالة الأنباء السعودية ذكرت أن وزير الخارجية الأمير سعود الفيصل استقبل دير والوفد المرافق له أمس، إذ حضر المقابلة مساعد وكيل وزارة الخارجية للشؤون الاقتصادية والثقافية الدكتور يوسف السعدون.

وكان دير قد ذكر في تصريحات أدلى بها في وقت سابق خلال زيارة قام بها الى الكويت أن شركته قدمت أفكارا حول الاستثمار في قطاع النفط السعودي سيتم مناقشتها بمزيد من التفصيل خلال زيارته الى السعودية، معتبرا أن المستثمرين الأجانب يمكن أن يساهموا بدور هام في صناعة الغاز السعودية.

ARTICLE 71

to keep silent	تكتم
treatment	خوض
accompanying	مرافق
cultural	ثقافي
view	فكر *pl.* افكار

«كونوكو» الأميركية للنفط تؤكد قدرتها على تحقيق أرباح بدون اندماج

● قالت شركة كونوكو الأميركية انه يمكنها ان تحقق أرباحا بدون الاندماج مع شركة أخرى رغم الانخفاض الحاد في أسعار النفط. ونقلت رويترز عن ارشي دونام رئيس كونوكو ومديرها التنفيذي قوله ان الشركة درست عدة بدائل قبل بيع دوبونت بمبلغ 4,4 مليار دولار في ما وصف بأنه أكبر اكتتاب أولي في الاسهم في تاريخ الشركات الأميركية.

وتابع «تقع على عاتقنا مسؤولية الامانة في بحث البدائل» في اشارة الى تكهنات اخيرة بان الشركة قد تندمج مع احد منافسيها.

وتابع «غير ان هدفنا المعلن كشركة هو النمو ومضاعفة قيمتها مع حلول عام 2003 . لقد نظمنا شركتنا ورشدنا محفظتنا وخفضنا التكاليف حتى يمكننا المنافسة وتحقيق ارباح عالية حتى مع انخفاض الاسعار دون حاجة الى الاندماج».

وقال دونام ان توقعات أرباح الشركة لعام 1999 تستند الى أن سعر خام برنت 13 دولارا للبرميل.

ARTICLE 72

substitute	بديل *pl.* بدائل
to continue	تابع
shoulders	عاتق *pl.* عواتق
trust	امانة
doubling	مضاعفة
to guide	رشد
portfolio	محفظة
need	حاجة

Chevron's president in Saudi to discuss investment opportunities in the oil sector

Riyadh - *Asharq al-Awsat*: The president of the US company Chevron, Kenneth Derr, arrived in Riyadh yesterday on a visit lasting several days during which he will discuss with Saudi officials ways of investing in the oil and gas sector.

Company sources in Riyadh said nothing about the discussions on the nature of the proposals that the company president is bringing to present to the Saudi officials. The Saudi News Agency said that the foreign minister, Prince Saud al-Faisal, met Derr and his accompanying delegation yesterday, when Dr Yousef al-Saudoon, assistant under-secretary of state for foreign and economic affairs, attended the meeting .

In statements made previously during a visit to Kuwait, Derr had said that his company had put forward ideas on investing in the Saudi oil sector. Recognising that foreign investors may play an important role in the Saudi gas sector, Derr will be discussing these ideas in greater detail during his visit to Saudi.

The US oil company, Conoco, confirms its ability to make profits without merger

The US company, Conoco, said that it was able to make profits without merging with another company in spite of the sharp fall in oil prices. Reuters reported Archie Dunham, president and chief executive of Conoco, as saying that the company had studied a number of alternatives before selling Du Pont for 4.4 billion dollars in what was described as the biggest initial share subscription in US company history.

In a reference to recent speculation that the company may merge with one of its competitors, he went on: "The responsibility of trust in discussing the alternatives falls on our shoulders. However, our stated aim as a company is growth and doubling its value by the beginning of 2003. We have structured our company, managed our portfolio and reduced our costs to allow us to compete and make high profits even with a drop in oil prices and without the need to merge."

Dunham said that forecasts for company profits for 1999 were based on the price of Brent crude of 13 dollars a barrel.

Exercises Articles 67 - 72

Exercise 1 Choose the best answer

١ تراجع قدم/واقع/قيام/فائض المبادلات التجارية بين البلدين.

٢ سيقوم البرنامج بتوفير أليات تتوافق مع متطلبات/اعتبارات/عمليات/مواصفات الشركات الصغيرة.

٣ يسعى البرنامج لتوسيع شبكة/اشارة/قاعدة/دعوة معلومات.

٤ حققت الشركة امكانيات/مشتقات/مستوردات/مبيعات قياسية.

٥ عزا هذا النجاح الى عدة قواعد/تفاصيل/عوامل/تكاليف.

٦ المرونة/المناسفة/الاولية/العملية القصوى كانت تعزيز الالتزام اتجاه متطلبات الابناء.

٧ يبحث مبان/سبل/طوابق/غرف الاستثمار فى مجال الغاز.

٨ قدمت الشركة احيا/اقدام/افكار/افاق حول الاستثمار.

٩ درست الشركة خسائر/بدائل/وسائل/ودائع قبل البيع.

١٠ يولى وزير الصناعة اهتماما خاصا بسير عملية/عملة/عميل/عامل التخصيص.

Exercise 2 Match the following pairs

١	يعود السبب فى ذلك	a	ان الصادرات بلغت ٤ مليار دولار.
٢	يوسع برنامج التجارة	b	مشتريات من الزيوت لم تتراجع.
٣	تفيد ارقام رسمية	c	قاعدة التمويل.
٤	يبحث البرنامج	d	الى انهيار.
٥	الجدير تسجيله ان	e	تطوير اساليب تمويلية جديدة.

Exercise 3 Match the following pairs

١	بهدف توفير	a	بتنفيذ مشروع اقليمى
٢	يقوم البرنامج	b	الصعبة
٣	من المقرر	c	المعلومات
٤	رغم الظروف	d	زادت المبيعات
٥	حسب الشركات فان	e	ان يجرى الوزير اتصالات

Exercise 4 Put these words into the following passage

امكانية	اتصالات	الفترة	الطاقة
اللاسلكية	اهتماما	العلاقات	اعضاء

وزير الصناعة الفرنسي يبحث في القاهرة مساهمة فرنسا في برنامج التخصيص

القاهرة: «الشرق الاوسط»

في اطار تنامي ____ التجارية الاقتصادية بين البلدين في الفترة الاخيرة يزور كريستيان بييريه وزير الدولة الفرنسي للصناعة القاهرة في ____ من 21 الى 23 فبراير (شباط) الجاري. وقالت مصادر السفارة الفرنسية بالقاهرة ان الزيارة تأتي تلبية لدعوة قدمتها السلطات المصرية للوزير ممثلة في الدكتور عاطف عبيد وزير قطاع الاعمال العام المصري خلال زيارة الرئيس مبارك لفرنسا في مايو(ايار) الماضي.

ومن المقرر ان يجري بييريه ____ مع عدد من ____ الحكومة المصرية حول مستقبل التعاون الفرنسي - المصري في مجالات التنمية الاقتصادية والصناعية، فيما تأتي قطاعات ____ والكهرباء والبترول والاتصالات ____ على رأس الموضوعات محل البحث، كما يولي وزير الصناعة الفرنسي ____ خاصا بسير عملية التخصيص في مصر و____ مساهمة الجانب الفرنسي في هذا المجال.

Exercise 5 These five passages are continuations of articles 67-72; match them

وعلى صعيد آخر يبحث بييريه مع وزير الصناعة المصري سبل استكمال التعاون المشترك الذي بدأ منذ عدة سنوات بين الهيئات المصرية الفرنسية التابعة لوزارتي البلدين والمعنية بالتنمية وتوحيد معايير المنتجات الصناعية وجودتها ومن المنتظر ان يقدم

ويتضمن هذا المشروع الذي ينفذ على مراحل تحليل التدفق التجاري بين الدول العربية لتحديد القطاعات والمنتجات الواعدة بالنسبة لتوسيع التجارة البينية، واجراء مسوحات للسوق في الدول العربية لتحديد واقع الاسواق وشروط التصدير والاستيراد في هذه الاسواق وعقد لقاءات دورية بين المصدرين والمستوردين يجمع الشركات العربية ذات الاهتمامات المتطابقة.

وحول أوضاع السوق ذكرت «نيسان» أنه على مدى السنوات الماضية، كان للأوضاع الاقتصادية تأثيرها الواضح على مبيعات السيارات بشكل عام. ومن المعروف أن سوق السيارات كانت دوماً تتأثر بتذبذب اسعار النفط. ومع حلول عام 1999 يبدو الوضع الاقتصادي أصعب مما كان عليه في السنوات الماضية، ولهذا فان الشركات العالمية المصنعة للسيارات تتوقع انخفاضاً في مبيعات السيارات، وذلك بسبب انخفاض أسعار النفط وهبوط قيمة الين مقابل الدولار.

وتابع «من الواضح ان السعر الان عشرة دولارات لذا فاننا نبدأ بتحد كبير لعام 1999».واضاف أن من المستحيل توقع سعر محدد للخام خلال العام، الا انه أعرب عن أمله ان تدرك الدول الاعضاء في أوبك وبصفة خاصة السعودية والكويت وايران وفنزويلا انه ينبغي عليها الالتزام بشكل جاد بخفض الانتاج. واعرب عن اعتقاده بان شركات النفط يمكن ان تحقق ارباحا بهذه الاسعار المنخفضة الا انه اضاف ان الدول المنتجة في اميركا الجنوبية والشرق الاوسط بحاجة الى اسعار اعلى للخام من عشرة دولارات للبرميل.

وتحتل فرنسا الموقع السادس على لائحة الدول المصدرة الى السعودية حيث تبلغ حصتها من السوق السعودية 4,5 في المائة، بعد الولايات المتحدة الاميركية (21,9 في المائة) وبريطانيا (10,3 في المائة)، اليابان (6,7 في المائة)، المانيا (5,5 في المائة) وأخيرا ايطاليا (4,6 في المائة).

والسعودية تمثل الوجهة الأولى للصادرات الفرنسية من بين مجموعة دول الشرقين الأدنى والأوسط السبع عشرة وهي، في الوقت عينه، المورد الأول لها من

محللون يستبعدون اتفاق المنظمة على الخفض اللازم لرفع الأسعار

لندن: «الشرق الأوسط»

من المقرر ان تعقد منظمة الاقطار المصدرة للنفط (اوپك) اجتماعها الوزاري في 23 من مارس (اذار) المقبل ومن المرجح ان تسيطر خلافات بين الدول الاعضاء حول وجبة جديدة من تخفيض الانتاج لدعم اسعار النفط المتهاوية على ذلك الاجتماع، خاصة في ظل تقارير تفيد بعدم التزام كامل من بعض الاعضاء بالتخفيضات التي اقرت في السابق.

وكان محللون قالوا انه يجب على (أوپك) ان تخفض مليون برميل يوميا اخرى من الانتاج لوقف هبوط اسعار النفط التي وصلت الى ادنى مستويات لها منذ منتصف الثمانينات.

الى ذلك، قال مصدر حكومي في المكسيك لرويترز ان المسؤولين النفطيين هناك مستعدون للاجتماع مع نظرائهم في السعودية وفنزويلا لبحث امكانية اجراء مزيد من تخفيضات الانتاج قبل اجتماع منظمة البلدان المصدرة للبترول (أوپك) الشهر المقبل.

وقال المصدر ان وزير الطاقة لويس تيليز كان على اتصال هاتفي مع نظيريه السعودي والمكسكي. واستدرك بقوله انه على الرغم من ان المسؤولين النفطيين لم يتفقوا على تاريخ للاجتماع فان المكسيك لا تمانع في حضور الاجتماع.

واضاف المصدر قوله «نحن اساسا في موقف الترقب والانتظار ومستعدون اذا وافق الاخرون جميعا». ولمح الى مشكلات بين المنتجين الذين اتفقوا على تخفيضات الانتاج العام الماضي في الوفاء بتعهداتهم.

وكانت المكسيك وفنزويلا والسعودية قادت جهود المنتجين في (أوپك) وخارجها العام الماضي لخفض المعروض العالمي من النفط بمقدار 3,1 مليون برميل يوميا لكن غياب الالتزام بتلك الاتفاقات حال دون اتخاذ خطوات اخرى.

وقالت امانة (أوپك) في احدث تقرير لها ان انتاج المنظمة في يناير (كانون الثاني) زاد 280 الف برميل يوميا الى 27,47 مليون برميل يوميا، الامر الذي يعني ان الالتزام بتخفيضات الانتاج بلغت نسبته نحو 80 في المائة.

وقال المصدر المكسيكي «ابلغنا الجميع اننا مستعدون لعمل المزيد لكننا لن نكون من يفعل هذا بانفسنا».

واذا تم الترتيب لعقد اجتماع فان تيليز على الارجح سيسافر خلال الاسبوعين المقبلين اذ ان مناظرة بشأن فتح قطاع الكهرباء لاستثمارات القطاع الخاص ستبقيه على الارجح في المكسيك في الاسبوعين الاخيرين من مارس. وقال المصدر ان المكسيك تشجعت باعلان فنزويلا انها ستلتزم اخيرا بتعهداتها بخفض الانتاج 525 الف برميل يوميا بحلول الاول من مارس.

وكان تيليز قال ان مشكلات فنزويلا في الوفاء بالتزاماتها ومشكلات الانضباط الاخرى تعرقل مساعي اجراء مزيد من الخفض في المعروض العالمي من النفط.

ARTICLE 73

to think unlikely	استبعد
telephone *adj.*	هاتفي
to supplement	استدرك
to object	مانع
to allude to	لمح الى
compliance	تعهد *pl.* ات
absence	غيابة
to prevent	حول دون
probably	على الارجح
dispute	مناظرة
to take heart	تشجع
to stick to	التزم
discipline	انضباط
to hamper	عرقل
effort	مسعى *pl.* مساع

Analysts think it unlikely that OPEC will agree to a reduction in production that is necessary to raise prices

London - *Asharq al-Awsat*: The Organisation of Petroleum Exporting Countries, OPEC, is scheduled to hold its ministerial meeting on 23rd March and differences between member countries over a fresh need to reduce production in order to support collapsing oil prices are likely to dominate this meeting, especially in the light of reports of the complete lack of compliance of some members to the reductions that had previously been agreed on.

Analysts had said that OPEC had to reduce production by a further million barrels a day in order to stop the fall in prices which had reached their lowest levels since the mid eighties.

Furthermore, a government source in Mexico told Reuters that oil officials there were ready to meet their counterparts in Saudi and Venezuela to discuss the possibility of increasing production cuts ahead of the OPEC meeting next month.

The source said that the energy minister, Luis Téllez, had been in telephone contact with his Saudi and Mexican counterparts. He made it clear that although oil officials had not agreed on the date for the meeting, Mexico would not be refusing to attend the meeting.

The source added: "We are basically in a wait and see position and we are ready if all the others agree." He alluded to the problems between the producers who had agreed to reductions in production last year over fulfilling their promises.

Mexico, Venezuela and Saudi Arabia had led the efforts of the producers, both within OPEC and outside it, last year to cut the world oil supply by 3.1 million barrels a day, but a lack of compliance to those agreements prevented other steps being taken.

In its latest report the OPEC secretariat said that the organisation's production in January rose 280 thousand barrels a day to 27.47 million barrels a day. This means that there was around an 80% compliance to reduce production.

The Mexican source said: "We all said that we were ready to do our utmost but we cannot do this by ourselves."

If there is agreement to hold a meeting, Téllez will most probably travel during the next two weeks because the dispute concerning the opening of the electricity sector to private sector investment will most probably detain him in Mexico in the last two weeks of March. The source said that Mexico was encouraged by Venezuela's announcement that it would finally abide by its commitments to reduce production by 525 thousand barrels a day from 1st March.

Téllez had said that the problems of Venezuela in abiding by its commitments and other discipline problems had hampered efforts to make greater cuts in the world oil supply.

وفد وزاري أردني يتوجه إلى السعودية اليوم لبحث العلاقات الاقتصادية والتبادل التجاري

عمان: «الشرق الأوسط»

يتوجه وفد وزاري اردني اليوم الى المملكة العربية السعودية برئاسة وزير الدولة لشؤون التنمية الدكتور طاهر كنعان في زيارة تستغرق عدة ايام يعقد خلالها مباحثات تتناول سبل تعزيز العلاقات الثنائية والتعاون الاقتصادي واستئناف التعاون المؤسسي. ويضم الوفد وزراء المالية الدكتور ميشيل مارتو والتخطيط الدكتور نبيل عماري والصناعة والتجارة والتموين محمد صالح الحوراني.

واكد الدكتور كنعان ان الزيارة تهدف الى بحث عدد من القضايا ذات الاهتمام المشترك وستركز على العلاقات الاقتصادية واقامة تبادل تجاري صحيح ومؤسسي اكثر من التركيز على البحث في المعونات او المساعدات.

وقال في تصريحات للصحافيين ان الاردن والسعودية تربطهما علاقات متميزة وان البلدين يحرصان على تعزيز العلاقات بما يعكس الاهتمام المشترك بالمصالح الثنائية. واكد ان الوفد الاردني سيبحث مع الجانب السعودي اسس الانفتاح التجاري وفي المجالات الاخرى ومنها حرية انتقال العمالة في ما بين البلدين.

من جانبه قال وزير المالية الدكتور ميشيل مارتو ان الوفد الوزاري سيعقد سلسلة اجتماعات مع المسؤولين السعوديين تتعلق بتعزيز التعاون الثنائي وتطوير العلاقات المتميزة بين البلدين في كافة المجالات واجراء مباحثات مع وزير المالية السعودي ابراهيم العساف استكمالا للمباحثات التي اجريت في عمان في التاسع من الشهر الحالي حول مجالات دعم الاقتصاد الاردني والتعاون بين البلدين. واعرب الدكتور مارتو عن امله ان تثمر المباحثات عن نتائج ايجابية تعود بالخير على البلدين.

على صعيد آخر قالت مصادر مطلعة اردنية ان المباحثات ستتناول امكانية فتح الاسواق السعودية للمنتوجات الزراعية الاردنية وتشغيل العمالة الاردنية واستئناف النشاط التمويلي للصندوق السعودي للتمويل واقامة مشاريع مشتركة في الاردن والتعاون الاقتصادي والتجاري في العديد من المجالات والتركيز على السوق العربي المفتوح.

وكانت المملكة العربية السعودية قد اكدت دعمها ومساندتها للاردن من خلال تقديم التسهيلات والمساعدات الاقتصادية والمالية.

ويذكر ان العلاقات الاقتصادية بين الاردن والسعودية شهدت نشاطا ملحوظا منذ عام 1996 في عهد حكومة عبد الكريم الكباريتي وان الميزان التجاري يميل حاليا لصالح السعودية حيث يستورد الاردن مواد البتروكيماويات والزيوت المعدنية والمواد الغذائية ويصدر الاردن المنتوجات الزراعية الموسمية.

ARTICLE 74

to deal with	تناول
resumption	استئناف
outstanding	متميز
to strive to	حرص على
transfer	انتقال
wages	عمالة *pl.* ات
series	سلسلة *pl.* سلاسل
produce	منتوج *pl.* ات
concentrating	تركيز
noted	ملحوظ
balance	ميزان *pl.* موازين

Jordanian ministerial delegation heads to Saudi today to discuss economic relations and trade exchange

Amman - *Asharq al-Awsat*: A Jordanian ministerial delegation is heading to Saudi Arabia today led by the minister of state for development, Dr Tahir Kanaan, on a visit for a few days during which he will hold discussions on ways to strengthen bilateral relations and economic cooperation and the resumption of commercial cooperation. The delegation brings together the ministers of finance, Dr Michel Marto, of planning, Dr Nabil Amari, and of industry, trade and supply, Mohammed Salah al-Hurani.

Dr Kanaan said that the visit aimed to discuss a number of questions of mutual interest and would focus on economic relations and establishing real commercial trade exchange rather than concentrating on discussing aid and assistance.

In statements to reporters he said that excellent relations linked Jordan and Saudi Arabia and that the two countries were intent on strengthening relations which reflected the common concern in bilateral interests. He said that the Jordanian delegation would discuss with the Saudi side the foundations for an opening up in trade and other fields, among them the freedom to transfer wages between the two countries.

For his part, the finance minister, Dr Michel Marto, said that the ministerial delegation would hold a series of meetings with Saudi officials concerning strengthening bilateral cooperation and developing the excellent relations between the two countries in all areas and holding discussions with the Saudi finance minister, Ibrahim al-Asaf, completing the discussions held in Amman on the ninth of this month on the areas of supporting the Jordanian economy and cooperation between the two countries. Dr Marto expressed his hope that the discussions would produce positive results that would bring benefit to both countries.

On another matter, informed Jordanian sources said that the discussions would deal with the possibility of opening Saudi markets to Jordanian agricultural produce, investing Jordanian salaries, the Saudi Financing Fund resuming its financial activities, setting up joint ventures in Jordan, economic and trade cooperation in a number of fields, and a focus on the Arab open market.

Saudi Arabia had confirmed its support and backing to Jordan through offering economic and financial facilities and assistance.

It is to be mentioned that economic relations between Jordan and Saudi Arabia have seen noticeable activity since 1996 under the government of Abdul Kareem al-Kabariti and that the trade balance now leans in favour of Saudi, with Jordan importing petrochemical products, mineral oils and food products and exporting seasonal agricultural produce.

دول آسيوية تتطلع لتعزيز علاقاتها التجارية مع دول الخليج

أبوظبي: «الشرق الأوسط»

تبدأ في دبي يوم الإثنين المقبل فعاليات معرض النمور الآسيوية في وقت تتطلع الشركات الآسيوية لمنطقة الشرق الأوسط كسوق بديلة قادرة على تعويض الخسائر التي لحقت بها جراء الأزمات المالية التي عصفت بأسواقها وذلك ضمن خطة جديدة لتفعيل نشاطها المعتمد على تطوير عملياتها في الأسواق الدولية النامية. وستمتد فعاليات المعرض من 22 ـ 25 فبراير (شباط) الحالي.

وستشارك في المعرض الذي ترعاه غرفة تجارة دبي مجموعة من الشركات العاملة في مختلف القطاعات التجارية في دول شرق آسيا تضم كلاً من سنغافورة، إندونيسيا، ماليزيا، هونغ كونغ وكوريا الجنوبية.

وتدل المؤشرات على تزايد إهتمام الشركات الآسيوية بأسواق المنطقة، فقد أظهرت إحصائية صادرة عن وزارة التجارة والصناعة والطاقة الكورية بالتعاون مع المركز التجاري الكوري في دبي إرتفاعاً في حجم الصادرات الكورية لأسواق دولة الإمارات بنسبة 11,4٪ في الشهور التسعة الأولى من العام الماضي مقارنة بالمعدلات المسجلة في نفس الفترة من عام 1997 بعد أن وصلت القيمة الاجمالية للصادرات الكورية الى أكثر من 1,140 مليار دولار.

وكانت الصادرات الكورية الى دولة الإمارات قد سجلت نمواً بنسبة 3,4٪ في عام 1997 بعد أن وصلت الى حوالي 1,424 مليار دولار. وشهدت صادرات المعادن إرتفاعاً بنسبة 130٪، والحديد 105٪، والآلات 90,5٪، والأحذية 83٪، والكيماويات 65,4٪ متصدرة بذلك القائمة على اعتبار أنها أكثر الصادرات الكورية نمواً في أسواق الإمارات. الا أن القائمة لم تخل من بعض الصادرات التي شهدت تراجعاً في معدلاتها، حيث انخفضت صادرات الآليات الدقيقة بنسبة 14,7٪ والإلكترونيات الإستهلاكية بنسبة 8,3٪ والأقمشة 4٪ والمنسوجات بنسبة 5,2٪.

وقد أعطى الإنجاز الكوري أملاً كبيراً للعديد من الشركات العاملة في دول شرق آسيا التي باتت تنظر إلى إمكانية تحقيقها لإنجاز مشابه يساعدها في التغلب على المصاعب المالية التي تواجهها حالياً. ومن المتوقع أن يوفر المعرض موقعاً متميزاً للعديد من العارضين الباحثين عن شركاء عمل وللشركات الجديدة التي تسعى لدخول أسواق المنطقة إضافة للشركات الباحثة عن شركاء في مشاريع إستثمارية للاستفادة من التسهيلات المتاحة في دولة الإمارات العربية المتحدة في مجال تجميع المنتجات المختلفة. كما يساهم المعرض في تشجيع العديد من كبرى الشركات الآسيوية على الاستثمار في المنطقة.

ARTICLE 75

to strive to	تطلع الى
to touch	لحق ب
to shake	عصف ب
to sponsor	رعى
heading	متصدر
not to be lacking	لا خلى من
fabric	اقمشة *pl.* قماش
to come to	بات
similar	مشابه
overcoming	تغلب
exhibitor	ون *pl.* عارض
assembling	تجميع
encouragement	تشجيع

Asian countries look to strengthen their trade relations with the Gulf countries

Abu Dhabi - *Asharq al-Awsat*: The Asian fair, Namur, will begin in Dubai on Monday at a time when Asian countries are looking to the region of the Middle East as an alternative market that can make up for the losses brought about by the financial crises that have swept through their markets. This is part of a fresh approach to channel their energies that relies on developing their operations in the expanding international markets. The fair will run from 22nd to 25th February.

A group of companies operating in various commercial sectors in East Asia, including Singapore, Indonesia, Malaysia, Hong Kong and South Korea, will participate in the fair sponsored by the Dubai Chamber of Commerce.

Indications point to an increase in the interest by Asian countries in the markets of the region. Statistics from the Korean ministry of trade, industry and power in collaboration with the Korean commercial centre in Dubai have shown an 11.4% increase in the size of Korean exports to the markets of the Emirates over the first nine months of last year, compared to the rates recorded in the same period for 1997, with the total of Korean exports topping 1.140 billion dollars.

Korean exports to the Emirates had recorded a 3.4% increase in 1997, to around 1.424 billion dollars. Exports of metals showed an increase of 130%, iron 105%, appliances 90.5%, shoes 83% and chemicals 65.4%, thereby heading the table in having the largest growth in the markets of the Emirates. However the table included some exports that saw a drop in their rates, with exports of precision instruments dropping 14.7%, consumer electronics by 8.3%, fabrics by 4% and textiles by 5.2%.

The Korean success has given great hope to the many companies operating in East Asian countries which have now come to look to the possibility of their achieving a similar performance that would help them to overcome the financial difficulties they are presently facing. The fair is expected to offer an outstanding opportunity for the many exhibitors looking for working partners, for new companies seeking to enter markets in the region, and also for companies looking for partners in investment projects to take advantage of the facilities available in the United Arab Emirates in the field of assembling various products. The fair is playing its part in encouraging many of the largest Asian companies to invest in the region.

إندونيسيا تسعى للحصول على مليار دولار قروضا إضافية من صندوق النقد

مونتيغو باي (جمايكا) - رويترز: قال وزير الاقتصاد الاندونيسي جينانجار كارتاساسميتا ان اندونيسيا في الطريق الى الخروج من ازمتها المالية الشديدة وتسعى الى الحصول على مبالغ اضافية تبلغ مليار دولار من صندوق النقد الدولي. وذكر جينانجار الذي كان يتحدث على هامش قمة الدول النامية الخمس عشرة المنعقدة في منتجع مونتيغو باي بجمايكا انه يتوقع عودة الاقتصاد الاندونيسي الى النمو في النصف الثاني من العام الحالي وان يشهد نموا متواضعا في العام القادم.

وقال «لقد شاهدنا الضوء في نهاية النفق. ولدينا ثقة كبيرة في اننا سنخرج قريبا جدا من هذا الوضع».

وكانت اندونيسيا من أول الدول التي وقعت ضحية للازمة الاقتصادية العالمية التي بدأت في تايلاند في يوليو (تموز) عام 1997 وامتدت الى اسيا وروسيا وأميركا اللاتينية. وحصلت اندونيسيا بالفعل على مليارات الدولارات من صندوق النقد الدولي والبنك الدولي والبنك الاسيوي للتنمية في اطار صفقة انقاذ عالمية قيمتها 43 مليار دولار. لكن جينانجار قال ان جاكرتا تتطلع الان الى مبلغ اضافي قدره مليار دولار من أموال صندوق النقد الدولي لتحرير مبالغ حصلت على وعود بها بموجب خطة ميازاوا في اليابان التي تتكلف 30 مليار دولار وتهدف الى اخراج الاقتصاديات التي أضيرت من جراء الازمة في اسيا.

وقال «اننا نحتاج الى مبالغ اضافية من صندوق النقد الدولي حتى نتمكن من الحصول على مزيد من الاموال من اليابان. وتصر اليابان في اطار خطة ميازاوا على مشاركة صندوق النقد الدولي في التمويل».

وذكر جينانجار ان اندونيسيا استكملت تقريبا خطاب نوايا الى صندوق النقد يتناول بالتفصيل خططها الاقتصادية المستقبلية وان كان أي اتفاق بشأن اموال جديدة يحتاج الى موافقة مجلس ادارة صندوق النقد.

وأضاف «وبحلول مارس ربما نعرف ان كان هذا الاقتراح حصل على موافقة مجلس ادارة الصندوق». ويحضر الوزير الاندونيسي القمة التي تعقدها هذا الاسبوع مجموعة الدول الخمس عشرة النامية التي تضم 17 دولة من اسيا وافريقيا واميركا اللاتينية.

ARTICLE 76

on the occasion of	على هامش
resort	منتجع
tunnel	أنفاق *pl.* نفق
victim	ضحايا *pl.* ضحية
deal	صفقة
promise	وعود *pl.* وعد
intent	نوايا *pl.* نية

Indonesia seeks to obtain an additional billion dollar loan from the IMF

Montego Bay, Jamaica - *Reuters*: The Indonesian minister of the economy, Ginandjar Kartasasmita, said that Indonesia was presently emerging from her severe financial crisis and was attempting to obtain an additional billion dollars from the International Monetary Fund. Ginandjar, who was speaking on the occasion of the summit of the fifteen developing countries held in the resort of Montego Bay, Jamaica, said that he expected the Indonesian economy to return to growth in the second half of the current year and that it would experience modest growth in the coming year.

He said: "We have seen the light at the end of the tunnel. We are confident that we will very soon be emerging from this situation."

Indonesia was one of the first countries that fell victim to the economic crisis that began in Thailand in July 1997 and spread to Asia, Russia and Latin America. Indonesia has indeed obtained billions of dollars from the IMF, the World Bank and the Asian Development Bank as part of an international rescue package of 43 billion dollars. But Ginandjar said that Jakarta was now seeking an extra billion dollars from the IMF's funds in order to release sums it had been promised for the Miyazawa project in Japan costing 30 billion dollars and which aimed to help the economy that had suffered because of the crisis in Asia.

He said: "We need extra funds from the IMF to allow us to obtain more money from Japan. Under the Miyazawa project Japan is committed to participating with the IMF in the financing."

Ginandjar said that Indonesia had almost finalised a letter of intent to the IMF detailing its future economic plans and that any agreement concerning new finances needed the agreement of the board of directors of the IMF.

He added: "By the beginning of March we will probably know whether this proposal has won the agreement of the board of directors of the IMF. The Indonesian minister is attending the summit held this week by a group of the fifteen developing countries that form part of 17 countries from Asia, Africa and Latin America.

وزير التجارة الكندي يبحث توسيع التبادل التجاري بين بلاده وبلدان الشرق الأوسط

الشارقة (الامارات) - ا.ف.ب: انهى سيرجيو ماركي وزير التجارة الدولية الكندي زيارة الى الامارات العربية المتحدة في اطار حملة اقتصادية في الشرق الاوسط تهدف الى تنويع وتوسيع التبادل بين كندا وبلدان المنطقة.

ورافق ماركي الذي زار السعودية ايضا، الشريك التجاري الاكبر لكندا في الخليج، 40 من رجال الاعمال وممثلون عن 32 شركة كندية. ومن المقرر ان يزور ايضا الضفة الغربية لافتتاح مكتب تمثيل كندي وتوقيع اتفاق للتجارة الحرة مع السلطة الفلسطينية قبل ان يتوجه الى اسرائيل.

وقال ماركي لوكالة الصحافة الفرنسية ان «التجارة هي محرك الاقتصاد الكندي باعتبار ان 40٪ من الناتج الداخلي الخام يعتمد على الصادرات» وتحدث عن نتيجة «ايجابية جدا» لاتصالاته في الخليج.

وافاد برتين كوتي المسؤول عن اوروبا والشرق الاوسط وافريقيا الشمالية في وزارة الخارجية الكندية والتجارة الدولية لوكالة الصحافة الفرنسية ان «زيارتنا الى السعودية والامارات كانت ايجابية جدا».

واضاف «لقد درسنا احتمالات تحسين تعاوننا في القطاعات الاساسية»، لا سيما في «مجال الاتصالات حيث تشارك اربع شركات كندية في تحديث شبكة الهاتف السعودية».

واوضح ان المناقشات تناولت ايضا التعاون في «مجالات الصحة والتعليم وقطاع المناجم».

وذكر كوتي ان التبادل مع السعودية بلغ 1,2 مليار دولار في عام 1998 ونصفه من الصادرات الكندية الى الرياض. من جهة اخرى قال ان «تعاوننا مع الامارات تقدم بشكل ملحوظ لا سيما مع مشاركة الشركات الكندية الخاصة في مجال الخدمات وبينها قطاع البناء وتصريف المياه والبتروكيماويات والصحة والتعليم».

ومن بين هذه الشركات ذكر كوتي «بي سي غاز انترناشيونال» التي تعهدت منذ يونيو (حزيران) 1998 اقامة شبكة لتوزيع الغاز الطبيعي في امارة الشارقة.

واضاف ان «التبادل الثنائي يبقى ضعيفا حيث بلغت قيمة الصادرات الكندية الى الامارات 200 مليون دولار في عام 1998».

واكد ماركي ان «كندا والامارات تستعدان لتوقيع اتفاقات عدة حول حماية الاستثمارات والازدواج الضريبي وتاشيرات الدخول».

وحسب السفير الكندي ستيوارت ماكدوال فان «الاتفاق حول تاشيرات الدخول سيسهل تنقل المواطنين ويعزز التبادل الثنائي والاستثمارات والسياحة».

وقال ان «كندا ستكون الدولة الوحيدة غير العربية التي ستسمح بدخول المواطنين الاماراتيين دون تاشيرات دخول وهو امتياز منح حتى الان فقط لجيراننا الاميركيين وبعض الدول الاوروبية».

ARTICLE 77

modification — تنويع

representation — تمثيل

motor — محرك

probability — احتمال

distribution — تصريف

to get ready — استعد

visa — تاشيرة *pl.* ات

double taxation — ازدواج ضريبي

migration — تنقل

tourism — سياحة

concession — امتياز *pl.* ات

neighbour — جار *pl.* جيران

The Canadian trade minister discusses broadening trade exchange between his country and the countries of the Middle East

Sharja, Emirates - *AFP*: The Canadian minister of state for trade, Sergio Marchi, ended a visit to the United Arab Emirates as part of a economic campaign in the Middle East that aims to alter and broaden exchange between Canada and the countries of the region.

Marchi, who also visited Saudi, Canada's largest trading partner in the Gulf, was accompanied by forty businessmen and representatives of 32 Canadian companies. He is also scheduled to visit the West Bank to open an office of Canadian representation and to sign a free trade agreement with the Palestinian authorities before heading to Israel.

Marchi told Agence France Presse: "Trade is the engine of the Canadian economy given that 40% of the gross domestic product relies on exports" and he spoke about "the very positive" results of his contacts with the Gulf.

The official for Europe, the Middle East and north Africa in the Canadian ministry of foreign affairs and international trade, Burtin Cuty, told Agence France Presse: "Our visit to Saudi and the Emirates was very positive."

He added: "We have studied the possibilities of improving our cooperation in the basic fields," especially in the "field of communications where four Canadian companies are participating in renewing the Saudi telephone network."

He indicated that the discussions had also dealt with cooperation in the field of health, education, and the mining sector. Cuty said that exchange with Saudi had reached 1.2 billion dollars in 1998 with half of it exports to Riyadh. He also said: "Our cooperation with the Emirates has developed noticeably, especially with the participation of private Canadian companies in the field of services, among them the construction sector and water distribution, petrochemicals, health and education."

Among these companies, Cuty mentioned BC Gas International, which committed itself since June 1998 to set up a network to distribute natural gas to the Emirate of Sharja. He added: "Bilateral exchange remains weak with Canadian exports to the Emirates totalling 200 million dollars in 1998."

Marchi said: "Canada and the Emirates are getting ready to sign a number of agreements concerning protecting investments, double taxation and entry visas."

According to the Canadian ambassador, Stewart MacDowall: "The agreement regarding entry visas will make travelling easier for nationals and will strengthen bilateral exchange, investments and travel."

He said: "Canada will be the only non-Arab country to allow the entry of Emirate nationals without entry visas, a privilege up to now granted only to our American neighbours and some European countries."

مجلس رجال الأعمال المصري ـ المغربي يبحث إعفاء 67 سلعة من الرسوم الجمركية

القاهرة: «الشرق الأوسط»

قرر مجلس الاعمال المصري المغربي عقد جلسته المقبلة في القاهرة خلال الاسبوع المقبل لمتابعة المشاورات بين المستثمرين المصريين والمغاربة لدعم التعاون التجاري بين البلدين، ومتابعة تنفيذ الاتفاقيات التجارية التي وقعها الجانبان في مايو (آيار) من العام الماضي والخاصة باعفاء 38 سلعة مصرية و29 سلعة مغربية من كل الرسوم الجمركية.

وقال يماني فلفلة منسق العلاقات الاقتصادية المغربية المصرية، ان مجلس الاعمال المصري المغربي سيناقش تفعيل التجارة بين البلدين وفقا لاستراتيجية متفق عليها بين الدكتور أحمد جويلي وزير التجارة المصري والعلمي التازي وزير التجارة والصناعة التقليدية المغربي، مؤكدا ضرورة انشاء مركز معلومات مشترك لتسيير حركة الاستثمار والتجارة بين القاهرة والرباط.

وتناقش الاجتماعات مد خط ملاحي ما بين الدار البيضاء وبنغازي الى الاسكندرية أو بورسعيد، وانشاء شركة نقل بحرية بين رجال الاعمال من البلدين. وتقوم الشركة بمد خط ملاحي الى دول الخليج ويتطرق الاجتماع الى موضوع الصيد البحري باعتبار ان المغرب من الدول المصدرة للاسماك كما أن مصر دولة مستوردة لبعض أنواع السمك.

ويبحث الاجتماع انشاء شركة تجارية مشتركة لتسويق الحاصلات الزراعية بين البلدين واقامة شركة قابضة وتيسير التنقل بين البلدين وسيعلن رجال الاعمال المصريون في الاجتماع تأييدهم لترشيح حسن أيوب «مغربي الجنسية» لمنصب مدير منظمة التجارة العالمية.

وشهدت الأيام الماضية تنسيقا على جميع المستويات بين المستثمرين المصريين والمغاربة في مجال الزراعة، ووقع د. سعد نصار وكيل وزارة الزراعة المصرية اتفاقية للتعاون الزراعي بين مصر والمغرب في مجالات تبادل المعلومات والحجر الزراعي ووقاية النبات ووقعها عن الجانب المغربي الطالب القرشي المفتش العام بوزارة الفلاحة والتنمية القروية والصيد البحري. كما وقعت اللجنة المصرية المغربية للتعاون في مجال الكهرباء اتفاقية للربط الكهربائي بين البلدين.

ARTICLE 78

exemption	اعفاء
duty	رسم *pl.* رسوم
consultation	مشاورة
promoting	تسيير
extension	مد
marine *adj.*	ملاحي
to touch on	تطرق الى
fishing	صيد
produce	حاصل *pl.* ات
holding	قابض
facilitating	تيسير
candidacy	ترشيح
ban	حجر
protection	وقاية
plants	نبات
inspector	مفتش

Egypto-Moroccan committee of businessmen discusses the exemption of 67 commodities from customs duties

Cairo - *Asharq al-Awsat*: The Egypto-Moroccan business committee agreed to hold its coming session in Cairo next week to continue consultations between Egyptian and Moroccan investors to support trade cooperation between the two countries, and to follow up the implementation of trade agreements which the two sides signed in May last year and in particular to exempt 38 Egyptian and 29 Moroccan commodities from all customs duties.

Yamani Falfala, coordinator of Egypto-Moroccan economic relations, said that the Egypto-Moroccan business committee would discuss conducting trade between the two countries according to the strategy agreed upon between doctor Ahmed Goweili, the Egyptian trade minister and Ilmi al-Tazi, the Moroccan minister for trade and traditional industry, confirming the need to build a joint centre of information to promote investment and trade activity between Cairo and Rabat.

The meetings will discuss extending the marine line between Casablanca and Benghazi to Alexandria or Port Said, and setting up a marine transport company between businessmen from the two countries. The company will establish the extension of the marine line to the countries of the Gulf and the meeting will discuss the subject of sea fishing, since Morocco is a country that exports fish and Egypt is a country that imports some types of fish.

The meeting will discuss the establishment of a joint trade company to market agricultural produce between the two countries, the setting up of a holding company and making transport easier between the two countries. In the meeting the Egyptian businessmen will announce their support to nominate the Moroccan, Hassan Ayoub, to the post of director-general of the World Trade Organisation.

The past days have witnessed a coordination on all levels between Egyptian and Moroccan investors in the field of agriculture. Doctor Saad Nasar, representative for the Egyptian ministry of agriculture, signed an agreement of agricultural cooperation between Egypt and Morocco in the areas of the exchange of information, the agricultural ban and the protection of plants. It was signed on the Moroccan side by Attalib al-Qurshi, inspector-general of the ministry of farming, rural development and sea fishing. The Egypto-Moroccan delegation for cooperation in the field of electricity signed an agreement to connect electricity between the two countries.

Exercises Articles 73 - 78

Exercise 1 Choose the best answer

١ تسيطر احتياجات/خلافات/محاولات/محفظات بين الدول على الاجتماع.
٢ لمح الى مشكلات بين المنتجين فى الاهتمام/الامكانية/الاقتراح/الوفاء بتعهداتهم.
٣ مناظرة بشان فتح قاعدة/طابق/قطاع/حاجة الكهرباء ستبقى الوزير فى المكسيك.
٤ مشكلات الانضباط تعرقل بدائل/تكاليف/اعطية/مساعى اجراء مزيد من الخفض.
٥ يساهم المعرض فى تجميع/تعليق/توفير/تشجيع العديد من كبرى الشركات على الاستثمار فى المنطقة.
٦ يوفر المعرض واقعا/موقعا/موضوعا/ميزانا متميزا للعديد من العارضين.
٧ الوزير كان يتحدث على هامش قيمة/كمية/قوة/قمة الدول النامية.
٨ ٤٠٪ من الناتج الداخلى الخام يعتمد على الايرادات/الاتفاقات/الصادرات/الواردات.
٩ تشارك اربع شركات فى تنسيق/تعزيز/تحديث/توزيع شبكة الهاتف.
١٠ الاتفاق حول تاشيرات/حاجات/مشتقات/احصائيات الدخول سيسهل تنقل المواطنين.
١١ يبحث الاجتماع اعفاء/اداء/ابقاء/انشاء شركة تجارة مشتركة لتسويق الحاصلات الزراعية.
١٢ شهدت الايام الماضية تسييرا/تكليفا/تفصيلا/تنسيقا على جميع المستويات.

Exercise 2 Match the following pairs

١	البلدان المصدرة	a	العالمى من النفط
٢	الخفض فى المعروض	b	نموا متواضعا
٣	تشهد فرنسا	c	على موافقة مجلس الادارة
٤	حصل الاقتراح	d	فى نهاية النفق
٥	شاهدنا الضوء	e	للبترول

Exercise 3 Match the following pairs

١	اعطى الانجاز	a	الاليات الدقيقة
٢	تدل الموءشرات	b	الثمانينات
٣	انخفضت صادرات	c	املا كبيرا
٤	منذ منتصف	d	من جراء الازمة
٥	الاقتصاديات اضيرت	e	على تزايد اهتمام

Exercise 4 Match the following pairs

١	حسب	a	ملحوظ
٢	بشكل	b	مع مشاركة فرنسا
٣	من جهة	c	اخرى
٤	لا سيما	d	حملة اقتصادية
٥	فى اطار	e	السفير

Exercise 5 Match this passage with one of the articles 73-78

ومن المقرر ان تعقد (أوپك) اجتماعها الوزاري في 23 من مارس ومن المرجح ان ترسل المكسيك غير العضو ممثلا لها في المحادثات.

هذا وقد أظهر مسح لخبراء صناعة النفط ان (أوپك) تحتاج الى خفض الانتاج بمقدار مليون برميل يوميا لكي يصبح لديها أي أمل في وقف تدهور اسعار النفط لكن من المستبعد ان تتوصل المنظمة الى مثل هذا الاتفاق عندما يجتمع وزراؤها الشهر القادم.

وقال محللون ان اعضاء منظمة البلدان المصدرة للبترول

Exercise 6 Match the following

١ أزمة آسيا عرقلت مساعي	a السعودية في الأسهم الآسيوية
٢ الأردن يتجه لخفض سقف البروتوكول التجاري	b إلى زيادة الرسوم والضرائب
٣ تحسن عائد صناديق البنوك	c تسويق الغاز اليمني
٤ محافظ «المركزي الإماراتي» يدعو	d الجارية الياباني للعام الماضي
٥ 139 مليار دولار فائض ميزان المعاملات	e مع العراق بنسبة 25% خلال 99

«اينتل» لصناعة المعلوماتية في مرمى القضاء بتهمة الاحتكار

ARTICLE 79

سان فرانسيسكو. ا.ف.ب: بعد ارجاء الدعوى على شركة «مايكروسوفت»، جاء دور شركة «اينتل» العملاق الآخر في صناعة المعلوماتية، لتكون في مرمى القضاء الاميركي ابتداء من غد الثلاثاء بتهمة الاحتكار. وستكون الدعوى على «اينتل» اقل ضوضاء واكثر تقنية من الدعوى المرفوعة على «مايكرسوفت» الشركة الاولى العالمية للبرامج المعلوماتية. لكنها ستكون محطة بارزة لانها ستتمحور حول مفهوم اساسي هو الدفاع عن الملكية الفكرية.

وقال شوك ميلوي المتحدث باسم «اينتل» ان اللجنة الفدرالية للتجارة تجازف «في سلوك طريق لم يطأه احد من قبل».

واضاف «تاريخيا، لم تصرح اي محكمة بأن الدفاع عن قانون مكافحة الاحتكار يجب ان يمر عبر التضحية بحقوق الملكية الفكرية».

وتتهم اللجنة الفدرالية للتجارة شركة «اينتل» التي تهيمن على ثلاثة ارباع السوق العالمية للحواسيب الصغيرة، بأنها ارادت ان ترغم ثلاث شركات هي «انترچراف» و«كومباك» و«ديجيتال اكويبمنت» التي اشترتها كومباك، بالتنازل لها عن تكنولوجيتها من خلال الغاء الاستفادة من منتجاتها والكف عن الإطلاع على اسرار منتجاتها الجديدة. ولا تنكر «اينتل» هذه التهم.

وقد طالبت «اينتل» التي نافست هاتين الشركتين بين 1995 و1997 باستعادة المعلومات الخاصة المتعلقة بمنتجاتها، مهددة بعرقلة الوصول الى منتجاتها الحالية ومنتجاتها المقبلة.

واوضح ميلوي «لا يشكك احد في شركة «اينتل» في حق هذه الشركات الثلاث بممارسة حقوقها المتعلقة بالملكية الفكرية». واضاف ان «اينتل» تطالب بالحق نفسه.

ولا تنظر اللجنة الفدرالية للتجارة الى الموضوع من هذه الزاوية. وهي تعتزم ان تثبت ان «اينتل» لم تكتف بالتحرك دفاعا عن تكنولوجيتها لكنها تحتكر سوق الحواسيب الصغيرة، مستخدمة موقعها القوي هذا للضغط على «انترچراف» و«ديجيتال» و«كومباك» بهدف تعزيز تفوقها على منافساتها.

لكن «اينتل» لم تكسب الرهان. ففضلا عن مسألة حصص السوق، يتعين على اللجنة الفدرالية للتجارة ان تثبت ان «اينتل» تتحكم في اسعار السوق وتمارس تأثيرا على الطلب الشامل للسوق وخصوصا من خلال عرقلة الابتكار والتجديد.

وقال مسؤول في شركة «كومباك» طلب عدم الكشف عن هويته ان «اينتل ستكون خصما اكثر شراسة من مايكروسوفت بالنسبة للجنة الفدرالية للتجارة».

IT	معلوماتية
goal	مرمى *pl.* مرام
judiciary	قضاء
accusation	تهمة
monopoly	احتكار
adjournment	ارجاء
legal proceedings	دعوى
giant	عملاق
noise	ضوضاء
to revolve	تمحور
intellectual	فكري
to plunge into	جازف
to tread	وطيء
court	محكمة
to control	هيمن على
processor	حاسب *pl.* حواسيب
transfer	تنازل
stopping	كف
to deny	نكر
retrieval	استعادة
threatened	مهدد
difficulty	عرقلة
angle	زاوية *pl.* زوايا
to fetter	كتف
ascendency	تفوق
bet	رهان
to be appointed	تعين
innovation	ابتكار *pl.* ات
adversary	خصم *pl.* خصوم

Intel of the IT industry to face the judiciary charged with breaking the anti-trust laws

San Francisco - *AFP*: After the adjournment of the case against Microsoft came the turn of Intel, the other IT giant, to face the US judiciary from tomorrow, Tuesday, accused of breaking the anti-trust laws. The case against Intel will cause less of a furore but will be more technical than the case against Microsoft, the largest company in the world for computer programs. But it will be a landmark because it will turn on a fundamental understanding of what is defending intellectual property.

Intel's spokesman, Chuck Milway, said that the Federal Trade Commission would be "venturing along a road nobody has trod before."

He added: "Historically, no court has shown that defending the anti-trust laws must mean sacrificing the rights of intellectual property."

The Federal Trade Commission is accusing Intel, which controls three quarters of the world's market for microprocessors, of wanting to force three companies - Intergraph, Compaq and Digital Equipment, which was bought by Compaq, to hand over their technology through not using Intel's products and because Intel stopped them becoming acquainted with the secrets of its new products. Intel does not dispute these accusations.

Intel, which was in competition with these two companies between 1995 and 1997, demanded the retrieval of information specifically linked with its products, threatened with the difficulty of reaching its present and future markets.

Milway said: "Nobody in Intel questions the right of these three companies to exercise their rights linked to intellectual property." He added that Intel requests the right itself.

The Federal Trade Commission does not look at the matter from this angle. It is committed to establishing that Intel did not restrict itself to defending its technology but that it monopolised the microprocessor market, using its strong position to pressure Intergragh, Digital and Compaq with the aim of strengthening its ascendancy over its competitors.

But Intel did not win the bet. Besides the question of market share, it was the Federal Trade Commission's task to establish that Intel was controlling market prices and influencing overall market demand, in particular by making innovation and renewal difficult.

An official for Compaq, who wished to remain anonymous, said: "Intel will be a more crafty adversary than Microsoft for the Federal Trade Commission."

دراسة لـ«فيزا» تتوقع بلوغ حجم التجارة عبر الإنترنت تريليون دولار بحلول 2003

دبي: «الشرق الأوسط»

بينت دراسة أجرتها مجموعة (WEFA) للدراسات والاستشارات الاقتصادية بتكليف من فيزا إنترناشونال أن حجم سوق التجارة الإلكترونية عالمياً يتوقع له أن يتجاوز تريليون دولار الأميركي بحلول عام 2003، مما يشكل نمواً سنوياً مركباً بنسبة 66 في المائة على مدار الأعوام الخمسة القادمة، إذ بلغ حجم التجارة الإلكترونية عبر الإنترنت ما يقارب 74 بليون دولار اميركي في عام 1998.

وهذه التوقعات هي أعلى بكثير من سابقتها، وهي تزيد عن توقع آخر لإنفاق المستهلكين عبر الإنترنت والتي قد تصل الى 100 بليون دولار اميركي بحلول عام 2002، ويشكل هذا التوقع الهام مؤشراً واضحاً على الطريقة التي ستمارس بها الشركات أعمالها خلال العقد القادم، كما يدل على أن التجارة الإلكترونية ستعيد تشكيل سوق الأعمال.

وتعتبر هذه الدراسة من أشمل تقييم لسوق التجارة الإلكترونية حتى هذا الوقت، وهي تتضمن تحليلاً مفصلاً لسبع عشرة سوقاً في العالم تشكل 85 في المائة من الحجم الإجمالي المحتمل لسوق التجارة الإلكترونية، وتتناول هذه الدراسة أيضا مجالات الأعمال التي ستعتمد أكثر من سواها على الإنترنت، وكذلك حجم الشركات التي تزاول أعمالها عبر هذه الشبكة، بالإضافة الى أنواع السلع والخدمات التي يتم التعامل بها.

ومن النتائج الهامة التي توصلت إليها الدراسة أن قطاع الخدمات والتصنيع ستكون أكبر المستخدمين لتقنيات الإنترنت في مزاولة العمليات التجارية، يتبعها في ذلك الحكومة، التعليم، والخدمات المالية، وتجارة التجزئة.

وتوصلت الدراسة الى أن الشركات والأعمال المتوسطة (50 – 249 موظفاً) والكبيرة جداً (أكثر من 500 موظف) هي التي لها سيكون لها الحجم الأكبر في التعامل مع الإنترنت، في حين أن الشركات والأعمال الصغيرة (1 . 49 موظفاً) ستحقق أسرع معدل نمو.

وأظهرت الدراسة أن 39 في المائة من المشتريات عبر الإنترنت ستكون من الأعمال التي تقدم خدمات الصيانة والتصليح والخدمات التشغيلية مثل الخدمات المؤقتة، وصفوف التدريب واللوازم المكتبية، بينما سيكون حوالي 12 في المائة مشتريات ذات علاقة بالسفر مثل حجوزات الطيران والفنادق.

وقالت الدراسة أنه بينما يتم 95 في المائة من نشاطات التجارة الإلكترونية حاليا عبر الإنترنت، فإنه بحلول عام 2003 سيتم 27 في المائة منها عبر شبكات الإكسترانت، وهي شبكات كومبيوتر تربط الشركة بالمورد أو بشبكة المورد مما يشكل مجتمعاً معيناً يضم مجموعة محددة من الشركات والموردين.

وقالت الدراسة ان 94 في المائة من حجم المشتريات ستكون متركزة في خمسة بلدان فقط هي: فرنسا وألمانيا واليابان والمملكة المتحدة والولايات المتحدة الأميركية من مجموع البلاد التي شملتها الدراسة والبالغة 17 بلداً.

وخلصت الدراسة إلى أن الولايات المتحدة الأميركية ستمثل 59 في المائة من حجم التجارة الإلكترونية، بينما تمثل كل من أوروبا وآسيا والمحيط الهادي حوالي 20 في المائة. وبالنسبة لڤيزا، فإن نتائج الدراسة تبين أن إمكانات كبيرة لاستخدام بطاقات الدفع التجارية كوسيلة الدفع المفضلة عبر الإنترنت.

ARTICLE 80

reaching	بلوغ
clear	واضح
separate	منفصل
to pursue	زول
maintenance	صيانة
temporary	موءقت
class	صف *pl.* صفوف
fixtures	لوازم

A study by Visa expects e-commerce to reach a trillion dollars by 2003

Dubai - *Asharq al-Awsat*: A study carried out by WEFA, the group for economic studies and consultancy, for Visa International reported that the market for e-commerce world wide is expected to exceed a trillion US dollars by 2003. This represents an annual compound growth of 66% over the next five years, with e-commerce on the internet at around 74 US billion dollars in 1998.

These predictions are far higher than the earlier ones, exceeding another forecast for internet consumer spending to reach 100 billion dollars by 2002. This significant forecast forms a clear indicator on the way companies will conduct their business over the next decade. It also shows that e-commerce will reshape the business market.

This study is considered to be the most comprehensive undertaken of the e-commerce market up to this time. It includes a separate analysis of seventeen markets in the world that make up 85% of the probable overall size of the electronic trade market. The study also looks at areas of business that will rely more on others on the internet, the size of companies which carry on their business on the network and the kinds of goods and services that are traded on it.

One of the significant conclusions the study reached was that the services and manufacturing sector will be the largest users of the internet in the pursuit of commercial business, followed by government, education, financial services and the retail trade.

The study concluded that medium-sized companies and businesses, 50 - 249 employees, and very large ones, more than 500 employees, are those that will have the largest business on the internet, while small businesses, 1 - 49 employees, will have the largest growth.

The study showed that 39% of purchases on the internet will be from businesses which offer maintenance and repair services, manpower services such as temporary services, training courses and office requirements, while around 12% of purchases will be connected with travel, such as airline and hotel reservations.

The study said that while 95% of electronic trade activity was now carried out on the internet, by 2003, 27% would be done on extranet networks, a computer network that links companies by supplier network to form a designated grouping that brings together a fixed group of companies and suppliers.

The study said that 94% of the purchases would be concentrated in only five countries: France, Germany, Japan, the United Kingdom and the United States from the group of the 17 countries included in the study.

The study concluded that the United States would represent 59% of e-commerce, while Europe, Asia and the Pacific Ocean around 20%. For Visa, the results of the study showed that there were great possibilities of using credit cards to pay as the preferred means of paying on the internet.

البنك الدولي: مشكلة الألفية الثالثة قد تؤدي إلى نكسة اقتصادية ثانية في آسيا

مانيلا - أ.ف.ب: حذر البنك الدولي امس في مانيلا من ان مشكلة الكومبيوتر لعام 2000 اذا لم يتم ضبطها قد تتسبب بانتكاسة ثانية مشابهة للازمة المالية الآسيوية التي اندلعت عام 1997.

وعلق تشيت ثارنتونج المسؤول عن دائرة المعلوماتية في البنك الدولي امام مئات المندوبين في اطار المؤتمر الدولي حول مشكلة العام 2000 ان «التعاون الاقليمي مسألة جوهرية لان عجز احد البلدان عن مواجهة هذه المشكلة قد ينتقل بسهولة الى سواه ولو كان هذا الاخير اكثر استعدادا».

وفي اشارة الى مدى هشاشة المنطقة حيال مشكلة عام 2000، شدد ثارنتونج على «النمو الهائل» للمعلوماتية في منطقة آسيا - المحيط الهادئ مقارنة بمعدل النمو الاقليمي في السنوات العشر الاخيرة.

واضاف ان الازمة المالية الاسيوية زادت من هشاشة المنطقة اذ حدّت من الموارد التي تحتاجها الدول لاتخاذ الاجراءات الضرورية بهدف تفادي مشكلة الالفية. واشار الى ان البنك الدولي يعيد حاليا درس اكثر من 300 مشروع تنمية يموله في المنطقة للتأكد من عدم تأثره بالمشكلة.

ويخشى في الاول من يناير (كانون الثاني) عام 2000 من ان لا تتمكن اجهزة الكومبيوتر القديمة والتي لم تعد برمجتها من الانتقال الى القرن الجديد لانها قد تعتقد انها لا تزال في عام 1900 مما قد يؤدي الى حال من الهلع في مجالات كالطب والدفاع والمصارف والمالية.

وقال ثارنتونج «لقد سبق ان شهدنا انتشار حالات من الهلع في المنطقة وهو ما نريد تجنبه». من جهته اعلن جو رايلي مدير مجموعة استشاريين استراليين ان «آسيا ستجتاز منعطفا خطرا» خلال الانتقال المحتم «وسيتأثر كل رجل وامرأة وطفل بهذه الظاهرة».

واشار بشكل خاص الى توزيع المياه والطاقة الذي قد يتأثر بالخلل الناتج عن المشكلة.

اما ممثل مجموعة «چارتنر» للابحاث في واشنطن فاشار الى ان 40 في المائة من الشركات في العالم ستتأثر بالظاهرة بشكل أو بآخر. الا انه اعتبر ان هذه النسبة ستكون «اكبر بكثير» في آسيا.

ونصح رايلي لتفادي وقوع الكوارث، دول آسيا لا سيما تايلاند والفلبين واندونيسيا «الاقل استعدادا في المنطقة» الى اعداد «خطط للطوارئ» لتجنب وقوع «كوارث ضخمة».

وقد صنف رايلي سنغافورة وتايوان وهونغ كونغ وكوريا الجنوبية بين الدول الاكثر استعدادا لمواجهة الانتقال الى عام 2000 في المنطقة.

وفي بدء اجتماع مانيلا الذي انهى اعماله مساء امس، قدّر امابلي اچويلوز مدير المجلس الرئاسي الفلبيني حول المشكلة نقلا عن خبراء ان التكاليف المباشرة والمترتبة على المشكلة الالفية ستبلغ ما مجموعه مليار و300 الف دولار.

واوضح انه يحتمل ان يخصص مبلغ 600 مليار دولار لاعادة برمجة برامج المعلوماتية في العالم ولتصليح الاعطال الناجمة عن المشكلة، بالاضافة الى 700 مليار للملاحقات القضائية الناجمة عن خلل التشغيل.

ARTICLE 81

failure	نكسة
relapse	انتكاسة
to break out	اندلع
fundamental	جوهرى
happiness	هشاشة
awesome	هائل
avoiding	تفادى
to fear	خشى
alarm	هلع
spread	انتشار
avoidance	تجنب
twist	منعطف
definitive	محتم
catastrophe	كارثة *pl.* كوارث
emergency	طارئة *pl.* طوارىء

The World Bank: The problem of Y2000 may lead to a second economic collapse in Asia

Manila - *AFP*: The World Bank yesterday in Manila warned that the computer problem of Y2000 if not controlled might cause a second downturn similar to the Asian financial crisis that flared up in 1997.

Tcheat Thanitung, an official for the department of information in the World Bank, told some hundreds of delegates as part of an international conference on the problem of Y2000: "Regional cooperation is a fundamental question because the inability of one country to face this problem may easily be transferred to another even if the latter is fully prepared."

Turning to the degree of complacency in the region with regard to the problem of the Y2000, Thanitung emphasised the startling growth in IT in the Asia-Pacific Ocean region compared with the rate of regional growth in the past ten years.

He added that the Asian financial crisis had raised the region's level of complacency as it had limited the income the countries needed to take the steps necessary to avert the problem of Y2000. He pointed out the World Bank was presently checking more than 300 development projects it was financing in the region to confirm it would not be affected by the problem.

It is feared that on 1st January 2000 the old computer systems whose programs have not been modified may not be able to change over to the new century because they may still think they are in 1900. This may lead to a panic situation fields like medicine, defence, banking and finance.

Thanitung said: "We have already witnessed the spread of panic conditions in the region and this is what we want to avoid." For his part, Jo Reilly, manager of the group of Australian advisers, said: " Asia will be on a dangerous bend" during the inevitable transfer, and "Every man, woman and child will be affected by this phenomenon."

He pointed specifically to water and power distribution which may be affected by a break resulting from the problem.

A representative for the Gartner research group in Washington pointed out that 40% of the companies in the world would be affected by the phenomenon in one way or another. However he considered that this rate would be "much greater" in Asia.

To avoid these catastrophes, Reilly advised Asian countries, especially Thailand, the Philippines and Indonesia, "the least prepared in the region" to prepare "emergency plans" to avert "huge catastrophes".

Reilly categorised Singapore, Taiwan, Hong Kong, and South Korea among the countries most prepared to face the transfer to the year 2000 in the region.

At the beginning of the meeting in Manila which finished its work yesterday evening, Amably Aguilos, director of the presidential Philippine commission on the problem, said that according to experts costs either direct or resulting from the millennium problem would reach in total around 1,300 billion dollars.

He made it clear that it might cost 600 billion dollars to reprogram software throughout the world and to repair the breakdowns resulting from the problem, in addition to 700 billion dollars for the legal cases resulting from an interruption in functioning.

البنك السعودي المتحد يرفع أرباحه 50% إلى 611 مليون ريال

الرياض: من محمد البسام

حقق البنك السعودي المتحد زيادة في ارباحه بنسبة 50 في المائة مقارنة مع العام السابق، حيث تضاعفت الارباح الموزعة على المساهمين مقارنة بنفس الفترة لعام 97، وهو اعلى نمو للارباح بين البنوك المحلية.

واكد رئيس مجلس ادارة البنك الامير الوليد بن طلال بان هذه النتائج تعكس وضعا ماليا قويا للبنك ومكسبا مرضيا لعملائه ومساهميه على حد سواء.

واشار البيان الذي وزعه البنك امس ان البنك ركز على تكثيف نشاطات لجني اكبر قدر ممكن من فوائد الاندماج مع بنك القاهرة السعودي.

وكان محور هذه النشاطات تخفيض المصاريف التشغيلية وتقليص عدد الفروع والمحافظة على عدد الموظفين واعلى انتاجية كما دل على ذلك ارتفاع تصنيف البنك.

واوضحت الميزانية الجديدة ان ارباح البنك قد قفزت من 406 ملايين ريال للسنة المالية 97 الى 611 مليون ريال للسنة المالية 98، اي بزيادة قدرها 5, 50 في المائة كما شهدت كافة بنود المركز المالي ارتفاعا ملحوظا، حيث ارتفع اجمالي الموجودات الى 3, 27 مليار ريال بنهاية 31 ديسمبر (كانون الاول) 98 مقارنة بموجودات 97 التي بلغت 6, 26 مليار ريال، كما ارتفع بند الاستثمارات من 5, 9 مليار ريال في نهاية 97 الى 11 مليار ريال بزيادة قدرها 5, 15٪.

واوضح البيان ان صافي القروض والسلف بلغت 11 مليار ريال، حيث سجل هذا الرقم زيادة قدرها 18 في المائة عن العام الماضي. واشار البيان الى ان سياسة البنك المتحفظة خلال السنوات الماضية قد ادت الى بناء مخصصات واحتياطات كافية لهذه القروض تعتبر نسبتها من اعلى النسب بين البنوك.

واوصى مجلس الادارة بتوزيع ارباح نقدية بواقع 32, 10 ريال لكل سهم، في حين كان ربح السهم الموزع قد بلغ 5 ريالات لنفس الفترة من العام الماضي.

وكان البنك السعودي الاميركي، والبنك السعودي المتحد قد اعلنا اتفاقا للاندماج بعد ان ابدى رئيسا مجلس ادارة البنكين، واعضاء مجلس الادارة، وادارتاهما اهتماما بالغا لتوحيد الشركتين ويتوقف اتمام عملية الدمج على موافقة مساهمي البنكين بعد الانتهاء من دراسات التقييم الجاري اعدادها الآن.

ARTICLE 82

to be doubled	تضاعف
gain	مكاسب *pl.* مكسب
equally	على حد سواء
consolidation	تكثيف
harvest	جنى
pivot	محاور *pl.* محور
branch	فروع *pl.* فرع
functionary	ون *pl.* موظف
classification	تصنيف
article, paragraph	بنود *pl.* بند
free loan	سلف
cautious	متحفظ
precautionary measures	احتياطات
to depend on	توقف على

The Saudi Bank Limited increases its profits by 50% to 611 million dollars

Riyadh *from Mohammed Albasam*: The Saudi Bank Limited raised its profits by 50% compared with the previous year, while shareholders' dividends doubled compared with the same period of 1997. This is the highest growth in profits among the national banks.

The bank's chairman, Prince al-Waleed bin Talal, said that these results showed the bank's strong financial position and a satisfactory return for its customers and shareholders alike.

The statement issued by the bank yesterday said it had focused on consolidating activities in order to reap the greatest possible advantages of a merger with the Saudi Cairo Bank.

The basis of these activities was to reduce operating costs and the number of branches, to control the number of employees and raise productivity. The rise in the bank's classification bore witness to this.

The new balance sheet showed that the bank's profits had jumped from 406 million riyals for the financial year 97 to 611 million riyals for the financial year 98, an increase of 50.5%. All the items of the financial position showed a considerable increase, with total assets rising to 27.3 billion riyals at the end of December 98, compared with 97 assets of 26.6 billion riyals, and investments up from 9.5 billion riyals at the end of 97 to 11 billion riyals, a 15.5% increase.

The statement indicated that net loans and interest-free loans totalled 11 billion riyals, this figure recording an 18% increase over last year. It said that the bank's prudent policy over the past years had led to the building-up of sufficient funds and reserves for these loans whose ratio is considered one of the highest among the banks.

The board of directors recommended a dividend of 10.32 riyals per share be paid, while the dividend per share had been 5 riyals for the same period last year.

The Saudi American Bank and the Saudi Bank Limited have announced an agreement to merge after the chairmen of the board of the two banks, members of the board, and their two managements showed a strong interest in merging the two companies. This course of action depends on the agreement of the shareholders of the two banks once the studies of the present setup currently being prepared have been completed.

6.25 مليون دولار صافي أرباح البنك الأردني ـ الكويتي عام 1998

عمان: «الشرق الأوسط»

ارتفع صافي ارباح البنك الاردني الكويتي في السنة المالية الماضية 1998 بنسبة 41٪ وبلغت في نهاية ديسمبر (كانون الاول) الماضي 4,43 مليون دينار (6,25 مليون دولار) مقارنة مع 3,13 مليون دينار (4,41 مليون دولار) للعام 1997.

واوضح رئيس مجلس الادارة رئيس الوزراء الاسبق عبد الكريم الكباريتي ان اهتمامات البنك تركزت العام الماضي بشكل رئيسي على مهام تنظيم وتفعيل خطط التغيير والتطوير الشامل واعادة الهيكلة التي شملت استراتيجيات البنك وسياساته ورؤيته المستقبلية بكافة اشكالها وحاجاتها.

واضاف ان ادارة البنك راعت الظروف الاقتصادية التي سادت وتمسكت بسياسة ائتمانية متحفظة وانتقائية مع تركيز الجهود على تنظيم وتنظيف المحفظة الائتمانية ومعالجة تحصيل الديون، مشيراً الى تعويض النمو المتواضع في التسهيلات المباشرة والبالغ 3,5٪ بالتوسع في انشطة مصرفية واستثمارية اخرى.

وأكد ان البنك عمل على تسوية كافة التزاماته الضريبية حتى نهاية عام 1997 مما ترتب عليه تسديد نحو 964 الف دينار (1,4 مليون دولار)، كما حقق البنك في صافي الفوائد العمولات زيادة مقدارها 3,35 مليون دينار عن عام 1997 أي بزيادة مقدارها 29٪. وتشير ارقام الميزانية العامة الى ارتفاع مجموعة الميزانية الى 346,6 مليون دينار بمعدل نمو مقداره 11,2٪ عن العام السابق، ونما صافي حقوق المساهمين بنسبة 7,7٪ ليبلغ 34,72 مليون دينار. كما تم دعم مخصص الديون لمستوى 7 ملايين دينار بزيادة بلغت 23٪.

وارتفع معدل كفاية رأس المال الى 20,3٪ وهو يزيد عن الحد الادنى المطلوب من قبل البنك المركزي والبالغ 12٪. وبالنسبة لمحفظة ودائع العملاء والبنوك فقد زادت من 251 مليون دينار الى 277 مليون دينار بنسبة نمو مقدارها 10٪. كما ارتفعت التأمينات النقدية من 12,5 مليون دينار الى 20,24 مليون دينار عام 1998 بزيادة بلغت 62٪.

ARTICLE 83

task	مهام *pl.* مهمة
view	رؤية
to frighten	راعى
to persist in	تمسك ب
credit *adj.*	ائتماني
selective	انتقائي
cleaning	تنظيف
settling	تسوية
payment	تسديد
commission	عمولة
sufficiency	كفاية

6.25 million dollars net profits for the Jordanian-Kuwaiti bank in 1998

Amman - *Asharq al-Awsat*: Net profits for the Jordanian-Kuwaiti Bank last year 1998 rose 41% to reach 4.43 million dinars (6.25 million dollars) at the end of December 98 compared with 3.13 million dinars (4.41 million dollars) for 1997.

The chairman of the board, the former prime minister, Abdul Kareem al-Kabariti, made clear that the bank's concerns last year were focused mainly on the tasks of organising and implementing the plans for comprehensive change, development and restructuring, including the bank's strategies, its policies and its future views in all its forms and needs.

He added that the bank's board was keeping an eye on the prevailing economic conditions and was following a cautious and selective credit policy by concentrating efforts on organising and clearing out the credit portfolio and the handling of debt collection, pointing to the offsetting of a modest growth of 3.5% in direct facilities with an expansion in foreign exchange and other investment activities.

He stated that the bank had taken steps to settle all its tax obligations up to the end of 1997, which meant paying around 964 thousand dinars (1.4 million dollars), as the bank had increased its net profits on commissions by 3.35 million dinars over 1997, up 29%. The figures of the general balance sheet show an increase of the total balance sheet to 346.6 million dinars, with a rate of growth of 11.2% over the previous year, with shareholdings increasing 7.7% to reach 34.72 million dinars. There was debt provision of 7 million dinars, an increase of 23%.

The capital adequacy ratio rose to 20.3%, more than the minimum 12% required by the central bank. The portfolio of customers' and banks' deposits rose 10% from 251 million dinars to 277 million dinars, with cash reserves rising from 12.5 million dinars to 20.24 million dinars, up 62%.

423 مليون ريال أرباح بنك قطر الوطني

الدوحة: صالح الأشقر

بلغت ارباح بنك قطر الوطني (اكبر البنوك القطرية) لعام 1998 423 مليون ريال قطري بزيادة نسبتها 11,5 في المائة عن عام 1997. وقرر مجلس ادارة البنك توزيع ارباح على المساهمين بنسبة 20 في المائة بالاضافة الى اصدار سهم مجاني لكل اربعة اسهم.

وقال سعيد عبد الله المسند نائب مدير عام البنك ان النتائج المالية تعكس التقدم المستمر الذي تحقق في العام الماضي على كافة المجالات.. موضحا ان عدد افرع البنك بلغ 24 فرعاً داخل قطر بالاضافة الى 32 صراف آلي الى جانب فرعي لندن وباريس اللذين يدعمان الاعمال المالية الخاصة بدولة قطر.

وقال المسند ان البنك كان المنظم الرئيسي لقرض مشترك بقيمة مائة مليون دولار لصالح شركة قطر الوطنية للفنادق بالاضافة الى مساهمة البنك مع 11 بنكا في ترتيب قرض مماثل بقيمة 510 ملايين دولار لصالح شركة البترول الوطنية للتوزيع (نودكو).. واكد المسند ان البنك سيستمر في مشاركاته التمويلية للمشاريع المتعلقة بتطوير صناعة الغاز المسال وتصديره الى جانب تمويل المشاريع الاخرى.

وفي ديسمبر (كانون الاول) قام البنك بدور المنظم المحلي والبنك القابض الوحيد لعملية الاكتتاب العام للنسبة التي طرحتها شركة اتصالات قطر (كيوتل) وقدرها 45 في المائة من اسهم الشركة.

وقد حافظت نسبة حقوق المساهمين على قوتها خلال العام الماضي وبلغت 16,32 في المائة مقارنة بنسبة 15,85 في المائة في عام 1997 مما رفع ترتيب البنك ضمن اول 25 بنكا في العالم من حيث حقوق المساهمين الى الاصول.

ويواصل بنك قطر الوطني المحافظة على نسبة كفاية رأس المال التي تتجاوز 50 في المائة والتي تحظى باهتمام متزايد نظراً للتحديات الاقتصادية التي تمر بها دول مجلس التعاون والتي تجعل القوة المالية وتدعيم قاعدة رأس المال من اولى اهتماماته.

وتبلغ موجودات بنك قطر الوطني 19,5 مليار ريال قطري والقروض والسلفيات 16,1 مليار في حين تبلغ ودائع العملاء 10,7 مليار ريال قطري. وكان عائد السهم في عام 1998 قدره 61,1 ريال قطري في حين كان هذا العائد عام 1997 قدره 54,8 ريال.

ARTICLE 84

sponsor	منظم
liquid *adj.*	مسال
to obtain	حظى
steadily increasing	متزايد
strengthening	تدعيم
cash advance	سلفية

423 million riyals profit for the Qatar National Bank

Doha - *Salah Alashgar*: Profits of the Qatar National Bank, the largest bank in Qatar, reached 423 million Qatar riyals in 1998, an 11.5% increase over 1997. The board of the bank decided to distribute 20% of profits to shareholders in addition to issuing one free share for every four.

The bank's deputy chairman, Abdullah al-Masnad, said the financial results reflected the continued progress made last year in all areas, pointing out that the number of branches totalled 24 within Qatar, in addition to 32 money changers Ali, and two branches in London and Paris, which promote financial operations specifically for Qatar.

Al-Masnad said that the bank had been the main broker of a joint hundred million dollar loan for the National Hotel Company of Qatar. The bank also participated with 11 other banks in arranging a similar loan of 510 million dollars for the National Oil Distribution Company, Nodco. Al-Masnad said that the bank would continue to take part in financing projects connected with the development and exportation of liquid gas as well as financing other projects.

In December, the bank undertook the role of local sponsor and the sole bank for carrying out the public subscription for the 45% of the shares offered by the Qatar Company for Telecommunications, Qatel.

It maintained the proportion of shareholdings at its last year's level of 16.32%, compared with 15.85% in 1997. This raised the bank's position to within the top 25 banks in the world as regards shareholdings to assets.

The Qatar National Bank continues to maintain a capital adequacy ratio of more than 50 %, which is the object of steadily growing interest in view of the economic challenges faced by the countries of the Gulf Cooperation Council, challenges that make financial strength and consolidating the capital base one of the bank's primary concerns.

The assets of the Qatar National Bank totalled 19.5 billion Qatar riyals, with loans and advances of 16.1 billion, while customers' deposits came to 10.7 billion Qatar riyals. Earnings per share in 1998 was 61.1 Qatar riyals as against 54.8 riyals in 1997.

Exercises Articles 79 - 84

Exercise 1 Choose the best answer

١ ستتمحور الدعوى حول مفهوم اساسى الدفاع عن الحكومة/العرقلة/الملكية/التهمة الفكرية
٢ تمارس الشركة تاثيرا على الاحتكار/الابتكار/الطلب/التنازل الشامل للسوق.
٣ تقدم كل الاعمال خدمات الوقاية/الصيانة/السياحة/التاشيرة والتصليح.
٤ يشكل هذا التوقع ابتكارا/بلوغا/وعدا/مؤشرا واضحا على طريق الاعوام القادمة.
٥ الدراسة تتضمن نجاحا/ميزانا/تحليلا/بديلا منفصلا للاسواق.
٦ المشكلة قد تتسبب بامكانية/باستجابة/باستعادة/بانتكاسة ثانية.
٧ التحصيلات/التكاليف/التذاكر/القيود المباشرة ستبلغ مليار دولار.
٨ هذه النتائج تعكس وضعا/وقفا/وفوعا/وقودا ماليا قويا.
٩ كان محور هذه النشاطات تخفيض الافكار/المصاريف/القواعد/التفاصيل التشغيلية.
١٠ دل على ذلك ارتفاع تصنيف/تكثيف/تعليق/تعويض البنك.
١١ ادارة البنك راعت الطرق/الطوابق/الظروف/الطاقة الاقتصادية.
١٢ البنك عمل على تسيير/تسجيل/تسويق/تسوية كافة التزاماته الضريبية.
١٣ البنك كان المنافس/المرافق/المنظم/المفتش الرئيسي لقرض مشترك.
١٤ حافظت نسبة عقود/حقوق/قروض/ظروف المساهمين على قوتها خلال العام الماضى.
١٥ اوضحت الكارثة/الاستفادة/العرقلة/الميزانية الجديدة ان ارباح البنك قد قفزت.
١٦ يتوقف اتمام عملية المحور/الاحتكار/الدمج/البند على موافقة مساهمى البنكين.

Exercise 2 Match the following pairs

١	لا تنكر الشركة	a	الراهن
٢	لا تنظر اللجنة	b	الكشف عن هويته
٣	لم تكسب الشركة	c	فى اسعار السوق
٤	لم يطلب عدم	d	هذه التهم
٥	لا تتحكم الشركة	e	الى الموضوع من هذه الزاوية

Exercise 3 Match the following pairs

١	انتقال	a	المعلوماتية
٢	الازمة	b	الاجراءات الضرورية
٣	دائرة	c	ستاثر بالظاهرة
٤	اتخاذ	d	المالية
٥	شركات	e	الى القرن الجديد

Exercise 4 Match the following pairs

١	صافى	a	متحفظة
٢	سياسة	b	النسبة
٣	تقليص عدد	c	الادارة بتوزيع ارباح
٤	اوصى مجلس	d	القروض
٥	اعلى	e	الفروع

Exercise 5 Match this passage with one of the articles 79-84

وقالت سيلفيا هاريس باين، النائبة الأولى للرئيس، لشؤون الخدمات والمنتجات التجارية، ڤيزا إنترناشيونال: تبين هذه الدراسة أنه يوجد سوق محتملة كبيرة ومهمة لجميع منتجات فيزا التجارية، بما فيها بطاقات ڤيزا للمؤسسات وللمشتريات والأعمال. ومن خلال تكامل التقنيات الجديدة وبرامج ڤيزا التجارية الحالية، فإننا نستطيع أن نلبي الاحتياجات المتنامية للعملاء التجاريين الذي يحتاجون خدمات آمنة يعتمد عليها في العالم. أما بالنسبة للبنوك الأعضاء في ڤيزا، فإن هنالك فرصة لإضافة المزيد من القيمة الى برامج البطاقات لديهم، وذلك من خلال تقديم منتجات البطاقات التجارية لديهم كأفضل طريقة للدفع والقبض عبر الإنترنت.

Exercise 6 Match the following

١ بنوك سعودية تنهي استعداداتها

a تعتزم فتح فروع إنتاجية في روسيا

٢ السعودية تحذر الدول الصناعية

b للصناعات البتروكيماوية في السعودية

٣ شركات صناعية ألمانية

c من فرض إجراءات حمائية إضافية

٤ تأسيس الشركة الوطنية

d لمواجهة مشكلة الألفية الثالثة

اليورو يتلقى دعما من صفقة ألمانية وتباين أداء البورصات الأوروبية

لندن: «الشرق الأوسط» ووكالات الأنباء

دعمت صفقة المانية بشأن الاجور التوقعات بأن البنك المركزي الاوروبي لن يخفض أسعار الفائدة، الامر الذي دفع الى ارتفاع اليورو امام العملات الرئيسية في معاملات امس بينما ساعدت نتائج جيدة لبعض الشركات الاسهم الاوروبية على مقاومة اثار هبوط الاسهم الاميركية. واستقرت أسواق السندات الاوروبية عند الفتح لكن أسواق النفط تتجه الى يوم صعب اخر بعد ان انخفضت أسعار النفط الخام الى أقل من عشرة دولارات للبرميل أمس الاول. وصعد الدولار الى مستوى مرتفع جديد في شهرين مقابل الين.

ودعم اليورو أمام الدولار الاعتقاد بأن البنك المركزي الاوروبي سيترك سعر الفائدة الرئيسي عند ثلاثة في المائة في اجتماع انعقد في وقت لاحق من يوم امس لاسيما بعد اتفاق اتحاد الصناعات الهندسية «اي جي ميتال» مع العاملين على زيادة في الاجور اكبر مما توقع كثيرون.

وقال نيل باركر الاقتصادي في رويال بنك أوف سكوتلاند «التسوية التي تم التوصل اليها مع اي جي ميتال ستعطي للبنك المركزي الاوروبي المبررات». وأضاف «لا يتوقع أحد حقا ان يخفض البنك المركزي الاوروبي أسعار الفائدة على أي حال. لكن تسوية اي جي ميتال بشأن زيادة الاجور كانت في الجانب الأعلى من التوقعات ولذلك يمكن ان يعطي ذلك للبنك المركزي الاوروبي أسبابا أخرى لعدم خفض اسعار الفائدة».

وبلغ اليورو اثناء التعاملات 1,1253 دولار مرتفعا من 1,1233 دولار في اواخر المعاملات امس الاربعاء وبنسبة واحد في المائة من اقل مستوى تدني اليه على الاطلاق عند 1,1155 دولار يوم الاثنين الماضي.

وبقيت العملة الاميركية قوية امام الين ووصلت الى أعلى مستوياته منذ شهرين ليصل الى 119,70 ين رغم انه تراجع في وقت لاحق عن هذا المستوى. وقال متعامل في بنك ياباني «الاتجاه هو ارتفاع الدولار لان السوق تدرك ان السلطات اليابانية ستقبل ينا أضعف».

وفي اسواق الاسهم الاوروبية تباينت الأسعار الاسهم حيث عوض خسائر الولايات المتحدة تقارير افضل من المتوقع عن ارباح الشركات. وكان مؤشر داو جونز لاسهم الشركات الصناعية قد اغلق منخفضا بنسبة 1,1 في المائة بينما تراجع مؤشر ناسداك المركب المؤلف من اسهم شركات التكنولوجيا 2,8 في المائة.

وفي لندن ساعدت النتائج الافضل من المتوقع لشركة «جلاكسو ولكام» وبنك «هاليفاكس» على الحد من خسائر مؤشر فايننشال تايمز الذي فتح على ارتفاع لكنه سرعان ما اتجه للهبوط.

وساعد أداء مماثل لواحدة من أكبر شركات بيع التجزئة في أوروبا وهي «كريفور» الفرنسية في ارتفاع مؤشر كاك المؤلف من 40 سهما بنسبة 0,2 في المائة. وصعد مؤشر اكسترا داكس في فرانكفورت بنسبة 0,4 في المائة. وصعدت السندات الحكومية الاوروبية في بداية التعاملات حيث اتجه تركيز السوق على اجتماع البنك المركزي الاوروبي.

وفي وقت سابق من يوم امس اغلق مؤشر نيكاي المؤلف من 225 سهما في بورصة طوكيو منخفضا بنسبة 0,1 في المائة.

ARTICLE 85

disparity	تباين
wages	أجور *pl.* أجر
resistance	مقاومة
bond	سندات *pl.* سند
belief	ات *pl.* اعتقاد
justification	ات *pl.* مبرر

The euro receives support from German deal and the difference in performance of the European markets

London - *Asharq al-Awsat and News Agencies*: A German deal on wages reinforced expectations the European Central Bank would not lower interest rates. This pushed the euro up against the main currencies in trading yesterday while excellent results of some companies helped European shares to withstand the effect of the fall in US shares. European bond markets opened firm but the oil markets face another difficult day after crude oil prices fell below ten dollars a barrel the day before yesterday. The dollar hit a two month high against the yen.

The euro strengthened against the dollar on the belief that the European Central Bank would leave prime interest rates unchanged at 3% in a meeting held late yesterday, especially after an agreement of the federation of engineering industries, IG Metall, with workers on a wage increase higher than what many had anticipated.

Neil Barker, an economist at the Royal Bank of Scotland, said: "The settlement agreed with AG Metall will provide the European Central Bank with justifications." He added: "No one really believes that the European Central Bank will reduce interest rates in any case. But the pay settlement of AG Metall was on the high side, and hence may give the European Central Bank other reasons not to lower interest rates."

During trading the euro reached 1.1253 dollars, up from 1.1233 dollars at the close of trading Wednesday and by one per cent from the lowest level it had ever sunk to of 1.1155 dollars last Monday.

The US currency remained strong against the yen and hit a two month high of 119.70 yen, although it dropped back later from this level. A trader at the Bank of Japan said: "The trend of the dollar is upwards because the market senses that the Japanese authorities will accept a weaker yen."

In the European stock markets share prices were mixed, where to make up for US losses there were better than expected reports of company profits. The Dow Jones industrial share index had closed 1.1% down, while the composite Nasdaq index made up of shares of technology companies fell back 2.8%.

In London the better than expected results of Glaxo Wellcome and the Halifax Bank helped to limit losses of the Financial Times index, which opened up but soon fell.

A similar performance of one of the largest retailers in Europe, the French company, Carrefour, helped the CAC-40 index to rise by 0.2% and the Xetra Dax in Frankfurt rose by 0.4%. European government bonds rose at the start of trading when the market focused on a meeting of the European Central Bank.

Earlier yesterday the Nikkei index of 225 shares on the Tokyo markets closed down 0.1%.

بورصات أوروبا تتراجع بسبب القلق من أسعار الفائدة الأميركية

لندن: «الشرق الاوسط» ووكالات الانباء

تراجعت الاسهم الاوروبية امس وخيم عليها عدم الاستقرار بسبب ارتفاع عائد السندات الاوروبية والأميركية ونتيجة للقلق بشأن التباطؤ الاقتصادي في الدول التي انضمت الى العملة الاوروبية الموحدة.

وارتفع الدولار الى مستوى اعلى من 120 ينا بدعم من تصريحات نائب وزير الخزانة الأميركي لورانس سومرز التي قال فيها ان اليابان ربما تحتاج الى اتخاذ مزيد من الاجراءات لمساعدة اقتصادها على الانتعاش.

وقال اكيم ماتسكي المحلل في كوميرس بانك بفرانكفورت «هناك ضغوط قوية على السندات الأميركية والاوروبية طويلة الاجل وهذا مؤشر على البيع». واضاف «تتأثر السوقان الأميركية والاوروبية بأسعار الفائدة وسيكون لذلك اثر سلبي على الاسهم». وفي المانيا تراجعت الاسهم بنحو واحد في المائة.

وفي لندن فتح مؤشر فاينانشال تايمز المؤلف من 100 سهم على انخفاض وافتقر الى اتجاه واضح. وتوقع متعاملون ان يحد من المكاسب القلق المستمر من ان الولايات المتحدة ربما ترفع اسعار الفائدة.

وانخفضت الاسهم الأميركية امس لان حدوث قفزة اخرى في اسعار الفائدة على القروض طويلة الاجل يؤثر على وول ستريت لكن رغم ان العائد على سندات الخزانة الأميركية يواصل الارتفاع الى مستويات لم تشاهد منذ اغسطس (اب) الماضي فان الاسهم استردت بعض خسائرها.

وأغلق مؤشر داو جونز لاسهم الشركات الصناعية امس الاول منخفضا 33,33 نقطة أو 0,35 في المائة عند 9366,34 نقطة بعد ان تعرض لخسارة بلغت 166 نقطة في اليوم الذي سبقه. وأغلقت الاسهم في طوكيو على انخفاض طفيف رغم الدعم الذي تلقته من قفزة الدولار امام الين نتيجة لتأثر السوق بموجة اقبال على البيع في اواخر المعاملات في سوق التعاقدات الاجلة. وهبط مؤشر نيكي الرئيسي المؤلف من 225 سهما 102,91 نقطة أو 0,17 في المائة الى 1436,54 نقطة.

واغلقت الاسهم في هونغ كونغ على ارتفاع شديد بعد صعود الاسهم الممتازة بسبب تقارير بأن شركة وولت ديزني على وشك اختيار الجزيرة موقعا لمدينة ملاهي جديدة. وقفز مؤشر هانغ سنغ 200,42 نقطة أو 2,08 في المائة ليغلق على 9858,49 نقطة.

وارتفع الدولار امام الين بعد تصريحات لسومرز خلال زيارة لليابان قال فيها ان سعر الصرف لا يمكن ان يصبح بديلا للسياسة النقدية. وفي اوروبا تم تداول الدولار عند 120,45/120,50 ين بالمقارنة مع 119,65/119,75 ين في اواخر المعاملات في نيويورك امس الجمعة. كما عاد اليورو ليرتفع عن 1,10 دولار مع اجتماع زعماء دول الاتحاد الاوروبي في برلين لبحث ميزانية الاتحاد.

وهبط اليورو امام الدولار بسبب ارتفاع العملة الأميركية امام الين.

ARTICLE 86

unease	قلق	to regain	استرد
to reign	خيم	close to	على وشك
to join	انضم	amusement *adj.*	ملاهي
negative	سلبي	to fluctuate	تداول
to lack	افتقر الى	leader	زعيم *pl.* زعماء
occurrence	حدوث		

European markets fall back on concern over US interest rates

London - *Asharq al-Awsat and News Agencies*: European shares fell back yesterday and unsteadiness prevailed because of the increase in the return on European and American bonds and because of the concern over the economic sluggishness in the countries that form the European single currency.

The dollar rose to over 120 yen buoyed by comments by Lawrence Summers, deputy secretary of the US treasury, that Japan would probably need to take additional measures to help its economy to recover.

Akeem Matksi, analyst at the Commerce Bank of Frankfurt, said: "There are strong pressures on long term US and European bonds and this is a sign to sell. He added: "The American and European markets are influenced by interest rates and hence will be a negative influence on shares." In Germany shares fell back by around 1%.

In London, the Financial Times 100 index opened down and lacked a clear direction. Traders expected that the continuing concern that the United States might raise interest rates would restrict gains.

US shares fell yesterday because another hike in long term interest rates affected Wall Street but despite the return on US treasury bonds continuing to rise to levels not seen since last August, share prices regained some of their losses.

The day before yesterday the Dow Jones industrial share index closed down 33.33 points, 0.35%, at 9366.34 points, after suffering losses of 166 points in the previous day. Shares in Tokyo closed down slightly despite the support they received from the jump in the dollar against the yen as a result of the market being affected by a wave of interest in selling in late trading in futures contracts. The main Nikkei index of 225 shares fell 102.91 points, 0.17%, to 1436.54 points.

Shares in Hong Kong closed sharply up after a rise in blue chips because of reports that the Walt Disney Corporation was on the point of choosing the island as a location for a new amusement park. The Hang Seng index jumped 200.42 points, 2.08%, to close at 9858.49 points.

The dollar rose against the yen after the comments of Summers during a visit to Japan in which he said that the bank rate could not become a replacement for a monetary policy. In Europe the dollar finished trading at 120.45/120.50 yen compared with 119.65/119.75 yen in late trading in New York yesterday, Friday. The euro fell back to close at 1.10 dollars with a meeting of the leaders of the countries in the European Union in Berlin to discuss the Union's budget. The euro fell against the dollar because of the rise of the US currency against the yen.

هدوء في البورصات الأوروبية والدولار يكافح للحفاظ على مكتسباته أمام اليورو

لندن: «الشرق الأوسط» ووكالات الأنباء

كافحت الاسواق الاوروبية للنهوض خلال معاملات امس غير انها لم تنجح في تحقيق مكاسب تذكر ومنيت بهبوط تجاوز في بعضها واحدا في المائة. وما زال الدولار يصارع للحفاظ على مستوياته مقابل الين واليورو في اعقاب هبوطه قبل نهاية تعاملات الاسبوع الماضي.

وتدنى اليورو عن 1,10 دولار بينما حامت العملة الاميركية حول 119 ينا متجاوزة ادنى مستوياتها خلال اسبوع والذي بلغته بنهاية الاسبوع الماضي. الا ان من المتوقع ان يواصل الدولار الهبوط بعد ان نقل عن نائب محافظ بنك اليابان المركزي يوتاكا ياماجوشي قوله ان اقتصاد اليابان لا يحتاج الى تخفيف اكبر لقيود الائتمان في الوقت الحالي.

وارتفع الجنيه الاسترليني بقوة امام الدولار واليورو بعد ان جاءت بيانات مؤشر مديري المشتريات في بريطانيا في شهر فبراير (شباط) اقوى مما هو متوقع. وارتفع المؤشر 45,5 في المائة في فبراير مقابل 44 في المائة في يناير (كانون الثاني) بينما كان الاقتصاديون يتوقعون صعوده 42,8 في المائة.

وفي طوكيو اغلق مؤشر نيكاي منخفضا اكثر من واحد في المائة، وعزا المتعاملون ذلك الى استمرار اتجاه الشركات المحلية الى اغلاق دفاتر الاسهم المتبادلة قبل انقضاء السنة المالية في 31 مارس (اذار).

ومع ضعف الدولار امام الين وهبوط اسهم قطاع التكنولوجيا في الولايات المتحدة يوم الجمعة تراجعت شركات التصدير اليابانية عن التعامل مما ساعد على هبوط المؤشر.

وانتعشت هونغ كونغ عند الاغلاق وزاد مؤشرها 161 نقطة ليتجاوز حاجز عشرة آلاف نقطة لأول مرة منذ 21 يناير. غير ان معظم البورصات الآسيوية هبطت اليوم لتضعف الآمال بالنسبة لاداء بورصات اوروبا.

وفي فرانكفورت سجل مؤشر داكس الالماني ارتفاعا قويا عند الفتح لكنه ما لبث ان سلك اتجاها معاكسا حتى بلغت نسبة هبوطه 1,3 في المائة. وفتح مؤشر فاينانشيال تايمز على ارتفاع طفيف ثم بدأ التراجع مسجلا هبوطا بلغت نسبته 1,17 في المائة.

وقال المتعاملون ان حجم التداول كان منخفضا وسط حذر قبل اجتماع لجنة السياسة النقدية في بنك انجلترا المركزي المقرر اليوم وجلسة تحديد اسعار الفائدة للبنك المركزي الاوروبي يوم الخميس.

ويتعرض البنك لضغوط من المانيا وبصفة خاصة وزير المالية اوسكار لافونتين لخفض اسعار الفائدة بهدف دعم الاقتصاد. غير ان بعض الاقتصاديين يتوقعون عدم تغيير اسعار الفائدة وان تظل عند ثلاثة في المائة عقب الاجتماع ولو لتجنب اعطاء انطباع بان البنك عرضة للتدخل السياسي. ومنيت ايضا بورصة باريس بهبوط وان كان اقل حجما.

ARTICLE 87

calm *n.*	هدوء
to struggle	كافح
gains	مكتسبات
rising	نهوض
to be affected by	مني ب
to struggle	صارع
end	اعقاب *pl.* عقب
to hover	حام
ledger book	دفاتر *pl.* دفتر
closing	اغلاق
traded	متبادل
expiry	انقضاء
hurdle	حواجز *pl.* حاجز
soon	ما لبث ان
to travel	سلك
counter-	معاكس
caution	حذر
object of	عرضة ل
interference	تدخل

Calm in the European markets and the dollar struggles to maintain its gains against the euro

London - *Asharq al-Awsat and news agencies*: The European markets struggled to rise in trading yesterday, however they were unable to make significant gains, with some suffering a fall of more than 1%. The dollar still struggled to maintain its levels against the yen and the euro after its fall before the close of trading last week.

The euro fell to 1.10 dollars while the US currency hovered around 119 yen, exceeding its lowest levels for a week which it had reached at the end of last week. Nevertheless the dollar is expected to continue to fall after the deputy governor of the Central Bank of Japan, Yutaka Yamaguchi, was reported as saying that the Japanese economy did not need to raise credit controls any more at the present time.

Sterling rose strongly against the dollar and the euro after reports of the Purchasing Managers' Index in Britain in February had risen more than expected. The index rose 45.5% in February compared with 44% in January, while economists had been expecting a rise of 42.8%.

In Tokyo the Nikkei index closed down more than one per cent. Traders attributed this to the continuing trend of local companies to close books of shares traded before the end of the financial year on 31st March.

With the weakness of the dollar against the yen and the fall in technology shares in the US on Friday, Japanese export companies retreated. This helped the market to fall.

Hong Kong recovered at the close and its index rose 161 points to break the 10,000 point barrier for the first time since 21st January. Nevertheless, most Asian markets fell today to weaken the hopes about the performance on the European markets.

In Frankfurt the German Dax index opened strongly but soon fell back to drop by 1.3%. The Financial Times Index opened slightly up then began to fall back recording a drop of 1.17%

Dealers said that trading was thin due to caution ahead of the meeting of the Monetary Policy Committee of the Bank of England scheduled for today and the committee that fixes interest rates of the European Central Bank on Thursday.

The bank faces pressures from Germany, in particular the finance minister, Oskar Lafontaine, to reduce interest rates with the aim of supporting the economy. However, some economists expect no change in interest rates and that they will remain at three per cent after the meeting, even if only to avoid giving the impression that the bank was subject to political interference. The Paris Bourse suffered a fall albeit smaller.

هبوط قياسي جديد لليورو أمام الدولار المتألق وارتفاع طفيف لبورصات أوروبا

لندن: «الشرق الأوسط» ووكالات الأنباء

هبط اليورو الى مستوى منخفض قياسي امام الدولار امس وسط مزيد من الادلة على ضعف النمو الاقتصادي الاوروبي. وارتفعت أسواق الاسهم الاوروبية بدرجة طفيفة بعد الفتح وبدأ المستثمرون يتطلعون الى بيانات الوظائف الاميركية اليوم (الجمعة) وهو الامر الذي يمكن أن يشير الى الاتجاه التالي لجميع أنواع أسعار الفائدة الاميركية المهمة.

وانخفض اليورو الى أقل من 1,0850 دولار بعد اعلان بيانات أكدت حدوث انكماش في الربع الاخير من اجمالي الناتج المحلي الالماني. وبلغ اليورو 1,0866/1,0869 دولار بحلول الساعة 09,15 بتوقيت جرينتش من 1,0886/1,0892 دولار في اواخر المعاملات الاوروبية امس الاول. وهبط اليورو صباح امس الى 1,0848 دولار. وتراجع نحو عشرة في المائة أمام الدولار منذ المستوى القياسي المرتفع عند 1,906 دولار الذي وصل اليه في اول يوم للمعاملات الرسمية فيه في الرابع من يناير (كانون الثاني) الماضي.

وبدأ البنك المركزي الاوروبي اجتماعا لبحث سياساته الائتمانية في فرانكفورت في وقت سابق امس ويتوقع صدور اعلان في وقت لاحق. وتوقع محللون استطلعت رويترز آراءهم عدم حدوث تغير في أسعار الفائدة عن النسبة الحالية التي تبلغ ثلاثة في المائة. لكن السوق مازالت تفضل الدولار لان المؤشرات الاقتصادية الاميركية القوية في الآونة الاخيرة اثارت تكهنات بأن مجلس الاحتياطي الفدرالي (البنك المركزي الاميركي) ربما يرفع أسعار الفائدة عن النسبة الحالية التي تبلغ 4,75 في المائة في الاجتماع التالي لتحديد السياسات في نهاية مارس (آذار).

ووصل الدولار الى أعلى مستوى في ثلاثة أشهر أمام الين في المعاملات الصباحية في أوروبا ولا يرى المتعاملون أن هناك شيئا يوقف ارتفاعه.

ومع انخفاض أسعار الفائدة اليابانية الى نسبة لا تذكر وصعود الدولار نتيجة لقوة الاقتصاد الاميركي انخفض سعر العملة اليابانية الى 123,14 ين للدولار في اوروبا قبيل ظهر امس وهو ادنى مستوى منذ اول ديسمبر (كانون الاول). واستقر سعر صرف الجنيه الاسترليني أمام اليورو الاوروبي دون المستوى القياسي الجديد الذي سجله أمس الاول وتراجع أمام الدولار عن أعلى مستوياته منذ أسبوع. وارتفع الاسترليني أمام الين لاعلى مستوى منذ أكثر من أسبوع مع التراجع العام الذي شهدته العملة اليابانية.

وفي اسواق الاسهم ارتفع مؤشر فاينانشال تايمز المؤلف من أسهم 100 شركة بريطانية كبرى 30 نقطة بعد عشر دقائق من بدء التعامل دون أي مؤشر واضح من وول ستريت أو الاسواق الاسيوية.

وصعد مؤشر اكسترا داكس الالماني بعد ان هبط نحو ثلاثة في المائة أمس الاول حيث يتوقع متعاملون معاملات فاترة بعد الاغلاق الضعيف لبورصة وول ستريت. وحد من ارتفاع الاسهم زيادة عائد السندات في الولايات المتحدة والمانيا. وكانت الشكوك السياسية في ما يتعلق بالاصلاح الضريبي المحلي في ألمانيا موضع اهتمام.

وتتطلع الاسواق الى بيانات الوظائف الاميركية خارج القطاع الزراعي التي ستعلن اليوم بحثا عن مؤشرات على نمو تضخمي في الاقتصاد وهو الامر الذي يمكن ان يؤثر على السندات ويعطي سببا قويا لمجلس الاحتياطي الفدرالي الاميركي لرفع اسعار الفائدة في الاجتماع القادم يوم 30 مارس.

ARTICLE 88

brilliant	متألق
sign	دلائل *pl.* دليل
degree	درجة
time	توقيت
issuance	صعود
to consult	استطلع
shortly before	قبيل
dull	فاتر

New record fall of the euro against the shining dollar and slight rise on the European markets

London - *Asharq al-Awsat and news agencies*: The euro fell to a record low level against the dollar yesterday on further signs of weakness in European economic growth. European share markets rose slightly after opening and investors began to study figures for US jobs today, Friday. This may indicate the direction of all the important US interest rates.

The euro fell to below 1.0850 dollars after the announcement of figures that confirmed that German GDP had contracted in the last quarter. The euro reached 1.0866/1.0869 dollars at 9.15 GMT down from 1.0886/1.0892 dollars in late European trading the day before yesterday. It has dropped 10% against the dollar since the record high of 1.906 dollars it reached on the first day of official trading on 4th January.

The European Central Bank began a meeting to discuss its credit policy in Frankfurt early yesterday and an announcement is expected later. Analysts who were asked by Reuters expected no change in interest rates from their present rate of 3%. But the market still prefers the dollar because the recent strong US economic indicators have fuelled speculation that the committee of the Federal Reserve, the US central bank, may raise interest rates from their present rate of 4.75% in the following meeting to fix policies at the end of March.

The dollar reached a three month high against the yen in morning trading in Europe and dealers do not see that there is anything to stop its rise.

With the fall of Japanese interest rates to an insignificant rate and the rise in the dollar as a result of US economic strength, the Japanese currency dropped to 123.14 yen to the dollar in Europe before noon yesterday, the lowest level since 1st December. Sterling stabilised against the euro below the new record level that it had recorded the day before yesterday and fell back against the dollar from its highest levels for a week. Sterling rose against the yen to its highest level for more than a week with the general retreat of the Japanese economy. On the share markets, the FT 100 index rose 30 points ten minutes after the start of trading without any clear indicator from Wall Street or the Asian markets.

The German Xetra Dax index rose after it had fallen around 3% the day before yesterday with dealers expecting dull trading after the weak close on Wall Street. An increase in returns on bonds in the US and Germany restricted the rise in shares. The political doubts concerning local tax reform in Germany was the subject of concern.

The markets are looking to the figures on US jobs outside the agricultural sector which will be announced today in the search for indicators of inflationary growth in the economy. This may affect bonds and give a strong reason to the committee of the US Federal Reserve to raise interest rates in the next meeting on 30th March.

بورصة «وول ستريت» تخطط للعمل 19 ساعة يوميا اعتبارا من عام 2000

ضمن السعي لمنافسة بورصتي لندن وفرانكفورت

لندن: «الشرق الأوسط»

تعتزم بورصة «وول ستريت» في نيويورك تمديد العمل بساعات الدوام الى 19 ساعة يوميا وذلك في اطار المنافسة مع البورصات الاوروبية. ووفقا لما ذكرته «يو.اس.توداي» فان المدير التنفيذي للبورصة ريتشارد چراسو مصمم على إحداث التغيير الذي يوصف بانه «دراماتيكي» لتمديد العمل في اكبر بورصات العالم.

والهدف المعلن تحفيز الطلب من قبل الشركات غير الاميركية لادراج نفسها في اطار المنافسة مع البورصات الاخرى التي نجحت خلال الاعوام القليلة الماضية باجتذاب استثمارات اجنبية اكثر من البورصة الاميركية التي اطلقت فكرة اجتذاب الاستثمارات الاجنبية.

ويواجه القرار معارضة شديدة من قبل المتعاملين بالبورصة حيث يعني تنفيذ القرار امتداد العمل من الساعة الخامسة صباحا ولغاية منتصف الليل اعتبارا من عام 2000. وتأتي خطوة چراسو في ظل الحديث عن قرب تنفيذ توحيد عمليات بورصتي لندن وفرانكفورت المتوقع مطلع عام 2000 ايضا.

ويدور الحديث عن كيفية تأسيس شروط الملكية بين اكبر بورصتين في اوروبا، الامر الذي يمهد لايجاد ما يمكن تسميته ببورصة اوروبا المقبلة التي يتوقع ان تنافس على اجتذاب الاستثمارات العالمية.

ومع ابقاء البورصة الاميركية عاملة لمدة 19 ساعة فان البورصة الاميركية تامل في اجتذاب بعض الصفقات التي تنفذ الكترونيا اثناء اغلاق البورصة الاميركية وبخاصة تلك التي تنفذ عبر خدمة الشركة البريطانية «رويترز»، كذلك يؤمل ان تزداد تنافسية البورصة الاميركية وبخاصة في لندن التي نجحت خلال السنوات القليلة الماضية باجتذاب العديد من الشركات الكورية الجنوبية مثل هيونداي، كذلك تم اجتذاب شركة غانا للتعدين وغيرها من الشركات.

يذكر ان ادراج الشركات في اميركا يخضع لشروط الرقابة الاميركية، اذ يتوجب على الشركات الوفاء بمتطلبات ومعايير المحاسبة الاميركية الصارمة، الا ان الشركات تقبل الوفاء بتلك الشروط مقابل الوصول الى اكبر اسواق رأس المال في العالم على غرار ادراج «سوني» و«كيبل اند وايرلس» البريطانية. الذي تم أخيرا حينما أدرجت كل من الشركتين أسهمها في البورصة الأميركية .

ARTICLE 89

prolonging	تمديد	manner	كيفية
working hours	ساعات الدوام	naming	تسمية
determined	مصمم	to be subject to	يخضع ل
creation	احداث	standards	معايير *pl.* معيار
inciting	تحفيز	accounting	محاسبة
register	ادراج	strict	صارم
opposition	معارضة	in the manner of	على غرار
as far as	لغاية		
beginning	مطلع		

Wall Street plans to open 19 hours a day from 2000 in an attempt to compete with the London and Frankfurt markets

London - *Asharq al-Awsat*: The New York stock market on Wall Street has decided to extend working hours to nineteen in order to compete with the European markets. According to US Today, Wall Street's executive president, Richard Grasso, is determined to carry out the change he described as dramatic to extend working hours in the largest stock market in the world.

The stated aim is to encourage demand from non-American companies to obtain a listing as part of the competition with other exchanges which have succeeded over the past few years in attracting more foreign investment than the US markets. This prompted the idea of luring foreign investments.

The decision is facing severe opposition from market dealers as it would mean extending hours of work from 5am up to midnight from 2000. Grasso's plan comes in the wake of the talk about how close the London and Frankfurt markets are to amalgamating their operations also expected by the beginning of 2000.

Discussion is focusing on how to establish conditions of ownership between the two largest markets in Europe, which will prepare the way for the creation of what may be called the future European market which is expected to compete in attracting worldwide investment.

With Wall Street remaining open for nineteen hours it hopes to attract some orders which are executed electronically while the US market is closed, in particular by the British firm, Reuters. It is also hoped that the US market will become more competitive especially in London, which has succeeded over the past years in attracting a number of South Korean companies like Hyundai, as well as a Ghanaian mining company and other firms.

It is to be noted that the listing of companies in the US will be subject to the US regulations for supervision, namely that it is up to the companies themselves to meet the strict requirements and standards of American accountancy. However, companies agree to comply with these conditions to gain entry into the largest stock market in the world in the way that Sony and Cable and Wireless have recently done when both these companies had their shares listed on the US market.

عمدة لندن: استعداد لمساعدة اللبنانيين في تنفيذ برامج التخصيص

بيروت: «الشرق الأوسط»

أعلن عمدة مدينة لندن اللورد مايور بيتر ليفين أن «حي السيتي» اللندني مستعد لمساعدة اللبنانيين في الاعمال المصرفية والتأمين وتمويل المشاريع وبرامج التخصيص، مؤكداً أن أسواق لندن جاهزة لمساعدتهم للاستفادة من الفرصة الجديدة التي يوفرها دخول اليورو الى الأسواق المالية وتأثيره على النظام المالي في العالم.

وقال اللورد مايور في محاضرة ألقاها في بيروت أول من أمس بدعوة من غرفة التجارة والصناعة «ان الصادرات البريطانية الى لبنان زادت 40٪ خلال الاعوام الستة الاخيرة. لافتاً الى أن قطاع الخدمات المالية في «حي السيتي» يمكنه مساعدة اللبنانيين في الاعمال المصرفية والتأمين وتمويل المشاريع وبرامج التخصيص منوهاً بشركات المرافق العامة البريطانية العاملة في الاتصالات والمياه والصرف الصحي التي خضع بعضها للتخصيص خلال الاعوام العشرة الاخيرة ولديها خبرة واسعة في ادارة مشاريع اعادة الإعمار والتحديث في العالم وخاصة في الشرق الاوسط».

واعتبر مايور الحديث عن التوقعات الاقتصادية العالمية، بأنه «موضوع دقيق في وقت يسعى اللبنانيون فيه الى إعادة بناء بلدهم على خلفية اجواء اقتصادية عالمية تضعف». واضاف «ان الاقتصاد الاميركي ما يزال محافظاً على قوته البالغة في اسعار الاسهم المالية. لكن الاشارات المستقبلية غير واضحة تماماً بالرغم من أن تعليقات آلان غرينسبان الاخيرة تشير الى اتجاه ايجابي نسبي. أما في منطقة العملة الأوروبية الجديدة (اليورو) فقد حدث هبوط في الثقة التجارية احدثته التأثيرات المتراكمة للازمات الاقتصادية في الاسواق الناشئة في أسواق الصادرات والمنافسة في الواردات، اضافة الى تقلب السياسات الاقتصادية. وهناك الكثير من التكهنات حول استجابة البنك المركزي الاوروبي الجديد اذا استمر تباطؤ التوقعات على الطلب».

وعن تأثيرات اليورو على الاقتصاد العالمي قال عمدة لندن «انه منذ انطلاقة اليورو في يناير (كانون الثاني) الماضي برز كعملة رئيسية في التجارة والاستثمار. وبالنظر لحجم العقود المالية المبرمة والتي كانت تتم بالمارك الالماني والفرنك الفرنسي وغيرها من العملات الاوروبية فإن اليورو سيستخدم في العمليات المالية اكثر من أي عملة اخرى باستثناء الدولار. ولا يعني ذلك ان وضع الدولار كعملة عالمية رئيسية هو وضع مهدد فهو لا يزال يمثل حوالي 60٪ من احتياطي العملات الاجنبية للبنوك المركزية و45٪ من الارصدة في المصارف الدولية. ولا تزال السلع تسعر به وليست لدى بورصة النفط الدولية أية خطط للتغيير باتجاه اليورو، بالرغم من ان عقود الكهرباء والغاز التي ستتم التجارة بها مستقبلاً قد تكون مسعرة باليورو».

ARTICLE 90

mayor	عمدة *pl.* عمد
readiness	استعداد
ready	جاهز
to turn to	لفت الى
alluding to	منوها ب (نوه)
healthy	صحى
air *n.*	جو
confirmed	مبرم
available funds	أرصدة *pl.* رصيد
to quote price	سعر

The Mayor of London: ready to help in implementing privatisation programmes

Beirut - *Asharq al-Awsat*: The mayor of London, Lord Mayor Peter Levene, said that the City of London was prepared to help the Lebanese in the banking and insurance business and in financing projects and privatisation programmes, saying that the London markets were ready to help them to take advantage of the new opportunity provided by the launch of the euro on to the financial markets and its influence on the world financial order.

In a lecture he delivered in Beirut the day before yesterday at the invitation of the chamber of commerce and industry, the Lord Mayor said British exports to Lebanon had grown 40% over the past six years. Turning to the financial services sector in the City he said it was able to help the Lebanese in the banking and insurance business and the financing of projects and privatisation programmes, alluding to British public utility companies working in communications, water and sewage - some of which were the subject of privatisation over the past ten years and have a wide expertise in the administration of reconstruction and renewal plans throughout the world and especially in the Middle East.

The mayor considered the talk about world economic expectations as "a sensitive topic at a time when the Lebanese are striving to rebuild their country against a background of a world economic climate that was weakening". He added: "The US economy is still maintaining its extensive strength on share prices. But the signs for the future are not completely clear despite the latest comments of Alan Greenspan pointing to a relatively positive direction. As for the region of the new European currency, the euro, there has been a fall in commercial confidence brought about by the accumulating influences of the economic crises in the emerging markets in export markets and the competition in imports, in addition to the vicissitudes of economic policies. There are numerous predictions about how the new central European bank will react if weakness in demand expectation continues."

Concerning the effects of the euro on the world economy the mayor of London said: "Since the launch of the euro last January, it has emerged as a major currency for trade and investment. Considering the size of the firm, financial contracts which were made with the German mark, the French franc and other European currencies, the euro will be used in financial transactions more widely than any other currency except for the dollar. This does not mean that the position of the dollar as a major world currency is threatened and it still represents around 60% of the reserves of foreign currencies of the central banks and 45% of the capital in the international markets. Commodities are still quoted in dollars and in the international oil market there are no plans to change to the euro, in spite of the fact that electricity and gas futures contracts may be quoted in euros."

Exercises Articles 85 - 90

Exercise 1 Choose the best answer

١ تحسين/تدعيم/تسوية/تسديد الارباح ستعطى للبنك المبررات على زيادة فى الاجور.
٢ بقيت العمالة/العمولة/المعاملة/العملة الامريكية قوية امام الين.
٣ المؤشر فتح على ارتفاع/اعتقاد/احتفاظ/احتياط لكنه سرعان ما اتجه للهبوط.
٤ ساعد افق/اطار/اداء/اجر مماثل من اكبر شركات فى ارتفاع المؤشر.
٥ تراجعت الاسهم الاوروبية نتيجة القلق بشان النظام/التباين/الانتشار/التباطوء الاقتصادى.
٦ حجم الدفاتر/السندات/التداول/الاجور كان منخفضا وسط حذر قبل اجتماع اللجنة.
٧ ادراج الشركات فى امريكا يخضع لشروط/لبنود/لاجور/لمرسوم الرقابة الامريكية.
٨ منذ احصائية/استعادة/امكانية/اقامة اليورو برز كعملة رئيسية فى التجارة والاستثمار.
٩ حدث ارتفاع/هبوط/اعتقاد/تكثيف فى الثقة التجارية احدثته التاثيرات المتراكمة للازمات الاقتصادية.
١٠ يتعرض البنك لضغوط من المانيا لتسديد/لخفض/لتجنب/لتنازل اسعار الفائدة بهدف دعم الاقتصاد.

Exercise 2 Match the following pairs

١	لا سيما	a	بعد الاتفاق
٢	فى اجتماع	b	اغلق منخفضا
٣	تسوية بشان	c	زيادة الاجور
٤	كان المؤشر قد	d	مستوى مرتفع جديد
٥	صعد الدولار الى	e	انعقد فى وقت لاحق

Exercise 3 Choose the best adjective

١ سعر الصرف لا يمكن ان يصبح بديلا للسياسة الهيكلية/الملحوظة/النقدية/النفطية.
٢ تتطلع الاسواق الى بيانات الوظائف الامريكية بحثا عن مؤشرات على نمو تجريبى/تضخمى/مئوى/تشغيلى فى الاقتصاد.
٣ يواجه القرار معارضة سلبية/فكرية/ثقافية/شديدة من قبل المتعاملين.
٤ على الشركات الوفاء بالمعايير الدورية/المتفائلة/المبكرة/الصارمة.
٥ هذه النتائج تعكس وضعا ماليا هيكاليا/قويا/منفردا/جويا.

Exercise 4 Choose the appropriate verb

١ هبط/اثر/تراجع/وصل الدولار الى اعلى مستوى فى شهرين.
٢ نكرت/نجحت/استعدت/حصلت بورصة لندن باجتذاب العديد من الشركات الكورية الجنوبية.

٣ ارتفعت/انخفضت/انتعشت/قفزت الاسهم الامريكية بسبب حدوث قفزة اخرى فى اسعار الفائدة.

٤ اهتمامات البنك تراجعت/تخلفت/تركزت/تحفظت على مهام تنظيم الخطط.

٥ يتوقع/يتخلف/يتطلع/يتوقف اتمام عملية الدمج على موافقة مساهمى البنكين.

Exercise 5 Match these two passages with articles 85-90

وفي وقت سابق من يوم امس اغلق المؤشر القياسي للاسهم اليابانية دون تغير يذكر في نهاية المعاملات في بورصة طوكيو للاوراق المالية. وقال السماسرة أن العوامل الايجابية المتمثلة في الين الضعيف واسعار الفائدة المنخفضة تبددت بسبب قيام شركات بتصفية مراكزها قبل نهاية السنة المالية في 31 مارس. وأغلق مؤشر نيكي المؤلف من 225 سهما ممتازا مرتفعا نسبيا 13,09 نقطة أو 0,09 في المائة الى 14183,45 نقطة.

يذكر ان خفض اسعار الفائدة في اوروبا يعتبر من المسائل الملحة التي تضغط على القائمين على البنوك المركزية وخاصة تلك التي ظلت خارج منطقة اليورو حيث يتسهدف الكثير منهم تقريب اسعار الفائدة من السعر السائد على اليورو.

Exercise 6 Match the following

١ المغرب والبرتغال يبحثان

٢ اليابان تؤكد أن أزمتها

٣ هدوء في تعاملات البورصات

٤ هبوط الأسهم في

٥ هدوء الطلب على

a السعودية والكويت وعمان

b الدولار

c تنفيذ مشاريع لإنعاش السياحة

d المالية توشك على الانتهاء

e الأوروبية وتراجع الدولار مقابل الين

اليابان في طريقها للتحول إلى أكبر مقترض في العالم

لندن: «الشرق الاوسط»

من المنتظر ان يتجاوز حجم سوق السندات الحكومية اليابانية سوق سندات الخزانة الاميركية لتصبح اكبر سوق سندات في العالم وذلك نتيجة لفورة الاقتراض التي تعتزم الحكومة اليابانية تطبيقها خلال العام الحالي.

وذكرت صحيفة «الفاينانشيال تايمز» البريطانية امس ان اليابان ستستحوذ على اكثر من 90 في المائة من الاصدارات الصافية للسندات الحكومية (وهي اصدارات الديون الجديدة ناقصا تسديدات السندات المستحقة) من بين اكبر 18 اقتصادا متقدما في عام 1999، وذلك طبقا لمؤسسة «جي بي مورچان» المصرفية الاستثمارية.

والنتيجة المتوقعة لذلك ستتمثل في اطلاق العنان لموجة بيع قوية في سوق السندات اليابانية خلال هذا العام وهبوط في عوائد السندات الحكومية الغربية التي تراوح الان حول اقل مستوياتها على الاطلاق.

ونقلت الصحيفة عن مات كينج، الاقتصادي في «جي بي مورچان» قوله «ان اليابان تسير في الاتجاه المعاكس لبقية العالم المتقدم. ويمكن لذلك ان يترك اثرا كبيرا على اسعار السندات في الاسواق المتقدمة». وتذكر الصحيفة ان خطط اليابان الاقتراضية تذكر بالارتفاع الكبير في مستويات ديون الحكومة الأميركية في الستينات والذي اعقب تصاعد الحرب الفيتنامية وادى الى نشوء تضخم منفلت. ولكن في حالة اليابان فان اقتراضات الحكومة تمثل محاولة يائسة لتجنب الركود الاقتصادي وذلك بعد اخفاق سلسلة من خطط التحفيز الاقتصادي في انعاش الاقتصاد.

وتعتزم اليابان اصدار ما قيمته 517 مليار دولار من سندات مقومة بالين خلال عام 1999، وهو ما يمثل زيادة صافية في ديون الحكومة اليابانية قيمتها 352 مليار دولار. ويخالف ذلك ما تشهده الولايات المتحدة حيث تعتزم خفض قيمة سندات الخزانة بنحو 112 مليار دولار في عام 1999 وذلك بفضل الفائض في ميزانيتها للعام الثاني على التوالي.

وحسب معدلات الصرف الحالية فان قيمة السندات الحكومية اليابانية غير المستحقة يتوقع ان ترتفع الى نحو 2500 مليار دولار هذا العام، في حين ستنخفض قيمة سندات الخزانة الاميركية الى اقل من 2200 مليار دولار. ومن المتوقع لعائدات سندات الحكومة اليابانية، التي ارتفعت من ادنى مستوى تاريخي لها يبلغ 0,7 في المائة في العام الماضي الى نحو 2,8 في المائة في الاسابيع الماضية، ان ترتفع اكثر.

والفرق الاساسي خلال العام الحالي يتمثل في أنه من غير المحتمل للحكومة اليابانية ان تشتري كمية كبيرة من ديونها. وسبب ذلك هو ان مكتب صندوق الائتمان الياباني سيبيع على الارجح حصة كبيرة من حيازاته من السندات على مدى العامين المقبلين وذلك بهدف تلبية الطلب غير العادي على الايداعات.

غير ان سالي ويلكينسون، من بنك «دايوا» تقول ان اليابان ستحافظ على معدل مرتفع للادخار من قبل القطاع الخاص. وهذه الحالة مشابهة لما يحصل في الولايات المتحدة.

ARTICLE 91

borrower	مقترض
treasury	خزانة
outburst	فورة
application	تطبيق
less	ناقص
giving free rein	اطلق العنان
free	منفلت
desperate	يائس
failure	اخفاق
difference	فرق *pl.* فروق
holding	حيازة
deposit	ايداع
saving	ادخار

Japan set to become the world's largest borrower

London - *Asharq al-Awsat*: The Japanese government bond market is set to overtake the US treasury market to become the largest in the world as a result of the Japanese government's planned borrowing spree this year.

The Financial Times said yesterday that Japan would account for more than 90% of the net government bond issuance (new debt minus redemption of maturing bonds) among the leading 18 developed economies in 1999, according to JP Morgan, the investment bank.

The likely result of this will be to trigger a strong wave of selling in the Japanese bond market this year and a fall in western bond yields, which are already at historic lows.

The newspaper quoted Matt King, economist at JP Morgan as saying: "Japan is going in the opposite direction to the rest of the developed world. This could have a far-reaching impact on bond prices among the leading markets." The newspaper said that the borrowing plans of Japan recalled the big rise in US government debt levels in the sixties which followed the escalation of the Vietnam war and led to runaway inflation. But in the case of Japan, government borrowing represents a desperate attempt to ward off depression after the failure of a succession of measures to revive the economy.

Japan plans to issue the equivalent of $517bn in yen in 1999, representing a net increase of $352bn in the government's debt. This contrasts with what has happened in the United States where it has been decided to reduce the amount of treasury bonds by $112bn in 1999 because of a second consecutive budget surplus.

At current exchange rates, the value of Japan's outstanding government bonds is expected to rise to almost $2,500bn this year, while US treasury bonds will fall to below $2,200bn. The yield on Japanese government bonds, which has risen from a historic low of 0.7% last year to around 2.8% in the past weeks, could rise further.

The key difference this year is that the Japanese government is unlikely to buy large amounts of its own debts because Japan's Trust Fund bureau is likely to sell a large proportion of its existing holdings over the next two years to meet an unusually high level of redemptions of its deposit accounts.

But Sally Wilkinson at Daiwa says that Japan will maintain a high private sector savings rate. This situation is similar to what is happening in the United States.

إنشاء صندوق استثمار برأسمال 3.8 مليار دولار

مسجل في البهاما ويستهدف تمويل المشاريع في الدول العربية والنامية

لندن: موسى مهدي

ابلغت مصادر مالية موثوقة «الشرق الأوسط» امس ان مجموعة مستثمرين من السعودية والخليج وماليزيا اسست صندوقا للاستثمار في المشاريع العربية ومشاريع الدول النامية برأس مال قيمته 3,8 مليار دولار.

ووفقا للمصادر التي تحدثت لـ«الشرق الأوسط» فان الصندوق تم تسجيله في جزر البهاما لاسباب ضريبية.

وعادة ما تستخدم الشركات مناطق «افشور» لتسجيل صناديقها المالية وشركاتها القابضة لتفادي الضرائب الباهظة التي تفرضها الدول الصناعية. وعلمت «الشرق الأوسط» ان الصندوق سيطلق رسميا وسيبدأ العمل في ابريل (نيسان) المقبل وسيكون مقر ادارته في لندن.

وقالت المصادر ان الممول الماليزي حاج محمد افندي بن محمد يتقلد منصب امين الصندوق. والحاج محمد افندي، من كبار رجال الاعمال الماليزيين الذين يصنعون السوق في بورصة كوالالمبور.

ويرأس الصندوق سعيد اختر فيما يحتل منصب نائب الرئيس المهندس احمد الرياطي.

وقال اختر في تعليقه لـ«الشرق الأوسط» حول خطط الصندوق أن مجموعة المستثمرين درست اوضاع الدول النامية ووجدت ان هنالك فجوة كبيرة في التمويل وان هنالك العديد من المشاريع المربحة التي ينقصها التمويل.

وطبقاً لوثائق انشاء الصندوق التي اطلعت عليها «الشرق الأوسط» فان الصندوق سيقوم بتمويل المشاريع الصغيرة التي تبدأ قيمتها من مائة الف دولار الى مشاريع كبيرة تتراوح قيمتها بين 50 مليونا الى مائة مليون دولار. من جانبه قال احمد الرياطي نائب رئيس الصندوق الذي سجل تحت مسمى «الصندوق العالمي للتنمية الاسلامية» ان الصندوق سيهتم بتمويل المشاريع في الدول العربية والاسلامية ذات الجدوى الاقتصادية المتميزة والعائد المجزي وبشروط اقراض مريحة وسهلة مع فترة سماح تمتد لعامين.

وتشير وثائق التأسيس الى انه في حال المشاريع الصغيرة فان الصندوق سيمنح التمويل بضمان المشروع نفسه، اي ان المشروع نفسه سيكون الرهن مقابل قرض التمويل. اما في حال المشاريع التي تتراوح قيمتها بين 50 مليونا الى مائة مليون دولار فان على صاحب المشروع ان يوفر 20٪ من كلفة المشروع في شكل ضمانان بنكية باسمه تكون مقبولة لدى الصندوق.

ويشترط الصندوق ان تكون دراسات الجدوى للمشاريع معترف بها من شركة تدقيق حسابات دولية.

وقال مؤسسو الصندوق ان القروض لانشاء المشاريع ستمنح لمدد تتراوح بين سبع الى 10 عشر سنوات مع فترة سماح في السداد تصل الى عامين. ويبدو ان هنالك مشاريع بنية اساسية في بعض الدول الخليجية تثير اهتمام الصندوق وان هنالك مشاورات اولية جرت حولها بين ادارة الصندوق والمسؤولين الا ان الرياطي رفض كشف تفاصيل حولها وقال ان الحديث حول هذه المشاريع سيأتي الحديث عنها حينما يبدأ عمل الصندوق وتنضج المفاوضات بشأنها.

ARTICLE 92

registered	مسجل
reliable	موثوق
heavy	باهظ
financier	ممول
to assume	تقلد
opening	فجوة *pl.* ات
profitable	مربح
document	وثيقة *pl.* وثائق
name	مسمى
benefit	جدوى
adequate	مجزى
owner	صاحب
acceptable	مقبول
to stipulate	اشترط
accuracy	تدقيق
to ripen	نضج

Establishment of investment fund with a capital of $3.8bn

Registered in the Bahamas to finance projects in Arab and developing countries

London - *Mousy Mahdi*: Reliable financial sources told the Sharq al-Awsat yesterday that a group of investors from Saudi Arabia, the Gulf and Malaysia had set up a fund to invest in projects in both Arab and developing countries with a capital of 3.8 billion dollars. According to the sources that spoke to the Sharq al-Awsat, the fund has been registered in the Bahamas for tax reasons.

Usually companies use the offshore areas to register their funds and their holding companies to avoid the heavy taxes that the industrialised nations impose. They told the Sharq al-Awsat that the fund would be launched officially and would begin work in April with its administrative headquarters in London.

The sources said the Malaysian financier, Hajj Mohammed Afnadi Bin Mohammed, would assume the post of trustee of the fund. Hajj Mohaamed Afnadi is one of the prominent Malaysian businessmen who are market makers on the Kuala Lumpur stock market.

Saeed Aktar heads the funds in which Engineer Ahmed al-Riati holds the post of deputy chairman. In his statement to the Sharq al-Awsat on the fund's plans, Aktar said that the group of investors had studied conditions in the developing countries and had found a large gap in financing and that there was a number of profitable projects for which financing was lacking.

According to the fund's memorandum of association disclosed to the Sharq al-Awsat, the fund will undertake to finance small projects starting from one hundred thousand dollars up to large projects of between fifty and a hundred million dollars. For his part, Ahmed al-Riati, deputy president of the fund which was registered under the name "International Fund for Islamic Development", said that it would be interested in financing projects in Arab and Islamic countries with outstanding economic benefit and adequate return, with satisfactory and easy conditions for lending with a grace period of two years.

The fund's memorandum of association indicates that in the case of small projects, the fund will permit financing with the guarantee of the project itself, that is the project itself will be the pledge against the loan for financing. In the case of projects between 50 and 100 million dollars, it is up to the owner of the project to provide 20% of the cost of the project in the form of two bank guarantees in his name that would be acceptable to the fund. The fund stipulates that there should be studies of the projects which must be approved by an international firm of auditors.

The fund's founders said that the loans to set up projects would be granted for periods ranging between 7 and 10 years with a grace period of up to two years. It appears that there are infrastructure projects in some Gulf countries that are interesting the fund and that initial consultations have been conducted on them between the fund's management and officials, but al-Riati declined to disclose details about them. He said that the discussions about these projects would come when the work of the fund began and discussions about them developed.

الدول المانحة تتعهد لمصر بمساعدات قيمتها 1.5 مليار دولار العام الحالي

باريس: من ميشال أبو نجم

تعهدت المجموعة الاستشارية للدول المانحة لمصر، بنهاية يومين من الاجتماعات التي عقدت في مقر البنك الدولي في باريس، برئاسة كمال درويش، نائب رئيس البنك، منح مصر مساعدات للعام الجاري بقيمة 1,5 مليار دولار. وتنقسم هذه المساعدات الى قسمين: الأول منحة ويشكل ثلثي المبلغ والثاني قرض بشروط ميسرة.

وبالاضافة الى ذلك، التزمت المجموعة تقديم قرض آخر بقيمة مليار دولار يخصص لمشاريع التنمية على المدى البعيد، غير انه ليس بالشروط التفضيلية عينها للقرض الأول.

وقد شارك في اجتماعات باريس ممثلون عن 16 دولة من بينها الولايات المتحدة الاميركية، اليابان، بريطانيا، فرنسا وسويسرا. بالاضافة الى ذلك حضر مندوبون عن المفوضية الاوروبية ومؤسسة التمويل الدولية وصناديق عربية منها صندوق التنمية السعودي وصندوق التنمية الكويتي والبنك الاسلامي للتنمية.

أما الوفد المصري فقد رأسه الدكتور عاطف عبيد، وزير القطاع العام وضم يوسف بطرس غالي وزير الاقتصاد، وظافر البشري وزير التخطيط، واسماعيل سلام وزير الصحة، اضافة الى السفير المصري في باريس علي ماهر السيد وآخرين.

ورغم اشادة كمال درويش بالاصلاحات التي حققتها مصر في الميدان الاقتصادي، الا انه لفت النظر الى التحديات الرئيسية التي لا تزال تواجهها في قطاعات التعليم والصحة والخدمات الاجتماعية المختلفة. والمعروف ان البنك الدولي قد منح مصر قروضا، منذ 25 عاما، تزيد على 4 مليارات دولار. وفي العامين الأخيرين، حصلت مصر من البنك على 130 مليون دولار (للعام 97) و240 مليون دولار (للعام 98). ويمول البنك الدولي حاليا، في مصر، مشاريع بقيمة اجمالية تصل الى 1,2 مليار دولار.

والواقع ان ما التزمت به الدول المانحة لمصر يقل بحوالي مليار دولار عما التزمت به العام الماضي. وتصر المجموعة المانحة على ان تعجل مصر من وتيرة اصلاحاتها في ميدانين اثنين: برامج التخصيص، بما في ذلك القطاع المصرفي، وخفض الرسوم الجمركية، بما يزيد من تحرير التجارة. فضلا عن ذلك، تدعو الدول المانحة الى ان تركز الحكومة المصرية برامجها على محاربة الفقر والاهتمام بالطبقات الشعبية الأقل قدرة على مسايرة الانفتاح الاقتصادي.

ومن جانبه، أكد الدكتور عاطف عبيد ان اجتماع باريس كان من أفضل الاجتماعات التي عقدت منذ عشر سنوات. وقال لـ«الشرق الأوسط» ان ما تم خلال الاجتماع الأخير «يعكس الثقة الكاملة للمستثمرين بقوة النظام السياسي في مصر وبنجاح برنامج الاصلاح الاقتصادي» معتبرا ان التحديات الرئيسية التي يواجهها الاقتصاد المصري هي أربعة: الانطلاق الى الاسواق العالمية، تطوير قطاع الخدمات المالية لتلبية احتياجات القطاع الانتاجي، توفير المهارات والكوادر ذات الاختصاص العالي ورعاية محدودي الدخل.

ARTICLE 93

part	اقسام *pl.* قسم
easy	ميسر
preferential	تفضيلي
commissariat	مفوضية
praise	اشادة
domain	ميادين *pl.* ميدان
speeding up	عجل
manner	وتائر *pl.* وتيرة
liberation	تحرير
combatting	محاربة
poverty	فقر
layer	ات *pl.* طبقة
adjustment	مساير
cadres *Fr.*	كوادر *pl.* كادر

Donor nations undertake to undertake to grant Egypt 1.5 billion dollars in aid in the current year

Paris - *Michel Abu Najm*: At the end of two days of meetings held in the headquarters of the World Bank in Paris and chaired by Kamal Drooish, vice president of the bank, the advisory group for the donor nations pledged to grant Egypt 1.5 billion dollars of aid for the present year. This aid will be split into two parts: the first grant consists of a third of the amount and the second a loan with easy terms.

In addition to that, the group undertook to make another loan of a billion dollars specifically for long term development projects, although not with the preferential terms of the first loan.

Representatives for 16 countries, which included the US, Japan, Britain, France and Switzerland, took part in the Paris meetings. Delegates for the European commissariat and the World Organisation for Financing and some Arab funds, among them the Saudi Development Fund, the Kuwaiti Development Fund and the Islamic Bank for Development also attended.

The Egyptian delegation was headed by Dr Atef Ebeid, minister for public enterprise, and included Youssef Boutros Ghali, economy minister, Dhafir al-Bashari, minister of planning, Ismail Sallam, minister of health, in addition to the Egyptian ambassador in Paris, Ali Mahir al-Saeed, and others.

While praising the improvements that Egypt has made in the field of the economy, Kamal Drooish focused on the major challenges that it still faced in the fields of education, health and various social services. It is known that the World Bank has granted Egypt loans, over 25 years, of more than 4 billion dollars. In the past two years, Egypt has obtained 130 million dollars (for 1997), 240 million dollars (for 1998). The World Bank is presently financing projects in Egypt totalling 1.2 billion dollars.

The fact is that the donor countries have pledged to Egypt about a billion dollars less than last year. The donor group is insisting that Egypt speed up the manner of its improvements in two fields: the privatisation programme, including the banking sector, and reducing customs rates to increase the freedom of trade. Beside that, the donor countries are calling on the Egyptian government to concentrate its programmes on combating poverty and concern for the lower classes that are least able to adjust to economic liberalisation.

For his part, Dr Atef Ebeid said that the Paris meeting was the best meeting that had been held for ten years. He told the Sharq al-Awsat that what had been achieved during the last meeting "reflects the complete confidence of investors in the strength of the political regime in Egypt and in the success of the programme of economic reconstruction." He considered that there were four major challenges that the Egyptian economy was facing: opening to the world markets, the development of the financial services sector to meet the needs of the manufacturing sector, the provision of skills and highly skilled cadres and a limited concern for return.

بنك إنجلترا يحذر من تباطؤ نمو الاقتصاد البريطاني هذا العام

لندن: «الشرق الأوسط»

حذر بنك انجلترا امس من ان اقتصاد المملكة المتحدة قد يخفق في تحقيق نمو يذكر خلال النصف الاول من العام الحالي، مشيرا في نفس الوقت الى ان التضخم سيبقى تحت السيطرة.

وتوقع تقرير التضخم الذي صدر امس تباطؤ نمو الاقتصاد البريطاني الى نحو يتراوح بين 0,5 و 1 في المائة خلال مجمل عام 1999، وهو معدل نمو ابطأ من المعدل الذي توقعه البنك في شهر نوفمبر (تشرين الثاني) الماضي. وعلى اساس فصلي يرى البنك ان النمو سيقترب من الصفر خلال النصف الاول من العام الحالي.

والجدير بالذكر ان عاملي ضعف النمو وضعف التضخم قد سمحا لتكاليف الاقتراض (معدلات الفائدة) بالهبوط حيث تم خفض اسعار الفائدة خمس مرات خلال خمسة اشهر الى مستواه الحالي البالغ 5,5 في المائة.

وفي حين يجاهد الاقتصاد البريطاني لتحقيق نمو في وجه ركود الطلب المحلي والخارجي، لا يزال صانعو السياسات الاقتصادية واثقين بقدرة المملكة المتحدة على تجنب الوقوع في احضان الركود. وقال ميرفين كينج، نائب محافظ بنك انجلترا، في مؤتمر صحافي امس «على ضوء تعريفنا للركود باعتباره انخفاضا خلال اربعة فصول متتالية فاننا ما زلنا نرى فرص (الركود) كنسبة واحد الى اربعة، اي بدون تغيير عن توقعاتنا الاخيرة».

من جهته قال امس متحدث رسمي كبير باسم الحكومة البريطانية انه لا توجد هناك خطط لخفض توقعات النمو الاقتصادي لعام 1999 والتي تتراوح بين 1 و 1,5 في المائة.

ومع تباطؤ النمو الاقتصادي، يعتقد بنك انجلترا ان التضخم سيبقى قريبا من المعدل الحكومي المستهدف عن 2,5 في المائة على مدى العامين المقبلين. ويرى بعض الاعضاء التسعة في لجنة السياسة النقدية ببنك انجلترا ان التضخم يمكن ان يكون اقل من مستواه الحالي خلال السنوات المقبلة. وفي حالة هبوط معدل التضخم عن المستوى المستهدف فان الاقتصاديين يتوقعون ان بريطانيا ستستمر في سياسة خفض اسعار الفائدة.

وكان معدل التضخم، باستثناء تكاليف القروض العقارية المتقلبة، قد استقر عند 2,6 في المائة في ديسمبر (كانون الاول) الماضي، الا انه من المتوقع له الهبوط خلال العام الحالي. ونقلت رويترز امس عن جيرمي هوكينز، الاقتصاد في بنك «اوف اميركا» قوله «هناك الكثير في تقرير (البنك) لهذا اليوم الذي يعزز الآمال بانخفاض سعر الفائدة الرئيسي الى 5 في المائة بحلول الصيف المقبل، والى 4,5 في المائة بحلول نهاية العام الحالي».

ويتفق عديد من المحللين مع هوكينز في هذا التوقع. اذ يقول جوناثين لوينز، الاقتصادي في مؤسسة «هونغ كونغ اند شنغهاي» المصرفية (HSBC) «التقرير يميل بشكل متواضع نحو الجانب المنخفض للتضخم وبالتالي لاسعار الفائدة».

ARTICLE 94

to fail in	اخفق في
seasonal	فصلي
confident	واثق
clutch, grip	احضان *pl.* حضن
definition	تعريف
successive	متتال
mortgage *adj.*	عقاري
variable	متقلب

The Bank of England warns of slowdown in UK economic growth this year

London - *Asharq al-Awsat*: The Bank of England yesterday warned that the UK economy might fail to achieve noticeable growth over the first half of the current year, at the same time pointing out that inflation would remain under control.

The report on inflation published yesterday expected a slowdown of UK economic growth to between 0.5% and 1% over 1999 as a whole. This is a slower growth rate than the bank had expected last November. On a quarterly basis, the bank thinks that growth will be close to zero for the first half of the current year.

It is worth noting that two factors, the weakness of growth and low inflation, have allowed the costs of borrowing (interest rates) to fall. They have fallen five times over five months to their present level of 5.5%.

At a time when the British economy is trying to achieve growth in the face of sluggish demand both at home and abroad, economists are still confident of the ability of the United Kingdom to avoid falling into the clutches of a recession. At a press conference yesterday, the deputy governor of the Bank of England, Mervyn King, said: "Given our definition of a recession as a fall over four consecutive quarters, we still think the chances of recession as one in four, unchanged from our last forecasts."

For his part, a senior official spokesman for the British government said that there were no plans to reduce the growth forecast for 1999 of between 1% and 1.5%.

With the slowdown in economic growth, the Bank of England believes that inflation will remain near the government's target of 2.5% over the next two years. Some of the seven members of the Bank of England's Monetary Policy Committee think that inflation may be lower than its present level over the coming years. In the case of a fall in inflation from the level targeted, economists expect that Britain will stick to a policy of lowering interest rates.

The inflation rate, not including cots of variable rate mortgages, stabilised at 2.6% last December, but it is expected to fall over the current year. Yesterday Reuters quoted Jeremy Hawkins, strategist at Bank of America: "There is much in the bank's report today to strengthen the hopes of a reduction in base rates to 5% by the summer, and to 4.5% by the end of the year."

Many analysts agree with Hawkins in this forecast. Jonathan Lewins, an economist at the Hong Kong and Shanghai Banking Corporation (HSBC), says: "The report leans slightly in favour of a reduction of inflation and consequently of interest rates."

ARTICLE 95

speeding up	اسراع
exhaustion	نضوب
to force	اضطر
to defend	دافع على
imploring	مناشد
conclusion	استنتاج
to the effect that	مفاد
existing	قائم
tangible	ملموس
adherence	تمسك
advice	نصيحة
postponement	تاجيل
change	تحول
respect	احترام
believer	مؤمن
discharge	ايفاء
living	معيشة
election	انتخاب
	pl. ات
criticism	انتقاد
	pl. ات
however	بيد ان

روسيا تطلب من صندوق النقد الإسراع في التوصل إلى اتفاق جديد

لندن: «الشرق الأوسط»

حذر وزير المالية الروسي، ميخائيل زادورنوف، امس الاول من ان روسيا قد تواجه نضوب احتياطياتها من العملات الاجنبية خلال الاسابيع القليلة المقبلة، مما قد يضطرها الى طبع مزيد من النقود الا اذا تمكنت من التوصل الى اتفاق جديد مع صندوق النقد الدولي. غير ان زادورنوف دافع عن اداء الحكومة الروسية منذ الانهيار المالي الذي شهدته البلاد في اغسطس (آب) الماضي، مناشدا مجموعة الدول الصناعية السبع الكبار تقديم دعم سياسي لمساعدة الصندوق.

وقال وزير المالية الروسي ان الاستنتاج الرئيسي من خبرة الاشهر القليلة الماضية مفاده «اننا حافظنا على الاوضاع الاقتصادية قائمة في حين خفضنا متأخرات الاجور غير المدفوعة». واضاف «ولكن من الواضح انه من دون هذا الاتفاق (مع صندوق النقد) فان مجمل سياسات الميزانية ستواجه اضرارا كبيرة وسنكون في وضع اقتصادي وسياسي مختلف جدا».

وذكر زادورنوف في حديث امام صحافيين ان الحكومة استطاعت تحقيق انجازات ملموسة من خلال التمسك بسياسة نقدية ومالية مشددة منذ اغسطس الماضي. وانخفضت ايرادات الضرائب الى 6,5 في مائة من الناتج المحلي الاجمالي في سبتمبر (ايلول) الماضي، الا انها تحسنت منذ ذلك الوقت.

وقد قبلت الحكومة الروسية نصيحة صندوق النقد الدولي بتأجيل اجراء تخفيضات في ضريبة القيمة المضافة بهدف تعزيز مصادر التمويل العام. وقال زادورنوف ان الحكومة تسعى الان الى تحقيق فائض اولي في الميزانية يزيد عن 2 في المائة من الناتج المحلي الاجمالي خلال العام الحالي، مقابل عجز اولي نسبته 1,5 في المائة في ميزانية عام 1998، الامر الذي يشير الى تحول كبير في السياسة المالية. وقد تم خفض معدل التضخم الشهري الذي بلغ 11,6 في المائة في ديسمبر (كانون الاول) الماضي الى 3,8 في المائة في فبراير (شباط) الماضي وذلك من خلال السيطرة على عملية طبع النقود. وقد اعربت روسيا عن استعدادها لاحترام التزامات الديون الاجنبية باقصى ما تستطيع وذلك من خلال تسديد 5 مليارات دولار خلال الفترة بين اكتوبر (تشرين الاول) الماضي ومارس (آذار) الحالي.

عجوز روسية تبيع بدلة تعود لحفيدتها املا بالحصول على دخل اضافي في هذه الأوقات الاقتصادية الصعبة التي يواجهها المواطنون الروس (أ.ب)

وقال زادورنوف، الذي يعد واحدا من قلة من المؤمنين باقتصاد السوق في الحكومة الروسية، ان روسيا ستسعى الى تلبية متطلبات الصندوق، لكنه قال انه من غير المجدي تقديم تعهدات لا يمكن الايفاء بها.

وتسى الحكومة الروسية الى دعم مستوى المعيشة للمواطنين وخصوصا خلال الفترة قبل موعد الانتخابات البرلمانية في ديسمبر (كانون الاول) المقبل. وخلال الايام الماضية استمر مسؤولو الصندوق بتوجيه الانتقادات الى سياسات الميزانية التي تتبعها الحكومة الروسية وخصوصا افتقارها الى برنامج اقتصادي طويل الاجل.

بيد ان اجوستو لوبيز ـ كارلوس، الاقتصادي المختص بشؤون اوروبا الشرقية لدى بنك «ليمان براذرز» الاستثماري الدولي، قال انه «متفائل بحذر» بشأن موافقة صندوق النقد الدولي على اتفاق مع روسيا قبل نهاية ابريل (نيسان) المقبل. وقال «على مستوى مجموعة السبع الكبار هناك استعداد للاستمرار في حوار مع روسيا ينطوي على استمرار الدعم المالي واعادة جدولة الديون من قبل نادي باريس».

Russia urges IMF to reach a new agreement soon

London - *Asharq al-Awsat*: Mikhail Zadornov, Russia's finance minister, warned the day before yesterday that Russia might face running out of its hard currency in the next few weeks and be forced to print more money unless it could come to a new deal with the IMF. Zadornov however defended the Russian government's performance since the financial crash which the country had experienced last August, and appealed to the Group of Seven industrialised nations to provide political backing for IMF support.

The Russian finance minister said that the main conclusion from the experience of the past few months was to the effect: "We have preserved the existing economic conditions while reducing wage arrears." he added: "But it is clear that without this agreement (with the IMF) the whole conception of our budget policies will face great harm and we will be in a very different economic and political situation."

Briefing journalists, Zadornov said that the government had been able to achieve tangible success through sticking to a tight fiscal and monetary policy since last August. Tax revenues had plummeted to 6.5% of gross domestic product in September, but had improved since then.

The Russian government had accepted the IMF's advice to delay further cuts in Value Added Tax to strengthen public finances. Zadornov said that the government was now striving to achieve a primary budget surplus of more than 2% of GDP this year, against a 1.5% primary budget deficit in the 1998 budget, representing a colossal switch in fiscal policy.

The monthly inflation rate, which reached 11.6% last December, had been cut to 3.8% in February, by controlling money printing. Russia had signalled its willingness to honour its foreign debt obligations as best it could by repaying $5bn between October and March.

One of the few liberal economists left in the government, Zadornov said that Russia would try to satisfy the fund's requirements, but he said that it would be futile to make promises it could not keep.

The Russian government is striving to raise the standard of living of the people, especially in the run-up to parliamentary elections in December. In recent days, IMF officials have continued to criticise Russia's budget policies and in particular, the lack of a long-term economic programme.

However the economist specialising in Eastern European affairs at the international investment bank, Lehman Brothers, Augusto Lopez-Carlos, said that he was "cautiously optimistic" the International Monetary Fund would agree on a deal before the end of April. He said: "At the G7 level there is a willingness to continue a discussion with Russia that involves continued financial support and a rescheduling of debts by the Paris club."

861 مليون دولار حصيلة برنامج التخصيص في تونس العام الماضي

تونس: «الشرق الأوسط»

ذكر تقرير اقتصادي تونسي ان عام 1999 سيشهد تزايد عمليات تخصيص المؤسسات ووسائل الانتاج الحكومية وذلك في اطار البرنامج الذي وضعته الحكومة التونسية منذ عدة سنوات والذي شهد خلال العام الماضي قفزة كبيرة شملت بيع 23 مؤسسة بقيمة مالية بلغت حوالي 492 مليون دولار.

وأشار التقرير الى ان عملية التخصيص في تونس منذ بداية البرنامج شملت 104 مؤسسات كانت حصيلتها الاجمالية حوالي 861 مليون دولار.

وأوضح التقرير ان الارتفاع في عوائد عملية التخصيص الذي شهده عام 1998 يعود اساسا الى بيع مصنعين للاسمنت بحوالي 409 ملايين دولار.

كما اوضح التقرير الاقتصادي ان عمليتي تخصيص مصنعي الاسمنت في منطقة النفيضة وجبل الوسط وفرت للحكومة التونسية ايرادات مهمة من العملة الصعبة مكنتها من تخفيض نسبة الدين الخارجي.

ويقول التقرير ان قطاع السياحة هو القطاع الذي شهد اكثر عمليات البيع حيث بلغ عدد المؤسسات التي تم بيعها 24 مؤسسة كانت حصيلتها المالية حوالي 158 مليون دولار تمثل 18,3 في المائة من الايرادات الاجمالية للتخصيص، فيما يأتي قطاع النقل في المرتبة الثانية حيث تم بيع 14 شركة نقل خاصة بالبضائع بحوالي 70 مليون دولار. وتوزعت بقية عمليات التخصيص على عدد آخر من القطاعات كقطاع الصناعات الميكانيكية والكيماوية حيث تم بيع 12 مؤسسة بايرادات مالية بلغت حوالي 50 مليون دولار يليه قطاع الصناعات الغذائية والصيد البحري بايرادات مالية بلغت حوالي 47 مليون دولار بعد بيع 14 مؤسسة. ويلي ذلك قطاع التجارة بتخصيص 14 مؤسسة وقطاع مواد البناء بتخصيص 10 مؤسسات وكذلك قطاع النسيج الذي شهد تخصيص 5 مؤسسات.

وأشار التقرير الى ان قطاعي النقل والنسيج سيشهدان خلال العام الحالي عمليات تخصيص واسعة تشمل بيع شركة كبيرة للنقل الجوي.

ويفيد التقرير ان وتيرة عمليات التخصيص في تونس سوف تتسارع خلال الفترة القادمة وذلك طبقا لبرنامج أعدته وزارة التنمية الاقتصادية في تونس اظهر اهمية عمليات التخصيص وانعكاساتها الهامة على الاقتصاد.

ARTICLE 96

revenue	حصيلة *pl.* حصائل
gradual increase	تزايد
to be distributed	توزع
to come	ولى
textile	نسيج *pl.* نسج
to hasten	سارع
repercussion	انعكاس

Receipts of 861 million dollars from the privatisation programme in Tunisia last year

Tunis - Asharq al-Awsat: A Tunisian economic report said that 1999 would see an increase in the process of privatising organisations and state means of production as part of a programme that the Tunisian government had set up a number of years ago and which last year witnessed a large jump that included the sale of 23 organisations with a value of 492 million dollars.

The report pointed out that the privatisation process in Tunisia since the beginning of the programme had included 104 organisations with total receipts of around 861 million dollars.

The report showed that the rise in receipts of the privatisation operation in 1998 stemmed basically from the sale of two cement factories for around 409 million dollars.

The economic report also showed that the two operations of privatising the cement factories in the region of al-Nadiqqa and Jabal al-Wasat provided the Tunisian government with important revenues of hard currency which allowed it to reduce the proportion of foreign debt.

The report says that the travel sector was the area which saw the most sell-offs, where 24 organisations were sold with revenues of around 158 million dollars, representing 18.3% of the total receipts from privatisation. In second place comes the transport sector where 14 goods transport companies were sold for around 70 million dollars. The remainder of the privatisations were spread out among other sectors like the mechanical and chemical industries where 12 organisations were sold, with receipts of around 50 million dollars. This is followed by the sector of food industries and sea fishing with receipts of around 47 million dollars after selling 14 organisations, the building products sector with the privatisation of 10 organisations and the textiles sector which saw the privatisation of 5 organisations.

The report pointed out that the transport and textiles sectors would see over the current year privatisation operations that include the sell-off of a large air transport company.

The report says that the manner of the privatisation process in Tunisia will speed up over the coming period, in accordance with a programme prepared by the ministry of economic development in Tunis which highlighted the importance of the privatisation process and its significant repercussions on the economy.

Exercises Articles 91 - 96

Exercise 1 Choose the best answer

١ عائدات/مكتسبات/مستوردات/ظاهرات سندات الحكومة اليابانية ارتفعت اكثر.
٢ اقتراضات الحكومة تمثل محاولة يائسة لتجنب الانتعاش/الاستهلاك/الركود/النمو الاقتصادى.
٣ عادة ما تستخدم الشركات مناطق " افشور" لتفادى المعايير/الضرائب/الطوابق/التفاصيل الباهظة التى تفرضها الدول الصناعية.
٤ هناك العديد من المشاريع المربحة التى ينقصها التسجيل/التاجيل/التقديم/التمويل.
٥ يشترط الصندوق ان تكون مكتسبات/تاشرات/مناسبات/دراسات الجدوى للمشاريع.
٦ تصر المجموعة المانحة على ان تعجل مصر من قدرة/وتيرة/وفاء/وقود اصلاحاتها.
٧ تركز الحكومة برامجها على مشاورة/منافسة/محاربة/مضاعفة الفقر.
٨ التضخم سيبقى تحت السلطة/السيارة/السيطرة/السيولة.
٩ فى حالة قفزة/هبوط/انتعاش/انماء معدل التضخم عن المستوى المتهدف بريطانيا ستستمر فى سياسة خفض اسعار الفائدة.
١٠ استطاعت الحكومة تحقيق انجازات ملموسة من خلال الاتنقل/الترقب/التحالف/التمسك بسياسة نقدية ومالية شديدة.
١١ تسعى الحكومة الروسية الى سهم/حجز/جهد/دعم مستوى المعيشة للمواطنين.
١٢ ارتفاع فى ارباح/نفقات/عوائد/احصائيات عملية التخصيص يعود اساسا الى بيع مصنعين.
١٣ اظهر البرنامج اهمية عمليات التخصيص وانتقاداها/وانعكاساتها/وانتخاباتها/واستنتاجاتها الهامة على الاقتصاد.
١٤ استمر مسؤولو الصندوق بتوجيه الانتخابات/الامكانيات/الالتزامات/الانتقادات الى سياسة الميزانية.
١٥ قبلت الحكومة نتيجة/مهارة/مرونة/نصيحة صندوق النقد الدولى بتاجيل اجراء التخفيضات.

Exercise 2 Match the following pairs

١	هبوط فى	a	فى الميزانية
٢	البيان تسير	b	السداد تصل الى عامين
٣	الممول يتقلد	c	عوائد
٤	بفضل الفائض	d	فى الاتجاه
٥	فترة سماح فى	e	منصب امين الصندوق

Exercise 3 Match the following pairs

١	الانطلاق	a	ذات الاختصاص العام
٢	تطوير قطاع	b	بالطبقات الشعبية
٣	توفير الكوادر	c	الى الاسواق العالمية
٤	اهتمام	d	بشروط ميسرة
٥	قرض	e	الخدمات

Exercise 4 Choose the best verb

١ تصدر/تعلق/تسعى الحكومة الى دعم مستوى المعيشة للمواطنين.

٢ ذكرت/قبلت/اعربت روسيا عن استعدادها لاحترام التزامات الديون الاجنبية.

٣ باشر/دافع/جاهد الوزير عن اداء حكومته.

٤ يرى/يحقق/يخفض البنك ان النمو سيقترب من الصفر.

٥ حذر المحلل من ان الاقتصاد قد ينجز/يخفق/يقفز في تحقيق نمو يذكر.

Exercise 5 Match these passages with articles 91-96

أما الدكتور يوسف بطرس غالي، فقد أكد لـ«الشرق الأوسط» ان «المساعدات الخارجية وان كانت مفيدة ومطلوبة، الا انها لم تعد تلعب الدور الذي كانت تلعبه في الماضي حيث كانت هناك ندرة من العملات الاجنبية اضافة الى ندرة من الموارد غير التضخمية».

وردا على سؤال لـ«الشرق الأوسط» حول تدني نسبة الادخار في مصر، الأمر الذي يعني عجزا في توفير الأموال اللازمة للحاجات الاستثمارية، اعتبر غالي ان هذا الواقع مقلق على المدى الطويل الأجل. وفي رأيه ان الوصول الى نسب نمو اقتصادي تتراوح ما بين 7 و8 في المائة يتطلب ان يشكل الادخار الوطني ما نسبته 25 الى 28 في المائة من الناتج المحلي. والحال، ان هذه النسبة هي في الوقت الحاضر، بحدود 19 في المائة.

وبناء على ذلك من المتوقع لمعدل التضخم واسعار الفائدة ان تنخفض الى ادنى مستويات لها منذ الخمسينات والستينات من هذا القرن.

والمعروف ان بنك انجلترا اقدم في الاونة الاخيرة على خفض اسعار الفائدة بهدف تأمين عودة النمو الى الارتفاع بعد تعثره خلال العام الحالي، وكذلك لتأمين عدم هبوط التضخم كثيرا عن مستواه المستهدف عند 2,5 في المائة.

ولكن على الرغم من هبوط تكاليف الاقتراض في بريطانيا خلال الاشهر الاخيرة، الا ان معدلات الفائدة البريطانية بقيت فوق مستوى 3 في المائة وهو معدل الفائدة في بلدان منطقة اليورو، الامر الذي يلحق اضرارا بالقدرات التنافسية البريطانية.

ويتوقع بنك انجلترا، الذي اصبح مستقلا عن سيطرة الحكومة في مايو (ايار) 1997، ان يعاود النمو الاقتصادي الارتفاع خلال العام المقبل ليعود الى معدل يتراوح بين 2,0 و 2,5 في المائة.

Exercise 6 Put these words in the correct order

١ يوم التحول لليورو لا حاجة للبنوك بنك فرنسي:

٢ سياسة العالمية لتطبيق تحرير الصين تواجه

أسواقها ضغوطا التجارة من منظمة

KEY TO EXERCISES

Articles	a,b etc. refers to the position of the word in the exercise
1-6	Ex. 1: 1b 2c 3c 4d 5c 6b 7a 8b 9d 10d 11b 12c 13d 14c 15d Ex. 2: 1b 2e 3a 4c 5d Ex. 3: 1d 2a 3b 4e 5c Ex. 4: 1f 2c 3a 4b 5e 6d Ex. 5: c a e b d Ex. 6: c i k f d e b g j h a
7-12	Ex. 1: 1c 2c 3d 4b 5c 6a 7b 8a 9a 10b 11c 12b Ex. 2: 1d 2a 3b 4e 5c Ex. 3: 1c 2e 3a 4b 5d Ex. 4: 1e 2c 3a 4f 5d 6b
13-18	Ex. 1: 1a 2d 3a 4c 5b 6c 7b 8a 9d 10c Ex. 2: 1e 2a 3f 4b 5d 6c Ex. 4: 1c 2b 3d 4f 5e 6a Ex. 5: 1c 2a 3b
19-24	Ex. 1: 1c 2c 3b 4c 5a 6d 7a 8a 9c 10b Ex. 2: 1d 2c 3a 4e 5b Ex. 3: 1b 2a 3a 4a 5c Ex. 4: 1d 2c 3a 4e 5b Ex. 5: 1c 2a 3e 4b 5d
25-30	Ex. 1: 1a 2d 3b 4a 5b 6d 7a 8d 9a 10b 11c 12a 13c 14b Ex. 2: 1d 2a 3e 4b 5c Ex 3: 1d 2a 3c 4e 5b Ex. 4: 1a 2b 3a 4b 5c 6c Ex. 5: 1g 2h 3f 4e 5c 6d 7b 8a Ex. 6: 1b 2d 3c 4a
31-36	Ex. 1: 1b 2d 3b 4a 5a 6a 7a 8a 9b 10d Ex. 2: 1d 2a 3e 4b 5c Ex. 3: 1a 2b 3b 4b 5a Ex. 4: 1f 2d 3c 4e 5b 6a Ex. 5: 1d 2a 3f 4c 5b 6e
37-42	Ex. 1: 1c 2b 3c 4d 5a 6d 7d 8b 9b 10d Ex. 2: 1c 2e 3a 4b 5d Ex. 3: 1b 2d 3d 4b 5a Ex. 4: 1b 2a 3d 4e 5c
43-48	Ex. 1: 1c 2c 3b 4b 5a 6a 7d 8c 9d 10c 11b 12b Ex. 2: 1e 2a 3d 4c 5b Ex. 3: 1e 2a 3d 4b 5c Ex. 4: 1b 2b 3b 4c 5c Ex. 5: 1 c e d b g f a 2 d c e b a 3 d a c b 4 c a f b g h e d i 5 d e c f b g a
49-54	Ex. 1: 1d 2d 3d 4c 5a 6c 7d 8c 9d 10d Ex. 2: 1d 2a 3e 4c 5f 6b Ex. 3: 1c 2b 3b 4c 5c 6a 7c 8a Ex. 4: 1 c a e f d b h g 2 g f b d a e c 3 d f b c e a Ex. 5: 1b 2e 3c 4a 5d
55-60	Ex. 1: 1b 2b 3c 4a 5b 6b 7b 8a 9b 10d Ex. 2: 1e 2a 3d 4c 5b Ex. 3: c e d k f h g a j i Ex. 4: 1 b d a c e 2 d f e c a b 3 b e d c f a Ex. 5: 1 59 2 60 3 57
61-66	Ex. 1: 1b 2b 3a 4d 5b 6c 7a 8d 9b 10b Ex. 2: 1b 2e 3d 4a 5c Ex. 3: 1b 2a 3c 4d 5c Ex. 4: 1b 2e 3a 4c 5d Ex. 5: 1c 2d 3b 4a
67-72	Ex. 1: 1d 2a 3a 4d 5c 6c 7b 8c 9b 10a Ex. 2: 1d 2e 3a 4c 5b Ex. 3: 1c 2a 3e 4b 5d Ex. 4: g c b h d e f a Ex. 5: 1 69 2 68 3 72 4 67 5 70
73-78	Ex. 1: 1b 2d 3c 4d 5d 6b 7d 8a 9c 10a 11d 12d Ex. 2: 1e 2a 3b 4c 5d Ex. 3: 1c 2e 3a 4b 5d Ex. 4: 1c 2a 3c 4b 5d Ex. 5: 73 Ex. 6: 1c 2e 3a 4b 5d
79-84	Ex. 1: 1c 2a 3b 4d 5c 6d 7b 8a 9b 10a 11c 12d 13c 14b 15d 16c Ex. 2: 1d 2e 3a 4c 5b Ex. 3: 1e 2d 3a 4b 5c Ex. 4: 1d 2a 3e 4c 5b Ex. 5: 80 Ex. 6: 1d 2c 3a 4b
85-90	Ex. 1: 1a 2d 3a 4c 5d 6c 7a 8d 9b 10b Ex. 2: 1a 2e 3c 4b 5d Ex. 3: 1c 2b 3d 4d 5b Ex. 4: 1d 2d 3b 4c 5d Ex. 5: 1 88 2 87 Ex. 6: 1c 2d 3e 4a 5b
91-96	Ex. 1: 1a 2c 3b 4d 5d 6b 7c 8a 9b 10d 11d 12c 13b 14d 15d Ex. 2: 1c 2d 3e 4a 5b Ex. 3: 1c 2e 3a 4b 5d Ex. 4: 1c 2c 3b 4a 5b Ex. 5: 1 92 2 93 Ex. 6: 1 d b c a 2 d f h g b a c e

Word List

A more extensive listing of words found in the articles. Words are listed under their roots. The number indicates the first occurrence of the word.

ا

اتى

	to come	18

اثر

	II to affect	31
اثر	influence	43
تأثير	influence	59

اجر

	II to hire out	25
اجر	pay	85

اجل

من اجل	because of	6
اجل	time	51
تأجيل	postponement	95
الآجلة	life to come	31

اخذ

	VIII to take	49

اخر

	V to be late	13
آخر	end	1
آخر	another	3
تأخير	delay	1

ادى

	II to cause	92
اداء	performance	2

ارخ

تاريخ	history	73

ازم

ازمة	crisis	11

اسّ

	II to found	47
اساس	basis	74
اساسي	basic	6
تأسيس	founding	89
تأسيسي	fundamental	36
مؤسسة	institution	10

اسر

اسرة	family	47

اسف

	to feel sorry	51
آسف	regret	51

اسمنت

	cement	4

اشر

تأشيرة	visa	77
مؤشرة	indicator	28

اصل

اصل	root	32
في الاصل	originally	22

اطر

اطار	frame	6

افق

	horizon	43

اقلم

اقليمي	regional	2

اكد

	II to assure	58
تأكيد	assurance	47

الف

ائتلاف	coalition	15
مؤلف	consisting	44

الكترونى

	electronic	9

الماس

	diamond	16

امر

امر	matter	7
مؤتمر	conference	35

امل

امل	hope	74

امن

امانة	reliability	72
تأمين	insurance	56
ائتمان	trust	83
مؤمن	believing	95

انس

ناس	people	47

انف

استئناف	resumption	74

اهل

اهلي	national	6
مؤهل	deserving	46

اول

اولية	priority	55

ان

اوان	time	51

ايد

	II to support	44
تأييد	support	44

ب

بئر

	well *n.*	41

بترول

	petroleum	4

بثّ

	to spread	26

بحث

بحث	search	59
مباحثة	discussion	17

بحر

بحر	sea	13

بدأ

بدء	beginning	56
ابتداء	start	79

بدل

بديل	substitute	72
مبادلة	exchange	9
تبادل	exchange	10
متبادل	traded	87

بدا

	IV to disclose	82

برّ

مبرر	justification	85
بري	land *adj.*	5

برز

ابرز	more marked	62
بارز	prominent	79

برق

بريق	glitter	64

برلمان

	parliament	14

برم

	IV to conclude	4
ابرام	conclusion	12
مبرم	confirmed	90

برنامج

	program	6

بشر

	III to pursue	15
بشري	human	43
مباشر	direct	59

بضع

بضاعة	goods	59

بطؤ

	V to be slow	23
	VI to be slow	63
ابطأ	slower	94
تباطؤ	slowness	23

بطاقة

	card	80

بطل

بطالة	unemployment	26

بعث

بعثة	delegation	12

بعد

	X to set aside	73
بعيد	unlikely	52

بقى

	IV to retain	73
	V to be left	67
بقية	remainder	91
بقاء	remaining	25
ابقاء	maintenance	50
باقي	staying	17

بكر

باكورة	first results	56
ابتكار	initiative	79
مبكر	early	29

بلغ

بلوغ	attainment	80
مبلغ	amount	1
بالغ	extensive	30

بن

	son, inhabitant	70

بند

article, clause 82

بنى

بناء building 3
بنية structure 1
مبني building 56

بهظ

باهظ oppressive 92

بورصة

stock exchange 22

بات

to get to 75

باد

بيد ان although 95

بيض

egg 37

بيع

to sell 69
مبيع sale 16

بين

II to show 48
بيان report 9
تباين difference 85

ت

تبع

to follow 80
III to follow 72
متابعة following 2
تابع following 78
متبع observed 56

تجر

تجارة trade 8
تاجر trader 68

ترك

to leave 44

تعب

متاعب troubles 11

تلا

to follow 17
بالتالي subsequently 57
متتالي successive 94

تمّ

تماما completely 90
اتمام completion 59

تاح

متاح given 10

ث

ثبت

II to prove 79
ثبات firmness 20
تثبيت strengthening 51

ثقف

ثقافي cultural 71

ثقل

ثقل weight 18

ثمر

استثمار investment 2
مثمر fruitful 4
مستثمر investor 4

ثمن

ثمن price 35

ثنى

اثناء during 11
ثنائي twofold 9

ثور

ثورة revolution 16

ج

جدّ

مجدد renewed 44

جدر

يجدر بالذكر worth saying 49

جدول

جدول الاعمال agenda 7

جدا

جدوى advantage 92

جذب

جذب attraction 55
اجتذاب attraction 36

جرب

تجريبي	experimental	15

جرى

اجراء	performance	39
جار	current	4
من جراء	because of	76

جزأ

جزء	part	36
جزئي	partial	21
تجزئي	retail	24

جزر

جزيرة	island	20

جزف

	III to risk	79

جعل

	to make	84
جعل	pay	39

جلس

مجلس الادارة	board of directors	5

جلو

	V to be clear	4

جمرك

	customs	17

جمع

	VIII to meet	2
جمعية	meeting	29
جميع	total	63
مجمع	meeting	15
تجميع	assembly	75
اجماع	agreement	44
اجتماع	meeting	2
اجتماعي	social	5
جامعة	community	50
مجموع	gathered	70
مجموعة	collection	54
مجتمع	assembly	47

جمل

بالجملة	wholesale	25
تجميل	beautification	38
اجمالي	comprehensive	16
مجمل	total	58

جمهورية

	republic	1

جنب

جانب	side	7
تجنب	avoidance	81

جنس

جنسية	nationality	78

جنى

جني	harvest	82

جهد

	III to strive	51
جهد	endeavour	58

جهز

جهاز	appliance	12
تجهيزات	equipment	31
جاهز	ready	90

جو

	air	90
جوي	aerial	60
الجوية	air force	39

جوب

استجابة	answering	60

جود

جودة	goodness	15
جيد	good	58

جور

جار	neighbour	77

جاز

	VI to exceed	16

جول

مجال	range	1

جوهر

جوهري	inherent	81

ح

حتم

محتم	determined	81

حجر

حجر	reservation	78

حجز

حجز	prevention	38
حاجز	obstacle	87

حجم

احجام abstention 27

حدّ

حدة sharpness 59
حديد iron 15
تحديد limitation 19
حاد sharp 16
محدود limited 15
محدد sharpened 10

حدث

IV to produce 90
حديث new 18
حديث speech 20
حدوث occurrence 88
محادثة discussion 13
احداث production 89
استحداث production 55
متحدث spokesman 34

حدو

تحد challenge 43

حذر

II to warn 81
حذر caution 87

حذا

حذاء shoe 75

حرّ

حر free 3
حراري thermal 15
تحرير liberation 93

حرب

محاربة struggle 93

حرص

to strive 24

حرق

حريقة fire 15

حرك

حركة movement 5
تحرك motion 63
محرك incentive 77

حرم

احترام respect 95

حسب

VIII to consider 33
فحسب only 50
حسب according to 29
حسبما according to 7
حساب account 21
على الحساب to s.o.'s debit 45
محاسبة accounting 89
حاسب computer 79

حسر

VII to disappear 51

حسن

تحسين improvement 10
تحسن improvement 47

حصّ

حصة share 18

حصل

to achieve 5
حصول occurrence 44
حصيلة yield 96
تحصيل attainment 33
حاصلات produce 78
محصول yield 13

حصو

احصائية statistics 21

حضر

حضور presence 4
محضر presence 48
تحضيري preparatory 7
مستحضر preparation 38

حضن

حضن arms 94

حط

محطة station 35

حظى

to obtain 84

حفز

تحفيز encouragement 89

حفظ

III to observe 95
V to preserve 61
VIII to maintain 32
محفظة portfolio 72
محافظة province 1
تحفظ caution 61
احتفاظ retention 57
محافظ governor 49
متحفظ vigilant 82

حقّ

II to carry out 57
X to claim 6
حق right 30
حقا really 85
حقيقي real 47
تحقيق realisation 43
مستحقات money due 41

حكر

VIII to corner 79
احتكار monopoly 79

حكم

V to be in control 79
حكم judgement 45
حكومة government 4
محكمة court 79

حلّ

VIII to occupy 54
حل solution 45
حلول beginning 41
محل place 69
محلي local 56
تحليل analysis 25
محلل analyst 22

حلف

تحالف alliance 34

حلو

حلويات confectionery 37

حمس

حماس enthusiasm 33

حمل

to carry 56
حملة campaign 38
احتمال probability 77
محتمل bearable 34

حمى

حماية protection 4
محام lawyer 77

حوج

VIII to need 45
حاجة need 72
احتياجات necessities 55

حاذ

X to usurp 55

حار

محور axis 82

حوض

basin 13

حوط

احتياط precaution 82
احتياطيات reserve funds 41
محيط ocean 80

حول

حالة condition 48
حالي present 2
حاليا at present 50
حول around 4
حوالي approximately 1
محاولة attempt 42
تحول change 95

حوم

حام to hover 87

حوى

to gather 56

حى

حي district 55
حياة life 47

حان

حينما while 89

خ

خام

raw 11

خبر

خبرة experience 4
خبير experienced 50
اختبار test 15

ختم

VIII to conclude 66

خدم

to serve 61
خدمة service 3
استخدام operation 48
مستخدم used 16

خرج

خروج exit 76
اخراج removal 48

خزن

خارجي	foreign	13

خزن

خزانة	treasury	91
خزينة	treasury	46
تخزين	storing	12
مخزون	stock	58

خسر

خسارة	loss	9

خشى

	V to fear	81

خصّ

خصوصا	in particular	3
تخصيص	specialisation	36
خاص	special	1
خاصة	in particular	13
مخصصات	credits	33
مختص	relevant	95

خصب

مخصبات	fertilisers	14

خصم

خصم	opponent	79

خضع

	to be subject to	81

خطّ

خط	line	60
خطة	plan	34
تخطيط	planning	1

خطب

خطاب	speech	19

خطر

خطر	dangerous	81
خطير	important	43
مخاطر	dangers	51

خطو

خطوة	step	49

خفّ

	II to reduce	68

خفض

	VII to decrease	11
خفض	reduction	39
تخفيض	reduction	40
انخفاض	reduction	11
منخفض	low	48

خفق

	IV to fail	94
اخفاق	failure	91

خلّ

خلل	gap	81
من خلال	through	46

خلف

	III to conflict	91
	V to stay behind	54
خلف	after	47
خلاف	difference	18
خلافة	other	67
خلفية	background	90
مختلف	different	1

خلاء

	to be free of	75

خوض

خوض	treatment	71

خوف

مخاوف	apprehensions	48

خير

خير	excellent	74
خيار	choice	10
اختيار	choice	9

د

دخل

دخل	income	53
دخول	entering	77
تداخل	interference	87
مدخول	revenue	48

درب

تدريب	training	80

درج

درجة	degree	88
ادراج	registration	89

درس

	to study	34
دراسة	study	15

درك

	IV to realise	85
	X to correct	73

دعم

دعمة support 6
تدعيم support 84

دعو

دعوة invitation 69
دعوي allegation 79
متداع collapsing 36

دفتر

ledger 87

دفع

III to defend 95
دفع repelling 46
دفعة burst 46
دفاع protection 79
دافع incentive 24

دقّ

دقيق precise 68
تدقيق accuracy 92
مدقق exact 30

دلّ

to show 60
دليل sign 85

دلع

VII to flare up 81

دلو

IV to deliver 71

دمج

VII to be merged 72
دمج merger 82
اندماج merger 33

دنو

V to be debased 53
ادني lower 26
تدن sinking 53

دور

دور role 43
دورة turn 43
دوري periodic 63
علي المدار throughout 80
ادارة administration 5
دائرة office 17
مدير manager 5

دول

VI to alternate 86
دولة state 2
دولي international 1
تدول circulation 29

دوم

دوام permanent 89

دوى

دواء medicine 36

دين

دين debt 33

ذ

ذا

بذا thereby 61

ذخر

ادخار storing 91

ذرو

ذروة summit 53

ذكر

يذكر considerable 88
تذكرة card 39

ذهب

ذهب gold 17

ذيع

اذاعي broadcasting *adj.* 35

ر

رأس

رأس head 69
رأس مال capital 3
رأس اميل capital 23
رئيس president 2
رئاسة presidency 2

رأى

رؤية inspection 83

رب

رب master 51
ربما perhaps 29

ربح

ربح profit 30
مربح lucrative 92

ربط

VIII to be related 68

ربط tying 5
رابطة tie 10

ربع

ربع quarter 52
مربع fourfold 48

رتب

V to be arranged 83
مرتبة step 54
ترتيب arrangement 32
مرتب organised 81

رجأ

ارجاء postponement 79

رجح

على الارجح probably 73
مرجح predominant 63

رجع

VI to retreat 67
تراجع retreat 17

رجو

رجا side 47

رحل

رحلة journey 39
مرحلة phase 1

رخص

ترخيص permission 56

ردّ

X to demand 86

ردف

رديف reserve 56

رسم

رسم duty 78
رسمي official 36
مرسوم act, decree 46

رشح

ترشيح candidacy 78
مرشح candidate 44

رشد

II to guide 72

رصد

رصيد available funds 90

رصف

رصف paving 12

رعى

III to supervise 83
رعاية attention 93

رغب

IV to force 79

رفع

VIII to rise 11
رفع lifting 19
ارتفاع increase 11
مرتفع rising 63

رفق

III to accompany 77
مرفق utility 90
مرافق companion 71

رفه

ترفيه luxury 55

رقب

رقابة supervision 89
ترقب expectation 23

ركب

مركب compound 88

ركد

ركود stagnation 48
راكد sluggish 25

ركز

V to concentrate 3
مركز centre 55
تركيز establishment 74

ركم

متراكم accumulating 86

رمى

مرمي goal 79

روج

ترويج spreading 68

روح

VI to fluctuate 6
مريح comfortable 92

روع

راع to frighten 83

ز

زجاج

	glass	15

زرع

زراعة	agriculture	3

زعم

زعيم	leader	86

زلّ

زلال	white of egg	37

زمع

مزمع	resolved	61

زمن

زمني	temporal	15

زهر

ازدهار	bloom	22

زوج

ازدواج	coupling	79

زور

زيارة	visit	1
زائر	visitor	38

زول

ما زال	to be still	34
	III to pursue	80
مزاولة	pursuit	80

زوى

زاوية	angle	79

زيد

	VIII to grow	10
مزيد	excess	58
تزايد	increase	96
متزايد	increasing	84

سأل

مسألة	question	18
مسؤول	responsible	6

س

سبّ

	V to be cause of	81
سبب	reason	6

سبق

سابق	previous	7

سبل

سبيل	way	18

سجل

	II to register	11
تسجيل	registration	57
مسجل	registered	92

سحق

مسحوق	grated	37

سحل

ساحل	coast	27
ساحلي	coastal	5

سخو

سخاء	generosity	54

سدّ

سداد	payment	42
تسديد	payment	83

سرّ

سر	secret	79

سرع

	III to hasten	96
سرعان ما	presently	85
سريع	quick	5
اسراع	acceleration	95

سعد

	III to help	64
سعادة	happiness	70
مساعدة	support	3
مساعد	assistant	13

سعر

	II to set price	90
سعر	price	6

سعى

	to strive	31
سعي	effort	45
مسعى	effort	73

سفر

سفر	departure	39
سفير	ambassador	10
سفارة	embassy	12

سقف

سقف	roof	67

سكن

سكان population 54

سلب

سلبي negative 86
اسلوب method 36

سلسل

سلسلة chain 74

سلط

سلطة power 14

سلع

سلعة commodity 22

سلف

سلف free loan 82
سلفية free loan 84

سلك

سلك travel 87
سلوك behaviour 79

اسم

اسمي nominal 53

سمح

to grant 45
سماح permission 6

سمد

سماد fertiliser 31

سمسر

سمسار broker 28

سمى

تسمية naming 89
مسمي named 92

سند

سند bond 85
مساند supporting 56

سهل

II to facilitate 77
سهل smooth 92
بسهولة easily 81
تسهيل facilitation 5

سهم

III to participate 5
سهم share 29
مساهمة participation 3
مساهم shareholder 30

سود

سواد majority 67

سود

سائد prevailing 48

سوس

سياسي political 4

سوق

سوق market 23
تسويق marketing 38
متسوق trader 55

سوى

VI to be similar 35
ليس..سوي only 59
لا سيما especially 77
تسوية settlement 83
متساني balanced 65
مستوي level 11

سيح

سياحة tourism 77

سير

سير course 69
سيارة car 9
تسيير dispatch 78
مسايرة adjustment 93

سيطر

to reign 65
سيطرة authority 66

سيل

سيولة liquid state 31

ش

شأن

matter 2

شبك

شبكة network 68

شبه

مشابه similar 75

شجع

V to take heart 73
تشجيع encouragement 75

شحن

شحن loading 46

شخص

شخص	individual	48

شدّ

شديد	strong	76

شرس

شراسة	wickedness	79

شرط

	VIII to stipulate	92
شرط	condition	42

شرع

مشروع	plan	1

شرف

مشرف	supervisor	49

شرك

شركة	company	2
شريك	partner	77
مشاركة	partnership	13
مشترك	joint	7
شراكة	partnership	4

شرى

شراء	purchase	27
مشتريات	goods	37

شعب

شعب	people	50
شعبي	national	93

شعر

	to realise	45

شغل

شغل	work	1
اشتغلال	occupation	4

شفى

مستشفي	hospital	56

شقّ

مشتق	derivative	67

شك

مشكوك فيه	doubtful	33

شكل

	V to be formed	59
شكل	form	41
تشكيل	formation	80

شمل

شامل	comprehensive	79
شمالي	northern	5

شهد

	to witness	25

شهر

شهر	month	15
شهرة	reputation	38

شور

	IV to signal	4
مشاورة	consultation	78
اشارة	sign	4
مستشار	adviser	6

شود

اشادة	praise	93

شيع

شائعة	rumor	29

ص

صحّ

صح	health	1
صحيح	genuine	74
صحي	hygienic	90

صحب

صاحب	owner	92

صحف

صحفي	journalist	13
صحافي	journalist	20

صدر

	IV to send	12
مصدر	origen	15
تصدير	export	5
صادرات	exports	11

صرّ

	IV to insist on	76
اصرار	persistence	42

صرح

تصريح	statement	1

صرع

	III to fight	87

صرف

صرف	money changing	57

مصرف bank 66
تصريف distribution 77
مصريف expenses 30

صرم

صارم harsh 89

صعب

صعب difficult 85

صعد

صعيد basis 61

صفّ

صف course 80

صفر

صفر zero 94

صفق

صفقة deal 76

صفو

مصفاة refinery 19
صاف clear 16

صقل

مصقول polished 16

صلح

مصلحة matter 61
اصلاح improvement 4
صالح proper 1

صمّ

مصمم determined 89

صندوق

fund 3

صنع

صناعة industry 3
مصنع factory 4
تصنيع industrialisation 80
صانع manufacturer 94

صنف

تصنيف sorting 82

صون

صيانة maintenance 80

صيد

صيد fishing 78

صيدلى

pharmacist 4

ض

ضبط

انضباط discipline 73

ضحى

ضحية victim 76
تضحية sacrificing 79

ضخم

ضخم huge 81
تضخم inflation 52

ضرّ

VIII to compel 95
ضرورة necessity 45

ضرب

ضريبة tax 36

ضعف

ضعف weakness 27
ضعيف weak 27

ضعف

VI to be doubled 82
مضاعفة doubling 72

ضغط

ضغط pressure 51

ضفة

bank 77

ضمّ

VII to unite 86
انضمام joining 59

ضمن

V to ensure 15
ضمن inside 39
ضمان security 6
مضمون guaranteed 51

ضوء

ضوء light *n.* 43

ضور

ضار to harm 76

ضوضاء

noise 79

ضيع

مضيع wasteful 42

ضيف

X to invite 7
اضافة addition 9

ط

طبّ

طب medicine 81
طبي medicinal 56

طبع

طبع printing 95
طبيعة nature 68
طبيعي natural 77
انطباع impression 87

طبق

طبقا ل according to 5
طبقة layer 93
طابق floor 56
تطبيق application 91

طرأ

طارئة emergency 81
طرح launch 36

طرف

طرف part 43

طرق

طريق road 5

طفّ

طفيف trifling 57

طفىء

اطفاء extinguishing 15

طلب

طلبية order 25
مطلوب wanted 45
متطلبات requirements 60

طلع

IV to acquaint 42
V to look at 75
X to explore 88
مطلع introduction 89
تطلع striving 59
اطلاع acquaintance 79
مطلع familiar with 15

طلق

VII to start 37
علي الاطلاق absolutely 54

انطلاق release 90

طوب

brick 15

طور

تطوير development 5
تطور development 23

طوع

تطوعي voluntary 46

طوق

طاقة ability 9

طول

طول length 5
طوال throughout 29

طوى

VII to contain 95

طير

طيران aviation 60

ظ

ظرف

circumstances 31

ظل

في ظل under protection 4

ظهر

IV to show 26
ظاهرة phenomenon 43

ع

عبأ

عبء load 59

عبر

II to declare 48
VIII to consider 37
عبر across 79
اعتبار respect 31
اعتبارا من effective from 89
باعتبار in terms of 50

عتق

عاتق shoulder 72

عثر

V to stumble 64

عجز

deficit 35

عجل

II to hurry 93
عاجل immediate 44

عجن

عجنة dough 37

عدّ

V to be numerous 29
X to be ready 77
عدة many 12
عدد number 19
عديد quantity 15
اعداد preparation 8
استعداد readiness 90
معدات equipment 12
متعدد multiple 37
مستعد prepared 35

عدل

III to be equal 58
عادلة justice 47
معادلة balancing 47
تعادل balance 31
عادل just 45
معدل average 6

عدم

عدم non- 19

عدن

معدن mineral 17

عرب

IV to express 44

عرض

V to face 29
X to consider 43
عرض display 37
عرضة target 87
معرض fair 37
معارضة opposition 89
اعتراض resistance 61
عارض exhibitor 75
معروض exposition 18

عرف

تعريف notification 94

عرقل

to hinder 73
عرقلة difficulty 79

عزّ

تعزيز strengthening 36

عزم

VIII to resolve 9
عزم determination 61

عزو

to attribute 23

عصر

عصير juice 12

عصف

to blow violently 75

عاصمة

capital 1

عضو

member 18

عطر

perfume 38

عطف

منعطف twist 81

عطل

عاطل unemployed 48
معاطل unemployed 41

عطو

عطاء gift 50

عظم

اعظم bigger 57
معظم majority 10

عفو

اعفاء exemption 78

عقب

IV to follow 91
عقب result 87
تعقيب comment 35

عقد

VII to convene 85
عقد contract 9
اعتقاد belief 85
معقد complicated 42

عقر

عقاري property *adj.* 94

عكس

انعكاس reflection 96
معاكس counter- 87

علج

معالجة treatment 15

علق

II to comment 81
علاقة connection 7
تعليق commentary 51

علم

علم knowledge 61
عالم world 59
علامة sign 16
عولمة IT 43
تعليمي educational 10
معلومات knowledge 10
معلوماتية IT 79

علن

اعلان announcement 28

عمّ

عمومي general 29
عام public 1

عمد

VIII to depend 80
عمدة mayor 90

عمر

عمر life 48
معماري architectural 12

عمق

تعميق deepening 10

عمل

عمل act 2
عملا ب according to 18
عملية process 55
عملة currency 64
عميل customer 70
عمالة wages 74
عمولة commission 83
معاملة transaction 28
تعامل business 27
عامل factor 21
متعامل dealer 86

عملاق

giant 79

عن

عنان rein 91

عنى

III to see to it 51
معني concerned 46

عهد

عهد time 74
معهد institute 25
تعهد undertaking 73

عوج

عاج ivory 27

عود

III to resume 64
عودة return 76
عادة habit, charges *pl.* 33
عادي customary 47
اعادة resumption 6
استعادة recovery 79
عائد profit 29
معتاد accustomed 42

عوض

عوض substitute 85
تعويض replacement 39

عول

عائلي domestic 50

عوم

عام year 2

عون

معونة help 54
تعاون cooperation 7
تعاوني cooperative 14
تعاونية cooperative spirit 56
معين helper 80

عير

معير measure 89

عيش

معيش living 95

غ

غاز

gas 4

غدر

مغادر departure 8

غذو

غذائي nutritional 10

غرّ

على غرار similar to 89

غرض

target 55

غرف

غرفة room 66

غرق

X to occupy, last 10

غضب

غضب rage 45

غطو

تغطية covering 41

غلّ

استغلال utilisation 15

غلب

اغلبية majority 34
تغلب overcoming 75

غلق

اغلاق closing 87
مغلق shut 50

غى

لغاية as far as 89
للغاية very 29

غيب

غياب absence 73

غير

متغير change 43

ف

فاتورة

bill 67

فأل

متفائل optimistic 64

فتح

VIII to open 2
فتح opening 85
افتتاح opening 38
انفتاح opening 74

فتر

فترة period 2
فاتر weak 88

فتش

تفتيش examination 42
مفتش inspector 78

فجو

فجوة opening 92

فدى

VI to avoid 92

فرد

منفرد solitary 61

فرص

فرصة opportunity 12

فرض

to impose 92
فرض prescribing 45

فرع

فرع branch 82

فرق

فرق separation 19

فرن

oven 15

فشل

to fail 42

فصل

تفصيل detail 61
منفصل separate 80

فضل

II to prefer 88
فضلا عن beside 3
بفضل thanks to 4
افضل better 59

فضى

IV to lead to 41

فقد

to lose 64

فقر

VIII to lack 86
فقر poverty 93
افتقار need 41

فقم

تفاقم	aggravation	48

فكر

فكر	thinking	71
فكري	intellectual	79

فلح

فلاحة	agriculture	78

فنّ

فني	technical	27

فندق

	hotel	80

فهم

مفهوم	understood	55

فور

فورة	flare up	91

فوض

	VI to negotiate	13

فوق

	V to be superior	52
تفوق	superiority	79

فيد

	IV to notify	30
استفادة	utilisation	66
فائدة	utility	51
مفيد	useful	68
مفاد	meaning	95

فيض

فائض	surplus	67

ق

قبض

قابض	holding	78

قبل

	X to meet	71
قبيل	shortly before	88
من قبل	on the part of	56
اقبال	approach	24
قابل	next	41
مقبول	acceptable	92
مقبل	next	2
مستقبل	future	31

قدر

قدر	extent	1
قدرة	faculty	33
مقدار	measure	46
تقدير	estimation	21
قادر	capable	75

قدم

قدم	foot	53
تقديم	dispatch	59
تقدم	advance	84
قادم	coming	13
مقدمة	front	56

قرّ

قرار	permanency	19
مقر	seat	2
تقرير	report	3
استقرار	establishment	43
قارة	continent	65

قرب

	VIII to approach	13
تقريب	approximation	18

قرح

اقتراح	proposal	10
مقترح	suggestion	72

قرض

	VIII to borrow	45
قرض	loan	5
اقتراض	loan	6

قرن

قرن	century	48
مقارنة	comparison	11

قرى

قروي	rural	78

قسر

قسرا	compulsorily	48

قسم

قسم	part	93
تقسيم	division	29

قشف

تقشيف	self-restraint	23

قصد

اقتصاد	economy	22
اقتصاديات	the economy	76
اقتصادي	economic	3

قصر

قصر shortness 57

قصو

اقصي most distant 70

قضى

قضاء judiciary 79
انقضاء expiry 87
بمقتضي according to 65

قطب

X to polarize 55

قطر

قطر country 73

قطع

قطاع sector 3
اقتطاع deduction 33

قعد

قاعدة base 68

قفز

to jump 22
قفزة jump 24

قلّ

قلة paucity 95

قلب

تقلب change 39
متقلب changeable 94

قلد

V to assume 92
تقليدي traditional 78

قلص

تقليص contracting 48

قلق

قلق disquiet 86

قمّ

قمة summit 23

قمح

قمح wheat 46

قمش

قمش fabric 75

قود

to lead 73

قوض

مقوضة exchange 4

قول

قول saying 9

قوم

قيمة value 6
قيام rising 63
مقاومة resistance 85
اقامة raising 4
قائم rising 95
قائمة list 37

قوى

قوة strength 24
قوي strong 4

قيد

قيد restriction 45
تقييد tie 18
مقيد registered 50

قيس

مقياس measure 52

قيض

مقايضة exchange 42

ك

كادر

cadre 93

كتب

مكتب office 34
اكتتاب registration 36

كتف

to shackle 79

كتل

تكتيل formation 43

كتم

V to keep silent 71

كثر

كثرة large quantity 50

كثف

تكثيف compression 82
مكثف condensed 41

كرث

كارثة disaster 81

كسب

	VIII to possess	24
مكسب	profit	82
اكتساب	acquisition	24
مكسوبات	gains	87

كشف

كشف	uncovering	79

كعب

مكعب	cubic	53

كفّ

كف	refraining	79
كافة	totality	47
كفاءات	capabilities	33

كفأ

تكافؤ	equivalence	63

كفح

	III to fight	87
مكافحة	struggle	79

كفى

كفاية	sufficiency	83
كاف	sufficient	82

كلّ

كلما	whenever	59
كلية	totality	50

كلف

	II to cost	56
كلفة	cost	15
تكليف	costs	41

كلم

كلمة	address	20

كم

كمية	amount	17

كمش

	VII to contract	20
انكماش	contraction	20

كمل

	VIII to complete	56
	X to complete	13
تكمل	integration	43
اكتمال	completion	56
استكمال	conclusion	49
بالكامل	completely	38

كهرب

كهرباء	electricity	12

كهن

تكهن	prediction	34

كون

مكون	consisting of	29

كيف

كيفية	manner	89

كيمياء

كيميائي	chemical	3

ل

لاسلكى

	wireless	69

لاءم

ملاءمة	adequacy	15

لبث

ما لبث	lost no time	87

لبى

تلبية	following	69

لجن

لجنة	committee	7

لحظ

ملحوظ	noted	74

لحق

	to touch	75
لاحق	subsequent	12

لزم

	VIII to adhere to	73
التزام	commitment	54
لازم	inherent	73
لوازم	necessities	80

لشى

	VI to disappear	52

لغو

	IV to nullify	19

لفت

	to turn	90

لقى

IV to address 90
لقاء meeting 67

لمح

II to allude 73

لمس

لمسة touch 13
ملموس tangible 95

لوز

almond 37

م

مئوى

per cent 28

متع

V to enjoy 18

مثل

تمثيل representing 77
مماثل similar 13
ممثل representative 10

مجن

مجاني free 46

مدّ

VIII to extend 42
مد extension 78
مدة period 6
تمديد lengthening 89
مادة matter 3

مدن

مدينة town 3

مدى

مدي extension 25

مرّ

X to last 17
استمرار duration 6
مرير persistent 51

مرأ

امرأة woman 81

مرس

III to pursue 79
ممارسة pursuit 79

مرونة

flexibility 60

مسّ

to touch 43

مسح

مسح survey 25
مساحة surface 36

مسك

V to persist 82
تمسك adherence 95

مضى

IV to spend time 47
ماض sharp 8

مكن

امكان capacity 44
امكانية possibility 69

ملح

ملاحي maritime 78

ملك

VIII to possess 36
ملكية ownership 56
مملكة kingdom 30

مليار

billion 10

منح

III to grant 14
منحة gift 46
مانح donor 54

منع

III to resist 73
VIII to abstain 35

منو

مني to be affected by 87

مهد

V to pave road 27
تمهيدا in preparation of 56

مهر

مهارة skill 93

موت

ميت lifeless 15

موج

موجة wave 24

موز

banana 45

مول

II to finance 1
مال property 50
مالي financial 2
مالية finance 2
تمويل financing 1
ممول wealthy 92

مان

تموين catering 60

ميد

ميدان square 93

ميز

امتياز benefit 77
متميز distinguished 74
ممتاز excellent 29

ميل

to bend 74

ن

انبوب

pipe 4

نبأ

نبأ news 8

نبت

نبات plants 78

نتج

نتيجة result 2
نتيجة because of 86
انتاج creation 3
استنتاج conclusion 95
ناتج product 20
منتوج product 74
منتجات products 13
انتاجية productivity 13

نجب

انجابي childbirth *adj.* 54

نجح

to succeed 89
نجاح successful 70

نجز

انجاز achievement 7

نجع

منتجع resort 76

نجم

منجم mine 29

نحا

نحاية side 42

نخب

VIII to choose 47
انتخاب election 95

ندب

مندوب deputy 81
منتدب appointed 38

ندو

ندوة club, meeting 66
ناد club 95
منتدي gathering 63

نزع

نزاع struggle 45

نزل

نزولي falling 30
تنازل yielding 79

نسب

نسبي relative 90
مناسبة occasion 44

نسج

نسيج fabric 96
منسوجات textiles 11

نسق

تنسيق arrangement 78
منسق coordinator 78

نشأ

انشاء construction 8
انشائي constructive 56
ناشيء growing 50

نشد

to implore 95

نشر

انتشار spreading 81

نشط

نشط lively 50
نشاط vigor 2

نصح

	to admonish	81
نصيحة	advice	95

نصف

نصف	half	48
منتصف	middle	26

نصب

نصوب	exhaustion	95

نضج

	to ripen	94

نطق

واسع ناطق	extensive	44

نظر

نظر	view	59
نظير	counterpart	9
مناظرة	dispute	73
انتظار	waiting	73

نظف

تنظيف	cleaning	83

نظم

نظام	arrangement	45
تنظيم	arrangement	83
منظم	arranger	84
منظمة	organisation	26

نعش

	VIII to recover	65
انعاش	boost	36
انتعاش	revival	16

نفذ

تنفيذ	execution	14
تنفيذي	executive	7

نفس

منافسة	competition	55
تنافسي	competitive	51
منافسي	competitive	79

نفط

	petroleum	18

نفق

نفق	tunnel	76
نفقة	cost	48
انفاق	spending	24

نقد

نقد	cash	6
نقدي	monetary	82
انتقاد	criticism	95

نقذ

انقاذ	rescue	18

نقش

	III to discuss	2

نقص

	to lack	92
ناقص	less	91

نقض

تناقض	contradiction	20

نقط

نقطة	point	28

نقل

	VIII to be carried	81
نقلا عن	based on	81
نقلة	model	55
تنقل	transfer	77
انتقال	transfer	74

نقو

انتقاء	selection	83

نكر

	to deny	79

نكس

نكسة	relapse	81
انتكاس	relapse	81

نمى

نمو	growth	11
انماء	expansion	5
تنمية	expansion	1

نهر

انتهار	rejection	19

نهض

نهوض	rising	87

نها

نهاية	end	30
انهاء	end	49

نوب

نيابة من	in place of	49

نوع

نوع	kind	37
تنويع	change	77

تنوع diversity 70

نول

VI to discuss 74

نوه

to allude 90

نوى

نية intent 76

ه

هبط

هبوط fall 16

هتف

هاتف telephone 77
هاتفي telephonic 73

هدّ

مهدد threatened 79

هدأ

هدو calmness 87
هادئ calm 29

هدف

هدف aim 7

هشّ

هشاشة gaiety 81

هلع

هلع impatience 81

هلك

استهلاك consumption 58
استهلاكي consumer *adj.* 75
مستهلك consumer 27

همّ

مهمة task 83
اهتمام concern 55
هام important 71
مهم important 18

همش

على هامش on occasion of 76

هندسة

engineering 25
هندسي technical 85
مهندس engineer 31

هو

هوية essence 79

هار

انهيار collapse 67

هول

هائل dreadful 81

هوى

to fall 53
متهاوي falling 73

هيء

هيئة commission 2

هيكلة

structure 59
هيكلي structural 63

هيمن

to control 79

و

ولو

even if 87

وأم

VI to agree 59

وتر

V to be strained 18
وتيرة manner 93

وثق

ثقة trust 33
وثيقة document 92
واثق trusting 94
موثوق trustworthy 92

وجب

X to deserve 59
وجبة meal 37
ايجابي positive 57
بموجب according to 46

وجد

وجود existence 10
ايجاد creation 45
موجود existing 19

وجه

VIII to point to 64
جهة side 38

وجه aspect 61
وجهة respect 18
مواجهة opposition 43
توجه attention 67

وحى

IV to suggest 63

وحد

وحدة unit 60
توحيد unification 82
اتحاد oneness 13
اتحادي federal 21

ودع

وديعة trust 32
ايداع deposit 91

ورد

X to import 67
مورد revenue 49
ايراد income 50
استيراد importation 19
واردات imports 17
مورد supplier 19
مستوردات imports 67

ورق

اوراق مالية bonds 50

وزر

وزير minister 1
وزارة ministry 9

وزع

II to distribute 96
توزيع distribution 29
موزع distributed 30

وزن

ميزان balance 74
ميزانية budget 2
توازن balance 31

وسط

وسط in middle of 51
وساطة intervention 62
اوسط middle 3
بواسطة through 58
متوسط middle 13

وسع

II to widen 68
توسيع widening 9
توسع widening 83

وسل

وسيلة means 55

وسم

موسم season 27
موسمي seasonal 21

وسك

IV to be close to 86

وصف

to describe 34
مواصفة explanation 55

وصل

III to continue 65
V to arrive 5
مواصلة connection 10
توصل attainment 18
اتصال link 10

وصى

IV to recommend 32
توصية advice 31

وضح

IV to explain 56
وضوح clarity 33
واضح clear 80

وضع

وضع *pl.* circumstances 48
موضع object 88
موضوع subject 43
متواضع small 16

وطىء

to tread 79

وطن

وطني national 19
مواطن compatriot 77

وظف

وظيفة post 51
موظف employee 82

وعد

وعد promise 76
موعد time 95

وفر

II to provide 75
توفير providing 49
متوفر abundant 15

وفق

	VIII to agree	52
وفقا	in accordance	21
موافقة	agreement	6
اتفاق	agreement	4
متفق عليه	agreed upon	45

وفى

وفاء	fulfilment	54
ايفاء	fulfilment	95

وقت

توقيت	timing	88
موقت	temporary	80

وقد

وقود	fuel	15

وقع

وقوع	occurrence	81
موقع	place	26
توقيع	signing	13
توقع	expectation	52
واقع	reality	66
بواقع	to the amount of	51
متوقع	it is expected	18

وقف

	II to stop	88
	V to be based on	82
وقف	stopping	73

وقى

وقاية	protection	78

وكل

وكيل	representative	38
وكالة	agency	2

ولى

	to follow	96
	IV to display	69
	V to occupy	44

وهم

	VIII to accuse	79
تهمة	accusation	79

ى

يئس

يائس	hopeless	91

يبس

اليابسة	dry land	49

يسر

ميسر	made easy	93
تيسير	facilitation	77